The Witch

A Pedagogy of Immanence

iowyth hezel ulthiin

ISBN 978-1-64504-287-7 (Paperback)

ISBN 978-1-64504-288-4 (Hardback)

ISBN 978-1-64504-289-1 (E-Book)

Library of Congress Control Number: 2022949321

Printed on acid-free paper

This book is part of the Critical Pedagogies Series

DEDICATION

This book is dedicated to my ancestors and to the women in my family who passed on their wisdom in whatever clandestine way they were able.

ACKNOWLEDGMENTS

First and foremost, I must acknowledge my mentor, Michael Hoechsmann, for whom helping others is such a commonplace event that, to him, it feels unexceptional. I have significantly benefited from his guidance. I would like to extend my appreciation to the staff and environment provided by Lakehead University, which made it easy and straightforward to complete this work. Their tireless efforts towards integrating Indigenous ways of being have helped me put myself back together again. Lastly, but perhaps most importantly, I acknowledge my mother's teachings in establishing the groundwork for my way of being. She gave me everything she could to help me rise above our family's trauma. I will take these gifts and the strength they have afforded me and use them to raise the next generation, to give freely of the wisdom that has been passed to me, owning nothing.

Table of Contents

List of Illustrations

Table of Contents

Preface

The Last Request

Crouching on the ground, my hands are pressed onto the earth with my face resting heavily on top of them. I am curled tightly into a ball, with the hands of a half-dozen members of my group tenderly stroking my back. I had never been touched with sensitivity and love in my entire life. I was tucked up like an animal awash in an unfamiliar experience, a fragment of stoneware pottery returning to the soil, with water falling out of my eyes and colours rotating like kaleidoscopes on the inside of my closed eyelids. There was the warmth of a dying fire and the sounds of the living forest all around us. I had opened up, perhaps for the first time in my life. The group had decided to perform a ritual right there and then, to hold my body and channel into me the love that I had been denied, to cradle my body as I was finally allowed to fracture, to break into pieces, to let down the walls built out of hardened muscle and to experience real human connection.

My first Witchcamp marks a turning point in the odyssey to reclaim my life from the crippling effects of childhood trauma. It was one of the first instances that I can remember feeling truly and fully myself, one of the first places where I learned that I could experience life without shame, and one of the most profound healing experiences of my life.

My Relations

At the age of 13, my grandparents all died within a year of one other. The only survivor was my Mother's father, a man who kicked my grandmother in the stomach while she was pregnant, who burned my uncle's hand on the stove, and who we didn't talk to anymore. So, little of our family's history was passed down to my generation, including our languages, Dutch, French, Michif, or Anshinaabemowin—all lost. I know little of my family's stories except the remnants I picked up over the years, stories told to me at dinnertime when the talk flowed, and my parents remembered.

Tracing the story back to its beginnings, this story must also be the story of my ancestors. It represents the coming together of two injured lines, each carrying a history of intergenerational trauma within their bodies. It has been difficult to stop blaming the people who have hurt me the most, but I understand now that the pain others give to you is a reflection of their own—that when people hurt you, it is because they have more than they can bear. My family's history—their pain—is my inheritance. So, in understanding my pain, I also begin to process and release the trauma of my ancestors.

Pulling up to my grandparent's farm in Sparrow Lake, there was a long drive lined with ancient trees forming near-perfect lines. Towering overhead, they dwarfed the ancient farmhouse. The front garden was planted with row on row of tulips, organized according to their glorious colours. On my father's side, they were Dutch survivors of the German occupation of Holland. They were POWs and members of the resistance. Yet, despite the absolute ubiquity of windmills and tulips at their farmhouse, I never spoke to them about their history. They were stern, religious—frightening. I remember one night when I was staying there, stealing downstairs in the cold of the night, I saw them in their front parlour on their knees, silently moving their lips in prayer over their rosaries. Their religion had made them inflexible; it created patterns of purity and simplicity, violence and fresh air. Staying with my grandparents was like entering a different time. They were a constant presence, impassive, quiet, and distant, but with moments and gestures of silent love and intimacy that felt fleeting and secretive.

My mother's mother was Métis-Anishinaabe from Penetanguishene. She died when she was 60 of a heart attack. She had inherited porphyria from her mother's side, which caused her to develop dementia at an early age. Her emphysema, which forced her to wheel around an oxygen machine, was from her chain-smoking. I remember that she used to sit under my cockatiel to smoke. My parents found it dead in its cage one day and told me that it had flown away. From what I remember of her, my grandmother had a warm nature and a deep laugh. She was prone to fits of sudden violence, which we laughed off while trying to duck since she was so tiny. She was incredibly generous and kind but was also haunted by her past. She lived with our family all through my childhood and would tell us stories when she would lose her mind. It was almost too terrifying for me to comprehend. My uncles say that at one time, our family lived on the Peninsula in Penetanguishene on a large parcel of land, which had been sold for some tiny amount, my uncle said flippantly, "to pay for more booze." From a very early age, I became aware of an unspeakable cruelty that could make life feel evil and heartless. It had happened to my grandmother and my mother after her and would soon happen to me as well.

The pain I felt from the women in my family was incapacitating, driving me for most of my life to seek healing in one way or another. It brought me home frequently to tend to and nurse my mother, who had been in and out of institutions for my entire life. I returned home until I couldn't do it any longer. I had become drained by the near-constant effort to help her. I accepted and grieved over the fact that I would never be able to save her, secretly fearing for my spirit under the weight of our collective heartache.

My mother's family has all but lost their links to our shared heritage. There is a Métis sash in our front hallway but little else. Yet, I have always suspected that something survived. We may not have known our name for the Creator, but we felt it nonetheless. Our worldview existed to us as water to fish, and it wasn't until leaving my family home that I began to unpack the latent cultural wisdom passed on by my mother. As children, my sister and I understood the world to be made up of a web of connections. We instinctively understood a respect for all life; we knew that we should attempt to understand different ways of life, learning from their unique approaches to the world, just as our own unique approaches to life could be understood to enrich the lives of others. As children, my mother told us that we had rights—rights to our knowledge and to our way of life, even if it was different from that of my parents or those around us. Before my grandmother died, she would bring people home that she met on the street to serve them tea and later, I would often lose my mother in public and find her talking to a stranger as though they were intimate friends. They treated other beings, both people and animals, like gifts to be cherished. The world was a magical place, full of sacredness and possibility.

As an adult, when I took the ACE (Adverse Childhood Experience) Test, I scored a 6 out of a maximum of 10. Many metrics that measure the correlation between ACE scores and incidence of alcoholism, suicidality, or liver disease have a final category of 4+ (Center for Disease Prevention and Control, 2015). Yet, when placed in relief to the trauma of my parents, my generation's trauma pales in comparison to theirs—and theirs, in turn, to that of my grandmother's generation. In each generation, I find a deeper well of misery, more profound violence, dislocation, and disease. I have little choice but to accept my inheritance; it runs in my blood, and thus, it is incumbent upon me and my generation to take it up, to not only find meaning in the pain of our ancestors but also to find healing through our stories. In my search for meaning, I have tried to find my place as both a White-coded person, identified female at birth, and the inheritor of the fall-out of cultural genocide. I experienced the felt reverberations of a world war and the inheritance of the colonizer and colonized both.

Yet, the dynamics of colonialism were also played out within my family system. My father, the White settler, became the outer authority to which we needed to bend and hide the way of life that was lived in secret when he was gone. His word was law, but the law contained no order other than his own. We were subject to an authoritarian rule that operated on instinct, on a whim and thus, we became habituated to living instinctually, engaging with the order that *was* rather than the order that *should be*. There was little justice in our home outside of the deep communion formed between my sister, my mother and me. We learned instead to accept life as a complex, sometimes joyous, sometimes sorrowful, unfolding process.

A correlative finding of those with high ACE scores is an incidence of repeated trauma in later life, a category into which I also unfortunately fell. I found many people to replace my father, keeping alive the repression and indignities of my youth as something that gave me a strange kind of comfort; after all, the bonding that occurs through shared trauma is as intensely negative as it is intoxicating. Like the messages sometimes came in the form of popular media. The media I discuss here have each served as integral pieces in the process of rediscovery and reclamation.

Inevitably, through Witchcraft, I have found the means to recast myself from a victim of trauma, not just to a survivor but a healer of trauma. I do not believe I will ever emerge into a world where the trauma I have experienced is firmly in the past, precisely because it lives within my body, and my everyday life involves interacting with and processing this trauma in relation to each unfolding situation, experience, and sensation. It is forever a part of me, but in lovingly attending to these fractures, I take up my role as healer, of myself, of my family, and in my small way, of humanity itself. A foundational document of Reclaiming Witchcraft, entitled *The Principles of Unity*, states, "Our ultimate spiritual authority is within, and we need no other person to interpret the sacred to us." It says, "We know that everyone can do the life-changing, world-renewing work of magic, the art of changing consciousness at will" (BIRCH Council, 2018, para. 5). In my coven, I began to understand my trauma, but more importantly, I began a decade-long search for a means of being in the world, with community, sharing my own wisdom with those who came after me, and of finding the authentic ground of my own unique experience. I have striven to take part in the work "to help to heal the wounds of the earth and her peoples" (BIRCH Council, 2018, para. 8). Circle was the place where I constructed my identity as a teacher, where I developed my pedagogy, where I engaged in leadership, healing, friendship, and forging connection with the natural world.

I believe that within settler culture, there are emancipatory clues, directions to another world. It has felt like I am re-learning a hidden language. Within the toxic mess we have found ourselves in, there exist the echoes of connection. There are hidden stories that hold the felt knowledge of our place on the Earth and it feels like if I listen closely enough, I can hear the voices of my ancestors speaking to me through lost fragments scattered throughout a culture that absorbs and eats whatever it comes into contact with. The stories of our shared legacy are there still, somewhere in the digestive tract of a Catholicism that ate early Indigenous cultures, in a politics that established itself upon the Iroquois Confederacy (Unites States Select Committee on Indian Affairs, 1988).

Embodiment: Writing into Being

How, then, does one engage with the texts of one's life to obtain meaning that might be transmuted to others in useful and meaningful forms? In revisiting the stories of my own becoming, I engage in texts that became a part of me precisely because of their nature as accessible and pleasurable. I attempt to engage with these texts as I did as a child, living in the feelings that they stir in me and also, in the act of playfulness as an adult, remembering being a child. Ott (2004) says that "children *create rules as a form of play*—rules that frequently change as quickly as do their desires" (p. 204, italics in original). In this way, I have sought to engage in a playful, formless method, reveling in what Barthes would refer to as the connotative (see Barthes 1972; Gómez, 2017), the symbolic, mythic level of language. It is in play and pleasure that emancipatory meaning is derived for I believe that pleasure is movement, novelty, creativity, joy. It is through an investigation of pleasure that each text is primarily consumed. This is as much an attempt to come to terms with my own latent and unspoken yearnings as it is a drive to play with, challenge, and entice the imaginary into engagement with an unknown that, perhaps, even I cannot admit to.

I engage with each text's connotative or mythic implications as a product in and of themselves. There is, primarily, a story but within that story is the DNA of meaning, the meme, the cultural knowledge held within the story. For Hall (2001), the discursive form ends in consumption only when the meaning has been derived. In elevating my meaning as well as the felt effect of those interpretations, I bring into prominence the felt reverberations of meaning-making, rendering the texts as complete artefacts through my processing of them.

Reading and attempting to comprehend popular media becomes critical to understanding certain types of reality (Storey, 1994). The felt experience of the daily may be acted upon as a text, one where one may enter into the mundane with an inward eye and open hands, welcoming meaning to emerge. As an Indigenous person, I look towards my own becoming as a study centred in my understanding of self. Yet, I also resist myself in my reading, attempting to undo and redo the process of learning that sees itself through the eyes and the mind of the patriarchy, the settler, as an-other, an alien, a beast, a woman. Instead, I seek to find in the texts of my own identity, a new kind of centre, a new locus for desire, one that finds its meaning in interiority existing with the other, not as a power over, but a power *with* (Benjamin, 1986). This is what I was looking for in these texts and what is I argue is buried within them, the seeds of a new humanity.

I engage here in a practice of embodied writing, a process of embodied research, where

> Nature feels close and dear. Writers attune to the movements of water, earth, air, and fire, which coax our bodily senses to explore. When embodied writing is attuned to the physical senses, it becomes not only a skill appropriate to research but a pathway of transformation that nourishes an enlivened sense of presence in and of the world. (Anderson, 2001, p. 83)

This is what I have done to embed the more theoretical aspects of the work into the felt, affective realm of the body, *my* body, de-centring the conceptual and cerebral process of theorization and coupling it with the processes of intuitive and spiritual knowing that may become manifest through felt sensation.

McIvor (2010), a member of the Swampy Cree nation, says that being in the body, "assists with a quest to connect with spirit and the spirit-world; many messages, gifts, and teachings are offered to us in non-verbal, non-cerebral pathways" (p. 143). We attune to the body when we wish to develop the kind of knowledge that comes from direct engagement with the world, which also involves the felt reality of spirit and all that entails. Spirit may not be adequately captured in words. It must be experienced directly and thus; the body becomes the primary site of engagement, the only means for attaining gnosis. It is in the act of translating the experience of bodily gnosis that one then attempts to reach out and to connect with other felt experiences, to achieve affective resonance through embodied, sensual narrative form and poetics.

This piece of writing is a "realist story" (Ellis, 2004), presented in a series of theoretical texts threaded with personal narratives. It was important for me to ground the work in a location piece, as suggested by Absolon and Willett (2005) in their chapter, "Putting Ourselves Forward," as well as by McIvor (2010), who asserts that Indigenous knowing centers on the self as the fulcrum of a web of relationships. The Western devaluation of "navel-gazing" is upended through the recognition that "the navel tells the story of our first connection to another" (Pelias, in Elis et al., 2010, p. 324). Telling our own stories need not result in a kind of empty solipsism. In looking at the self as a relational being, a crossroads, we begin to see the potential for autoethnography to reveal a deeper sense of the interrelatedness of the self within a world. Anderson (2001) suggests that, "Relaying human experience *from the inside out* and entwining in words our senses with the senses of the world...affirms human life as embedded in the sensual world" (p. 83, italics in original). In this way, embodied inquiry helps to ground through this process of coming to know, speaking to a deeper sense of interconnectedness, a larger web of being. McIvor (2010) states that his story "is one of an untold generation—a generation that may feel that they have nothing useful to say because we do not have the language..." saying that he hopes his story "will bring voice to a generation lost. Lost without our language. Lost without our grandparents and their teachings. Lost without land and traditional food to nourish our mind-body-spirit. But especially for those who have not lost hope. (p. 148) We, both Western and Indigenous alike, tell our stories to connect to larger forces, to draw emphasis towards broader connections. However, in the case of Indigenous communities, we may subsequently become dislocated and groundless in the loss of our language, our stories, and our lands of origin. What does it mean to be Indigenous when one does not know or understand the land from which we came? In telling my own story through the lens of those narratives that have shaped my life, I hope to speak to one experience of the relational world, shedding light on my discovery of a path back to the land, and perhaps giving hope to those who have a similar path to walk.

Methods of Inquiry and The Limits of Knowledge

Beyond understanding the whys and wherefores of my personal experience, I want to delve into the potential for these experiences to sow the seeds of future connection. I wonder how my experiences can be transformed into a methodology. In transpersonal psychology and its focus on "embodiment and integration" (Davis, 2003, p. 7) and critical realism (Oliver, 2012), I look from the subjective to the intersubjective. There are aspects of the personal that become something more through a *shared* ground of being. I seek connection through the collective inheritance of Western subjects, of the oppression endemic to a modern, capitalist, and industrial order. I engage in a reading that draws upon and aligns with a psychoanalytic feminist recasting of desire, of understanding feminine eroticism, being, and power (Benjamin, 1986) within my own approach to the world as a web of relationships.

I have attempted to centre my body as the fundamental ground of discovery, of gnosis as a means of resisting, in particular, the Western tendency towards strict intellectualization (Thanasoulas, 1999). In this pursuit, I seek a way of testing the boundaries of personal experience, pursuing the notion that if I go deeply enough within, I may begin to encounter the space in which I am touched and may touch upon the other. Yet, gnosis here also suggests a connection to the inexplicable or a-rational at the heart of this pedagogy. So, while I may be able to point toward common feelings in the experience of humanity, there will always be an unknown at the edge of our comprehension, which I may only hint at and which one may only experience directly. It is this I reach for with my hands waving out before me in the darkness, which I will never find because it is destroyed in being found. Thus, I hint and suggest engaging in a dance with the unknown that exists as an invitation to curiosity.

Throughout this process, I have followed Strauss and Corbin (1994) to maintain "an openness of the researcher, based on the 'forever' provisional character of every theory" (p. 279). Instead of concrete meanings, I have tried to become sensitized to connections, not strictly through a process of coding per se, but in an embodied sense of relationality. I attempt to seek out fellow feelings in my studies, my time becoming a window wherein "serendipity" (Konecki, 2019, p. 17) may occur. Conversations within my community, meditative insights, dreams, and chance encounters all become woven into a process of coming to know. Conceptual shapes hit upon an embodied resonance, suggesting an affective pairing and connections are made, unmade, and made anew.

In this process, my body becomes the matrix through which materials flow and become processed. Konecki (2019) says that our bodies may give us clearer and more immediate insight into what is happening both inside and outside of us, but more importantly, what is happening in the space where those two worlds meet. He goes on the state that the body itself is the determining factor in how we relate to and perceive the world around us. Yet, the body's wisdom is much like the mind's intellect, useless without practice, honing, experience. Conceptual understandings from my readings become activated through praxis by engaging with and through the concepts into relationships through the lived instances of connection. The process of discovery involves a sensitization to the body as a means of detecting and processing instances of serendipity, making connections, and drawing conclusions from spontaneous instances of personal gnosis. It becomes a process of rooting, a deep interrogation of the self and conceptions of the self. Therefore, the body leads the way in an engagement of non-self, of looking towards the connective matrix of being and attempting to move beyond the particularities of what is *me*. It is in process where the pedagogy lies. In undoing myself, by coding, processing, and re-narrativizing my own being, I bring myself into relation and thus reveal a way of learning into relation through and with the stories of the self. I attempt to lay the groundwork for a perspective that orients one towards a direct encounter with *the world*, all the while recognizing, as Oliver (2012) suggests, that:all description of that reality is mediated through the filters of language, meaning-making and social context. It is impossible to step outside our own perspective-ism and so the gap between the real world and our knowledge of it can never be closed. (p. 374)

I maintain the perspective that there *is* something to be known, a substance or spirit that unites all matter and energy into a single, unmediated reality. This reality may be grasped in instantaneous moments of halting insight that exist as a shimmer, escaping the ability to look back through memories that are mediated by language and analogy. However limited our grasp may be, however limited the language we have to explain it, I contend that in our personal and sensual engagement with the world, we may experience a more profound understanding than what may be expressed in words, one that may be able to unite humanity with the more-than-human across the divide of individual consciousness through of ground of immanent emergence from a shared whole.

Social Structure and Emancipatory Narratives

On a practical level, I seek to engage with and describe the social world in which we live, especially the structures of power and control within which we enact our social relationships. Through the social imaginary (Taylor, 2004), our practical ability towards agency is either buttressed or thwarted by what we imagine to be possible and what we imagine to be possible is largely structured upon what we have seen but also what we have been told. It is in this space of the possible that we begin to engage with the social mechanisms that take root within our lifeworlds and thus within the pre-figurative imagination (Johnson, 1987; Ezzy, 1998). It is this space that is referred to when I speak about how our bodies mediate our sense of the world around us.

There is an embodied sense of the real and within that, the potential for what may become real. I seek to reach beyond even my own limitations and thus attempt to utilize my body as a means of reaching beyond it, to engage in a contemplative and engaged social praxis rooted within the body that may serve to process the social imaginary, to hint towards the potential for something more, not in a reality that transcends this one but that expands upon it, giving meaning and depth to the lived connections within a felt, material matrix of interconnection. In transcendence, I see a letting go of constructs, allowing instead for a grounding down, a sacralisation of the body and its connections. In seeking this ground, Oliver (2012) points to the process of "retroduction" to explain how one may reaches towards an answer to the question, "what must be true for this to be the case" (p. 379)? He says that we may take what we know and try to understand the pediment upon which it stands, to follow the structure to the limit, to attempt to abstract a truer understanding of the way the world operates. As Oliver suggests, "It allows the theorizing to go beyond what is immediately knowable but maintains an obligation to test that theorizing in the crucible of real-world experience and against competing theories" (Oliver, 2012, p. 375). Thus, in attempting to reach back into a history that has not only been lost but utterly obliterated with a violent will, I must seek resonance within the present moment that infers a past that used to be present. Yet, in an engagement with the present moment, one brings the abstraction back into praxis, into relation through the felt material of the senses and into the space of serendipity. One may then be able to build upon current affective categorizations, grounding into the immanent.

Transcendence and immanence operate in this piece of writing as functions as much as they are states. Transcendence occurs in the breaking down of structures that may have once appeared to be fundamental, thus thrusting one into a transcendent realm that is also immanent. In transcendence, therefore, we are merely exceeding limits, coming deeper into connection with more fundamental principles. If everything is, in fact, united and continuous, one may never emerge into a separate reality but rather, simply into a deeper confrontation of that same reality, without the protective shell of mediated socially constructed boundaries and limits.

Thus, when delving into the texts embedded in this work, it is not only the description of phenomena that is important, but the emancipatory meanings behind them. It is not just an attempt to know the mechanisms by which I have my own relationship with the more-than-human world but also a theorizing of how we may come to know the world again as human beings. Yet, I agree that "The best we can hope for is to uncover approximate evidence of tendencies rather than proofs allowing prediction" (Oliver, 2012, p. 375). What I attempt to create here is not *the* means, but rather *a* means for a return to nature, *my* means.

Proper representation of the means for attaining spiritual gnosis or of direct connection with the natural world may be impossible to represent in language, but I hope in utilizing personal, embodied tools, I may inspire a shared affective resonance that may lead to a common understanding, one that may point to a potential opening, to seduce into relation through re-enchantment. I attempt to avoid a show of intellectual force that comes from a strict rationalist paradigm. I cannot possibly fit my spiritual knowledge into a neat package, but I can hint towards a way where others may feel inspired to walk.

The methods I have utilized here are deeply personal, grounded largely in serendipity and personal gnosis. In the search for meaning through the self and in the environment, I begin by bringing myself into communion with the web and framework within the relations that surround me. When I engage in research in relation, I begin to follow the threads of my own connection to larger worlds that make up the *reason* of connection. I believe it is through the world that we may begin to find ourselves and in asking the world to reveal itself, of waiting patiently within the present moment for a hint of life to make itself manifest, that we may live in connection. It is the reason of connection I am attempting to articulate here, the reason of my life and the foundations of my own identity as brought forth into the world by the texts of my world, by the stories that have become my own. It is only then, in the process of discovery, I begin to seek the roots of these connections and in following them down into the habitus and systemic, I begin to theorize towards an embodied methodology of resistance that comes from a radical shift in the centre, in occupying a new space of being. This is the space that we reach from, into the new, reaching into connection with our relations and becoming a tether whereby to ground the world.

The Territory of Return

Without a community structure or access to Elders, it became incumbent upon me to find my own way back into connection to what Absolon and Willet (2005) lay out as the foundations of Indigenous research, to revise, research, re-claim, re-name, re-member, reconnect, and re-cover. My family has lost our shared language, and our stories and I, therefore, have the project of trying to resolve the tensions of my identity as both a White settler and Anishinaabe, an identity that may be understood in our language as non-binary, queer, and neuro-diverse while rejecting orientational boundaries that serve to restrict the emergent principles of Eros.

One of the most compelling sources in my attempts to make sense of and transform my family's story has been found in the pagan community and occult philosophy, particularly within the Reclaiming tradition of Witchcraft and in Chaos Magic as expressed through oral tradition. In these practices, I saw for myself a process of transmuting trauma into resilience as a way to re-write the story of my childhood and my family's struggle to survive poverty, trauma, addiction, and mental and physical illness. In paganism, I found a love for the world I had not felt in my Roman Catholic upbringing. In the pagan path, the manifest world is sacred, the body sacred. There is no separation between mind and body, sacred and profane, except that which humans make for our own benefit. The body is not something to be transcended but rather something to be understood and enjoyed. The world is not a veil of tears; instead, we may look through the veil, beginning the understand the gift of life and celebrate it through our pleasure and worship.

Austin Osman Spare (2001/1913) says in his work *The Book of Pleasure*, "Riding the Shark of his [sic] desire he crosses the ocean of the dual principle and engages himself in self-love." (p. 36) Desire is a principle by which living beings operate. It is harmful to deny it, but rather, one must seek harmony with it, use it as a tool, embrace and ride it, live with it as a companion. It is a knowledge of desire and pleasure that bring the self to the limit, into a confrontation with the other, and in this confrontation, the web of interdependence becomes manifest. I argue that pursuing pleasure to its ultimate end leads one to mutual aid, to pleasure through care, love, and stewardship. I cannot shut out the suffering of my relatives, no matter how high the wall— even if it only exists in my nightmares. I am at the greatest peace, ease, and happiness when justice is manifest, the greatest good for all beings.

It is through occult and mystical understandings I began to learn how to process the story of my life, unglue it from false cultural tethers, and to dive down into the process of grounding myself within the world of relations. In modern reconstructions of shamanism, through trance and vision work, I have been able to reach backward, looking towards a time when my own Whiteness would have been colonized, to separate the Whiteness itself from the disease it carries. In reconstructions of Norse paganism, I can begin to see the road that led me here and expand my imaginary to include a time when my ancestors would have been free of the illness that makes you want to consume the world, leaving nothing for your children or grandchildren. We have such a rich inheritance of stories, living within the belly of a story-eater. This culture is a devourer of worlds and as fellow subjects of this hunger, we ruminate with the imaginaries of untold generations, sifting through the fertile excrement of a monster to find the jewels of the ancients.

A Pedagogy of Immanence

Towards the end of my first Witchcamp, one of my newfound friends and I ventured up onto the ritual ground to do a ritual with just the two of us. It was a grey day and there was a wind that ruffled the billowing fabric in my dress. Earlier that day, I had taught him a playful way of dispelling energy by running around, wiggling our bodies, shrieking, and giggling like children. When no one was watching us, we ran around the field until we lost our breath and I remember looking at him. At that moment, I could see myself the way another person saw me. In one startling moment, I was the person I might become, the fear and trauma were gone and nothing was left but the wild and uncontained power of my true personality, alive like an animal. It was one of the few moments in my life when I was able to sit within myself, needing absolutely nothing, feeling utterly complete. It was in being seen as a wild and beautiful being of the world I was able to complete the circle of becoming. I had begun to remake myself and in that moment, I discovered the power of being uncovered by the loving eyes of a friend.

I believe that the texts in this book have carried me towards these moments of wholeness, and is why I wish to document them here. The texts I cite are not monuments to be studied and pried apart for meanings to be applied to all but as momentary relations that occurred within my life and that served as the wedges to pry me open. In studying the meaning of these texts, I document the processes that have embedded me within my body, which is within a world. It is not transcendence from the world I sought, but rather, the transcendence of the oppression embedded within my body, that kept me from reaching towards pleasure and imprisoned me within relations of non-consent at the whims of those in power. It is not a transcendence of, but a rooting through and in, that is presented here, a freedom that comes from being connected within and with the world. The theories I present here stem from the most important texts of my life. I attempt to create a kind of embodied theory, a pedagogy of immanence that illustrates an inward journey into the centre not just of the self, but of the self within the web-of-being that encompasses all life.

The pedagogy of immanence is a denial of an individuation that finds itself through a severing of connection (Benjamin, 1986). Rather, it seeks to recast humanity as *of* the world, that in being with the world, we find ourselves revealed. We find ourselves through the world as we are, an emergent quality of the Earth and in embracing our immanence, we may take our place within a network of relations. The pedagogy of immanence is a realization of what is, a reawakening to the deeply felt, resonant relationships between living and moving beings. It is a remembering of the indebtedness we have to the Earth itself, one that requires us to replenish and restore it through a habitual reinvestment of energy into its systems and harmonies, but which also involves the embrace of human pleasure as another form of ecological health. The pedagogy is a push towards witnessing all life *in* and *of* the world as fundamental and inextricable from human happiness. It is a realization that our health *is* the health of the world; I am the world and it is me, and it is only through the world, in conversation with the world, that I may become the truest embodiment of my authentic and individual self.

As I come to know myself more and more profoundly, I have continually found my relations close by. It is through a process of inner discovery I may attempt to create a guide for thinking and, more importantly, of feeling through this path, to suggest, entice, and enchant. I have intentionally avoided closure in the thoughts and feelings presented here as they are not meant to present a completed process but rather an invitation to a journey. It is through my words that I attempt to evoke an opening in the mire, the oppression, and the blindness of our indoctrination into materialist-capitalism both as a system and a way of life. I don't suggest that I have found a way out, but rather suggest that there *is* a way out and that we can look for it collectively.

References

Abram, D. (1996). *The spell of the sensuous: Perception and language in a more-than-human world*. Pantheon Books.

Absolon, K., & Willett, C. (2005). Putting ourselves forward: Location in Aboriginal research. In L. Brown & S. Strega (Eds.), *Research as resistance: Critical, Indigenous and anti-oppressive approaches* (pp. 97-126). Toronto: Canadian Scholars Press.

Anderson, R. (2001). Embodied writing and reflections on embodiment. *Journal of Transpersonal Psychology*, *33*(2), 83–98.

Barthes, R. (1972). *Mythologies* (A. Lavers, Trans.). The Noonday Press.

Benjamin, J. (1986). A desire of one's own: Psychoanalytic feminism and intersubjective space. In T. de Lauretis (Ed.), *Feminist studies/critical studies* (pp. 78–101). Palgrave Macmillan UK. https://doi.org/10.1007/978-1-349-18997-7_6

Bietti, L. M., Tilston, O., & Bangerter, A. (2018). Storytelling as adaptive collective sensemaking. *Topics in Cognitive Science*, *114*, 710–732. https://doi.org/10.1111/tops.12358

BIRCH council. (2018, February 28). Principles of Unity. *Reclaiming*. https://reclaimingcollective.wordpress.com/principles-of-unity/

Davis, J. (2003). An overview of transpersonal psychology. *The Humanistic Psychologist*, *31*(2/3), 6–21.

Ellis, C. (2004). *The ethnographic I: A methodological novel about autoethnography*. Alta Mira Press.

Ellis, C., Bochner, A., Denzin, N., Goodall, H. L., Pelias, R., & Richardson, L. (2008). Let's get personal: First-generational autoethnographers reflect on writing personal narratives. In N. K. Denzin & M. D. Giardina (Eds.), *Qualitative inquiry and the politics of evidence* (pp. 309-333). Left Coast Press.

Ezzy, D. (1998). Theorizing narrative identity: *The Sociological Quarterly*, *39*(2), 239–252. https://doi.org/10.1111/j.1533-8525.1998.tb00502.x

Gómez, J. (2017). *An analysis of Roland Barthes's mythologies*. CRC Press.

Hall, S. (2001). Encoding/decoding. In M. G. Durham & D. M. Kellner (Eds.), *Media and cultural studies: Keyworks* (revised edition). Blackwell.

Johnson, M. (1987). *The body in the mind: The bodily basis of meaning, imagination, and reason*. The University of Chicago Press.

Kahnawake Mohawk Elders. (2006). *The eagle and the condor*. Montreal, QC.

King, T. (2003). *The truth about stories: a native narrative* . House of Anansi Press.

Konecki, K. (2019). Creative thinking in qualitative research and analysis. *Qualitative Sociology Review, 15*(3), 6–25. https://doi.org/10.18778/1733-8077.15.3.01

McIvor, O. (2010). I am my subject: Blending Indigenous research methodology and autoethnography through integrity-based, spirit-based research. *Canadian Journal of Native Education, 33*(1), 137–155.

Oliver, C. (2012). Critical realist grounded theory: A new approach for social work research. *British Journal of Social Work, 42*(2), 371–387. https://doi.org/10.1093/bjsw/bcr064

Osman Spare, A. (2001). *Ethos*. I.H.O Books. (originally self published in 1913)

Ott, B. L. (2004). (Re)locating pleasure in media studies: Toward an erotics of reading. *Communication and Critical/Cultural Studies, 1*(2), 194–212. https://doi.org/10.1080/14791420410001685386

Storey, J., & Storey, J. (1994). Cultural theory and popular culture: A reader. New York: Harvester Wheatsheaf.

Strauss, A., & Corbin, J. (1994). Grounded theory methodology. *Handbook of Qualitative Research, 17*(1), 273–285.

Taylor, C. (2004). *Modern social imaginaries*. Duke University Press.

United States Select Committee on Indian Affairs. (1988). H. Con. Res. 331.

Chapter 1

A Pedagogy of Immanence

We have stories upon stories in layers built up like sediment and are tasked with the role of becoming in a fashion much like Tzara, a Dadaist artist, may have construed it, picking up stray bits of tattered paper from the floor to form an assemblage. Lacking intelligible grand, centralizing narratives for identity formation or life path, we must sift through a narrative detritus to pick out fragments that may express an authentic sense of inner truth. Western culture in the 21ˢᵗ century presents the nascent adult with an impossible hallway full of doors, offering insight into the many ways a life could be lived, and yet, none of those doorways leads to *my* life. As such, the individual must take cues from the ways and means that are presented to them, somehow constructing a way and means of being themselves that is both walking with the traditions of the past and, at the same time, forging new paths within an, as of yet uncharted web of social and ecological relations in extremity.

For the marginalized among us, the problems of alienation create an even greater task, to craft an identity in resistance to the flow, one that expresses a reality that *cannot* or rather, *must not* be known and yet, which cannot be other, thus cutting-out new exits onto a once fixed barrier. In the increasing marginalization and alienation that one may call the modern condition, marginalization operates like ripples in a pond. As those once at the center become pushed into an ever-expanding periphery, the center of relevance becomes increasingly narrow and diffuse by the effect of this. As those whose dreams matter become increasingly rare, those of us who share, at the very least, the status of the outer rings, more or less marginal in status but collective in our alienation, begin to look around ourselves at a new world, a wilderness without inherent value or sense principally because it contains no center. In this terrain, we begin the struggle for identity, for a storied existence amongst the beasts, who, after being rejected from a paradise of cultural connection and purpose, may begin to seem more alike, more a potential ally, than a tool. For, how may those increasingly without capital buy and sell an animal's life like a piece of chattel? Instead, *I* am bought; I am owned.

It is in this space where identities that embrace and thrive within the marginal, the outcast, and the abject may form the strength of a new center, one that embraces a radical centrality that is radical precisely due to its multiplicity, an individuality *with* and in collaboration with the other in this new ecosystem. The Gutenberg Parenthesis (Pettitt, 2012) suggests that in the era of modern media communications, there is a departure from a culturally mediated center of truth, from the orderly, storied world in which a hierarchy of being descends from the angel to peasant, in which our means to gather truth emerges in a secondary orality, a culture whereby we must navigate truth in the instantaneous and temporary realm of online discourse and interaction and its subsequent touch on the lived experience of communication and what may be a common understanding of reality. As such, we are thrust from the nest and the protection of our collective mythologies and into a new position of individual reckoning and responsibility. In Yates Sexton's (2020) *American Rule*, he says that the mythos of America:

> …has grown more complicated and contradictory, distorting reality and tearing our understanding of the world to pieces. Now, trapped in a cycle of self-mythology and atrocity, Americans feel immobilized and confused, incapable of change, and troubled by a moment inundated with inconsistencies, contradictions, and outright nonsense. (Prologue, para. 23)

I would posit that we could extend this narrative to include the notion of human exceptionalism under the umbrella of a dizzying unravelling of truths coming to fruition through our collectively staring down the barrel of total global environmental collapse. How exceptional can we possibly be when we live in such a state of imbalance that our very lives and livelihoods are threatened through the acts of our apparent genius? The proof of our own ignorance is staring at us from the abyss, and it is within this condition that a global populace must collectively take stock, finding our bearings as the dust from the death of a cultural empire begins to settle around our feet, and yet, whose core machinations remain startlingly pristine. Hall (1986) warns us that, "You can't live another century constantly confronting the end of the world" (p. 48). As it stands, the myths by which we unconsciously organize and understand our lives have a shifting and uncertain sense of solidity, one that may easily "melt into air" as in Berman's (1982) famous reflections on the experience of modernity. Yet, we are tasked with living through the end of a world that will not end, continually encountering the next moment as it unfolds, demanding us to chart a course through this unending end, to find solid ground.

Zuboff (2019) says in a talk for the Alexander von Humboldt Institute for Internet and Society, that there has been a "focal shift from ownership of the means of production to ownership of the production of meaning." (25:10), which she speaks of in relation to surveillance capitalism. In this newly dawning world, she says, "human futures" become a commodity that becomes brought into meaning under capitalism through commodification. In harnessing information, new systems of capitalist surveillance are able to both predict and manifest human action, organizing this knowledge into a commercial marketplace wherein the human mind, will, and spirit become goods to be bought and sold. If we are to locate ourselves within this brave new world, we must wrest back the creation of meaning as a radical and transformative act. We have been given an inheritance of what Forbes (2008), a prominent activist of Powhatan-Renapé and Lenape descent, calls "Wetiko," which is a disease brought to North America by White settlers. He defines Wetiko as *the consuming of another's life for one's own private purpose or profit* (p. 32, italics in original). We may understand the commodification of human futures as nothing else but cannibalism, the capture, and exploitation of human potential for the purposes of private profit. Forbes says that "the wealthy exploiter 'eats' the flesh of oppressed workers, the wealthy matron 'eats' the lives of her servants, the imperialist 'eats' the flesh of the conquered" (p. 33). So, if the food of the conqueror is had through the imposition of meaning, acts of myth-making construe new and, perhaps, unpredictable centres through which new actions and patterns of action may emerge. In decentering external truth, in the balance, to consider and reflect without succumbing, we may set our sights on flows that come from and emerge into a relationship with a real and tangible worldliness, looking to and responding along with the natural world.

In a talk for the National Center for Collaboration in Indigenous Education, Robinson (2021) speaks of the dual relationships between learning within the classroom and learning on the land, saying that each requires totally different skillsets and yet, experiences on the land may become part of the inner world, creating a rich tapestry of meaning that can emerge as a locus of knowledge in other contexts. She tells the story of a river with two branches. Her understanding of riding on the river, its movements and currents help her understand her place within two systems, as integrating the waters into one flow. I speak about this inner tapestry as a testing ground, a means for reflecting upon and expanding the realm of the possible; as Deleuze (2001/1965) states, "In reflecting on the passions, the imagination liberates them, stretching them out infinitely and projecting them beyond their natural limits" (p. 47). Whatever our inheritance and the impulses, desires, and drives it has engendered, it is within us to stretch beyond the limits of the temporal and spatial worlds that we have encountered thus far. We may exist equally within the timeless and limitless, to see beyond but also to see into and with the space around us. We may inhabit the rivers and forests of our minds and use those rivers to inform our lives. Forbes (2008) says that an Indigenous way of understanding religion that it:

> is not prayer, it is not a church, it is not theistic, it is not atheistic, it has little to do with what white people call 'religion.' It is our every act. If we tromp on a bug, that is our religion; if we experiment on living animals, that is our religion; if we cheat at cards, that is our religion... *All that we do, and are, is our religion.* (p 25-26, italics in original).

This is not the mind or imagination existing separately from life, but rather, the expansion of possibility within the imaginal and also within the minutiae of act and action, gives the possible material expression. Deleuze (2001/1965) says that "Transcendence is always a product of immanence' (p. 31), that in attempting to rise above, we must also look within or perhaps *be* within the world, and only in this way may we begin to engage with an immanent humanity. In the exploration of the possibilities of immanence, I interrogate the archetypes of the wolf (Raphael, 1997), witch, and cyborg (Haraway, 1990; 2016) as points along a spectrum of nature and culture, as sub-categories of liminal, shapeshifting, transformative forces that present potential for social transformation. Within each point, there exists the resonance of the other. I argue that the witch exists as a pole at the center between nature and culture as a mediating force, drawing forth from nature to inform culture and vice versa. The witch as an identity, is that of a crucible, a place at the boundary wherein the unknown, feral, chaotic, and untamed world may find coherence in a grounding and evolution of the civilized. Yet, order cannot sustain itself without a constant engagement of that which is without, which is the ground from which order emerges. To exist without connection to the unknown universe can only be an inward-looking state of contraction and decay. The witch as an archetype and identity is a bridge from the known to the unknown, developing techniques and powers to deal with this transaction.

Narrative Identity and Archetype

Identity as a structure, a concept, or ideal is an emergent principle presupposed first by a somatic experience of being. The somatic realm is the affective state of being, of feeling before the mind as intelligence of body and mind engaged in present moment awareness. This somatic realm of experience resembles what Heidegger (1953) refers to as the *DaSein*, as an experiential alive-ness that prefigures the conscious or thinking state of being. Deleuze and Guattari (1987) describe identity as a hazy nucleus from which certain configurations of desire emerge that presuppose action in the world. These desires create a gravity that coalesces into machinic structures that serve to carry out tasks in relation to what has *become* a self within a moment of desire and its consequent action. This may then suggest that identity comes into being as a response to movements and configurations within the somatic as a mirror to a configuration that shifts and adapts to newly emerging pressures, yearnings, and drives.

Within this pre-thematic and miasmic-ly frothing reality, we may understand the process of coming to be in the moment through Ricoeur's (1983; 1991) concept of the hermeneutical process of narrative and identity. Ezzy (1998) describes this as operating through three stages, "prefiguration, configuration, and refiguration" (p. 244). First, there comes the experience of being which, after the first moment of life, becomes continually prefigured through previously established symbolic connections that serve as the building blocks of the narrative imagination. These connections become configured and refigured through a process that is both personally and communally mediated and continually narrativized to cohere a sense of self-continuity over time. One may also understand the prefigured symbolic imagination through Bourdieu's' (1977) concept of the habitus, wherein external political and cultural values become rooted within the body, becoming activated through momentary interactions between the individual and the social world. This prefigurative imagination becomes ossified through experience and, in times of novel crisis or deep transformational upheaval, requires plasticity to invent radical new orders of being.

Goffman's (1961) work on identity as occurring within asylums and penitentiaries describes how our institutions affect identity by placing individuals within narrow environmental affordances that restrict how a person's identity may be acted out. The crux between affordances and our range of expression within them, exemplifies the interstice of affordances and the habitus and serves as the theatre for Laing's (1967) philosophical thoughts on the 'real'. He reflects on the political nature of *reality* as systematically asserted hierarchically, moving from those identified as sane to those identified as insane by the social order of the day. He argues that distinctions such as these lead to realities in which an individual is classified as insane, or their experience as *not real*, due to overarching power structures such as in the case when normative human emotions, identities, and even cultures become rejected and thus, pathologized (see Bell, 2007; Pupavac, 2002; Wagner, 1994; De Block & Adriaens, 2013).

In my own experience, when traumatic events occurred, I was unable to escape, change, or even process my experiences. This led to an incredible amount of stress and consequent symptoms, which manifested as depression, insecurity, and anxiety that were pathologized–at the age of thirteen–as a chemical imbalance rather than a logical response to a traumatic childhood. I, the individual, was not considered a product of my relationships but rather a lone entity who must remain integrated despite lacking the required emotional, social, and spiritual foundations for survival. The fallout from extreme life experiences requires lengthy processing, healing, reconnection, contemplation, and coming to terms with a new reality. As I connect with and experience new somatic states, my narrative must adapt to and process these states, bringing them into the realm of civilization, story, and meaning. Yet, I have often struggled to find the resources to engage in this process within the current configuration of our social world and have been required to make exceptional contortions to take the space to heal by force. I ask, what is a 'normal' reaction to insane circumstances? The question itself points towards the fissures in the classification of insane and sane, irrational and rational, weird and normal.

Without requiring the firsthand experience of institutionalization, other social structures, from schools to political affiliations, can be seen to create affordances, embedding the habitus of the human world within the individual bodies of its denizens, thus shaping the daily actions and, eventually, their very identities. We have all been shaped by the social world in which we live, and this world touches upon our imaginations, creating the boundaries around what we consider possible. If I am to believe the authorities in my story, I am inherently chemically imbalanced and will never be well again. In the stories that I was told, my experiences of abuse and neglect were not instances to be understood, processed, and healed, but rather incidental and unspectacular subjective elements to an otherwise unexceptional diagnosis. To medicalize alone does not take into account the thirst of the human spirit for meaning. In order to process and heal the fragments of my soul, harmed by circumstances outside of my control, I was required to take upon myself the process of understanding, without community, without stories, without a guide. Those in poverty are not afforded the luxury of narrative integration, of exploring the meaning of their experiences. It is a luxury to confront and understand our worlds, which harkens back to Zuboff's (2019) analysis of surveillance capitalism. She says that an increasing epistemic inequality comes from the capture of meaning-making. This has been long understood within marginalized communities, whose stories simply could not be "known," could not be real, could not be realized within the structures of settler culture.

In trying to reach into and perhaps bring back descriptions from the edges of the unknown, one assembles aspects of the familiar into new formulations, new descriptions of the somatic being-ness that one knows to be true simply because one feels it. Jameson's (1991) concept of the pastiche is a fragmented imitation, an assemblage of referents used without an awareness of their origins as a method of mixing and matching cultural signifiers without the added baggage of context or history. Within the increasing dislocation of the modern, within this placeless-ness, Borden (2001) says. "The innate nomadic nature of the individual in today's society is provided for by the reactionary relationship dependent upon the ever-increased speed of participation, interaction and consumption" (p. 253). The land and ourselves in relation to it are predicated instead upon our ability to flexibly adapt to a placelessness within which our relationship to consumption becomes the operative mode under which our identity becomes construed. Within a world where the people have no land, there can be no identity outside of the machinic operation of Capitalism which would arrest our lives, meanings, and futures within its cycles of capture and commodification. The process of pastiche allows for the flexible use of cultural signifiers without the need for tethers, which is ideal for a landless people, to assemble witch's hats and hieroglyphs like one would a poem, juxtaposing and working with the implied or emotional value of each symbolic reference to describe something unseen. Yet, in the age of Wetiko, the act of pastiche may also be considered a mode of cannibalism, especially for those who have remaining ties to the land, meaning, and identity. As those who have been taken from the land and given endless and meaningless space in return, one can easily participate in the Wetiko by grasping for meaning from within an empty territory, addressing a full one. To fill the endless void requires endless energy and the world cannot sustain the scope of this imaginary and the hunger it creates.

Winczewski (2010) warns us that identity constructed via a process of postmodern pastiche, when gone awry, can result in the dissolution of that identity through a loss of interiority. A person may lose touch with who and what they are through the process of taking up referents from the outside world. By looking to the placeless landscape of the modern for one's meaning, one may become a person without an inside, without center, without ground. Winczewski (2010) refers to identity pastiche as a form of assemblage that lacks orientational boundaries, which in schizophrenia is exhibited as a loss of interiority through the subsequent loss of internal cohesion. Yet, in thinking of certain states of madness as constructs in and of themselves, one may contemplate the cross-cultural conditions of schizophrenia, which suggests that, for example, "those in India and Ghana...were more likely than the Americans to report rich relationships with their voices and less likely to describe the voices as the sign of a violated mind" (Luhrmann, Padavati, Tharoor, & Osel, 2015, p. 41). One might understand the loss of orientational boundaries, also, as a failure of narrative, of one's society's failure to acknowledge, elevate, and integrate the lived experiences of its individual members. If psychosis and other forms of madness could be folded into the social world, there could be created a more inclusive reality, one that engages with the real in the ways that Laing (1967) suggests, without the harsh delineations between external and hierarchically imposed states of normalcy that exclude diversity.

Deleuze and Guattari's (1987) *A Thousand Plateaus*, complete with an apt subtitle, *Capitalism and Schizophrenia*, look at the dissolution of identity structures as favouring the emergent quality of self that co-alesces through desiring motivations in differing configurations across time. These structures coalesce in concert *with* the undulations of an environment equally emerging into being, not as entities split from the place but as movements emerging from place and time. In their work, Schizophrenia exists on the boundaries of capitalist production of coherence. In the mind of one who engages with the world as emerging intensities, a sense may be created that fails to conform to expected, orderly, and productive *common* sense that allows for the tidy structuring of social order. Through direct experience of the world, madness finds different outlets and connections, which may place the mad person in conflict with a world that relies on and orchestrates sense-making as an integral part of a production cycle. Deleuze and Guattari's (1983) notion of a "minor literature" offers the potential for spontaneously formed cohesions to emerge as assemblages made out of the referents of what they call a "major literature." Such literature would encompass, for example, the stories, tropes, imaginaries, and dreams of Western Culture, the collective common sense and shared, consensus reality as enforced by a status quo. Yet, a minor literature becomes a rhizomatic cohesion, rooted within this larger body but more than that, emerging from it in a chaotic coherence that escapes definition, presenting one with a narrative that provides potential routes of escape and that abhors closure (Deleuze & Guattari, 1983). A minor literature could be considered a language of outcasts, the hunted, the despised, the abject, and the invisible. This lack of closure is described by Deleuze and Guattari (1987) as allowing for definitions to be created that escape definition, and thus, there is an opening for selfhood that may elude the devouring maw of Western colonialism. We are not only trying to construct identities on the margins but also attempting to create identities that cannot be captured, disassembled, and repackaged as consumer products. Under this framework, pastiche can serve as a means of constructing a coherent sub/counter-narrative. Identity fragments allow for forms of identificatory cohesion that might have been otherwise excluded by structures that prohibit an authentic sense of being for cultural outsiders, the colonized, or the mad. Access to radical new avenues of expression allows for authentic identities to emerge. From the point of view of a minority within a majority, the insane may become sane, the irrational rational. Alternately, one may create routes of escape from the insanity, irrationality, and pathology contained within an ecocidal, hegemonic social order. Such configurations may allow for minority sentiments, among them the development of biophilia that overarching distinctions between humankind and nature would otherwise extinguish as a series of objects in instrumental service to 'man.' These escape routes propose a methodological path for "third-order change" (Bartunek & Moch, 1994) to take place, change that occurs on the deepest levels, beyond even the schemata, instead of happening on the level of cellular coherence.

The narrative structure I am proposing is based on shifting ground, an ecological perspective that emerges from the felt moment, from a sense of exile from current narratives of meaning and sense while still being semiotically moored within them. Morton (2007) says, "If we could not merely figure out but actually experience the fact that we were embedded in our world, then we would be less likely to destroy it" (p. 64). This perspective not only emphasizes the being-ness of ecological relation but also a flattening of the divide between humans and nature, an ecology of all that excludes nothing. This sentiment is encompassed by Deleuze and Guattari's (1987) plane of immanence, which rejects the distinction between human and more-than-human, locating humans within a network of moving parts, desires, motivations, and actions, all emerging and becoming within a protean messiness that becomes and undoes itself across the limits of time and space. It is not merely that we must become moored within the more-than-human. Still, we must become habituated to the shifting and continuous dialogue between beings and forces within the more-than-human world. A situatedness-in-relation may not become ontologically stagnant. Instead, it necessitates a lively engagement with a continually evolving desiring impetus within a present moment encounter. Within the limits of our current cultural constructions, words may be harnessed to signify these shifts in perspective. The seeds have been planted by those who came before us and tended by generation upon generation, waiting for hidden sacred narratives to emerge, to be embraced by a new generation and brought to fruition within a newly emerging world-relation.

Ultimately, while words and stories may help us navigate the world, Buber's (2008) I-Thou relationship lays the foundation for how one might begin to engage in a lively way of being in those spaces where words fall away, bringing a theory of immanence into praxis. The I-Thou relation is where an individual may come up to the more-than-human, approaching from a sense of the unknown, becoming present to the moment until such a time that the thinking mind can become suspended within the engagement. At this moment, two being-nesses may come into the conversation, acknowledging the inter-being's separate but continuous nature. Buber believed it possible to engage in a mode of present-moment attention that engaged with the prefigurative sense of being-ness in such a way that any conscious sense of both narrative and subjective or literary distinctions melted into a shifting and dynamic somatic experience of the other refracted through the experience itself. This form of being becomes situated at the level of sense-perception, which gives way to a direct experience of the 'thou' of the world as a relationship in which there is no distinct boundary and to which time may shape, change, and evolve a living relationship between horizontal feeling and perceiving subjects. Here, one becomes open; one's imagination becomes attuned to the possibility latent within each infolding moment. Csikszentimihliyi's (2008) notion of the flow state captures the subjective personal experience of this type of engagement, which in itself, he describes as a complete loop or an "autotelic experience" (p. 67), an end in itself. Adrift in the stream of sensuous experience, within a present moment sensation of direct relation, we can achieve a measure of wholeness. There is an interweaving of the sensual and direct experience of the world without judgement and the storied world of culture and civilization. In the interstice between the two, the transformative potential of noticing and integration occurs. One may observe the world and its movements, opening the self up to the potential of a non-narrative experience of present moment awareness, and at this moment, there is the potential for radical reformulations of symbol and story to emerge in new and fresh ways. In traversing the river of awareness, one may emerge reborn into a consciousness of new connections, new paths, and new routes of escape. There is in the observation of the world around us the potential of learning to emerge from felt experience, itself becoming a new ground for individual and social life.

It is a being-in-relation that is the ultimate purpose of an eco-pedagogy of immanence, and this state of being is expressed through the archetype of the witch, not only as a narrative element but an identity fragment, an archetype that has the potential to create an egress from settler culture and its consequent illness and degradations. This isn't to say that there is a formulated praxis behind the word, a concrete philosophy that would carry one to the threshold of a relationship with nature. Instead, it presents a wedge, a crack, an invitation to step outside the paradigm of Western hegemony .

Definitions of the word 'witch' still largely carry the stigma of malignancy, which in and of itself is indicative of social discomfort with a femininity of flows, power, and independence. The witch is a natural and social figure, one who holds the power to touch and direct reality itself, through growing in direct relationship with the world and its beings, through present-moment awareness, an autotelic act of engaged attention. The act of transmutation may be *super*-natural in the sense of being extremely natural. It does not occur outside of nature but within it. Sitting with alert, open attention to the world, one may discover previously unexplored territories of the mind and spirit. It is possible to shift and transmute the narrative of a world lain over the world itself, shaping, cajoling, and caressing reality into a pleasing shape, a liberatory form.

Furthermore, when thinking about Bandura's (1971) notion of social learning, of how we internalize both problems and possibilities acted out in our environments in lieu of personal experience, we may consider archetypes themselves as an aspect of narrative pedagogy as a way of understanding of one's place within the world through what Bartunek and Moch (1994) call analogical communication, which is central to second-order change, change that takes place on the level of schemata. Stories help to expand our sense of the possible by showing us potential paths of engagement. Yet, we require more than the ability to shift our schemata through demonstrated possibilities. To truly engage the transformative potential required to reshape human engagement with the more-than-human world, we need to rise above the schemata into the transconceptual, to see beyond the edges of what *is*, into what *may* be. Transconceptual communication, according to Bartunek and Moch, allows one to reach into a deeper level of change, one that eludes rigid classification precisely because it reaches into unknown territories as they begin to take shape; living in the limit between self and other, human and nature, we may begin to grasp our connections through our ability to ground, to pay attention to those experiential moments that allow for direct contact and experience, direct knowledge of our connection. And although the transconceptual hints at the notion of transcendence, it is not a transcendence of the material world but rather the transcendence of rigidly imposed internal boundaries erected within the social mind, that we engage more deeply in the now-ness of relation, where we emerge more directly into contact with the immanent world, which is the mother of all.

The Witch Archetype: Alienation and Re-Enchantment

In his book, *Archetypes of the Collective Unconscious,* Jung (1981) refers to archetypes as complete concepts. They point to something beyond the individual experience that may be passed down through our collective stories, embedded within them, and carried within the dreams of generations. Archetypes represent intensities stored within the prefigurative imagination as forms of deep humanity. They are, perhaps, another attempt to encapsulate something that cannot be otherwise bounded within language, of those things that may only be understood somatically, pointed to by the poets. In this way, I wield the archetype of the witch but resist making it into something fully fleshed or pinned down. I allow the concept of the witch to flexibly adapt, remaining semiotically open-ended, hinting towards a reality that can never be fully encapsulated by words or even grasped by human intelligence. I ground the theory of the witch within Strengers' (2012) new animism, a theory that eschews narrative closure in favour of an open-ended and living thought. I wield the stories that I present here as illustrations of the potential of the archetype, as puzzle pieces, fragments, or pastiches that may be embodied as identities or used as tools for the expansion of the imagination, which may serve to create new potentials within an unfolding present moment reality. The archetype of the witch is juxtaposed with other archetypal imaginaries in order to explore their semiotic richness, each image becoming another fragment caught in a web, a relationship of meaning pointing towards something more. Cixous's (1986) notion of the sorceress and the hysteric is one such example. In the *Newly Born Woman*, Cixous discusses these two archetypes as forms of transgressive feminine identity. Both figures bring forth an aspect of that which has been effectively repressed by the Western mentality, namely the identificatory power of nature (via the sorceress) that may serve to heal the trauma of the schism between human and nature (via the hysteric). The very existence of these archetypes is transgressive for Cixous in that their natures confront the blindness of Western rationalism towards the emotional, subjective, and a-rational world and the perceived chaos of a natural order that remains beyond the capacity of the human mind to conceptualize and, therefore, to capture and control. The sorceress carries within herself the potential of feminine power, linked with a nature that is beyond capture. Her power hints toward the mystery of semiotic uncertainty, profound transformative potential, and the power to upend the social order in the face of more profound orders, deeper orders, and orders of nature and time. As the yin to her yang, in the hysteric, we see the embodied physical and psychological effects of modern dissociation brought into the light through the inescapable insistence of her disorder. In the two poles, we have the two outcomes of the process of identificatory pastiche: the individual's empowerment to recreate reality and the dissolution of the individual into madness. In this way, I posit that the witch is a sorceress, a hysteric, a wolf, and a cyborg. The imagination of the witch exists within a tradition of liminal beings, existing between, underneath, and within.

Taylor (1995) asserts that the modern is something we assume to be a-cultural, resulting from a process of getting rid of old beliefs in favour of a purer form of rationalism, whittling down the nonsensical traditions of our past in a march of progress. The problem in this, he says, is that we then assume that the West lacks a kind of moral framework or standpoint, misattributing scientific understandings of fact with speculation about moral value within the modern imaginary. In this way, I believe that discussing the role of outsiders brings forward the subjective Western lens, allowing one to consider and reflect upon the implicit values embedded within a secular-materialist paradigm. The witch archetype has the power to subvert the so-called and false 'logic' of the modern by tapping into something deeper and more essential to the experience of *human-ness* as an embodied essence. This 'essence' is not akin to a totalizing force asserted by hierarchical, materialist thinking, but rather, it is a core power that manifests differently in all. Its essential-ness comes from access to the universal force, the creator, the center of all, as something that we have in common; it lies within or underneath the social conditioning, the stories, the imaginaries of our worlds. In opening up and developing a capacity for direct contact and communication with the more-than-human world, one may become open to a transpersonal experience of interbeing, intimacy and immediacy that, I argue, may bring about a biophilic revolution. It is not so much an acknowledgement of a creator God that is required in this understanding, but a common source of all life, a connecting logic that is beyond human comprehension but that exists nonetheless.

The witch occupies the mythic imagination as someone who can connect with unknown sources of power that emerge from within the body. The archetype could be described as iconoclastic, yet it is also represented as participating in rites with fellow practitioners. In the relations of the witch, we have a model for a new society, a new individuality, elevating the desires of the individual while simultaneously succumbing to the flows of nature. We have the fanciful descriptions of the Witches Sabbat contained in Sprengers (2009/1487) Malleus Maleficarum or *The Hammer of the Witches*, where they gather together to make a paste out of the bones of children and baptismal water. The figure of the witch balances between the precipice of individualism and community but in a way that manifests as dangerous to the status quo of the society in which they reside, her baptism a death, the destruction of the collective social order. She represents a potentially fruitful genesis of power that originates from within individual and exiled group identity. In Said's (2013) notion of the exile, they remain alienated from the social order, becoming protective of their state as one of the only things that they have control over and special claim to. Yet, exile is also identified through the intensity of the love of the place from which they have been ejected. The witch thus exists on the periphery but need not be an outsider; instead, they serve a vital function as a bringer of exalted chaos, of direct confrontation with the mystery of the world and its movements. The figure of the witch can bring change, acting as the midwife to the painful process of third-order transformation. While privileging their position as an outsider, the witch also demonstrates a deep well of caring for the world, demonstrating this through an association with healing as the doula, the sage, the mystic. The coming biophilic revolution need not represent a hatred of human order but may instead embrace a deep love for the state of humanity as a natural emanation of the living world and a fierce protectiveness over the birthing of an interdependent human existence. I use the archetype of the witch as a lens, a fulcrum point. Because the witch engages in both the material and the not-yet-imaginable, they become situated at the gateway between what is and what may be. As such, the archetype suggests the potential to live as an exile, both on the periphery and in connection, capable of looking towards the expanding horizon opening up with each step, into a new flexion of the imaginary.

In the Colony

The dislocation one many feel within the modern state can be, at least partially, understood through Habermas' (1987) apprehension of colonization, which posits that due to the sheer complexity of the human world in which we live, we become inherently colonized by it. Not able to comprehend the machinations of the very worlds that we inhabit, we see no way to interact with, affect, or change our worlds. Thus, we become awash in history as it plays out before us, helpless to act, sure only of our mutual destruction. As such, anyone who confronts this alienation has the potential to become exiled from their own culture, to come to a realization of the State as an 'other,' a force seeking to colonize the self, not an extension of the self (as a nation would be to a citizen). To achieve an embedding of ecological being within culture, we become exiles first by confronting our alienation not only from our culture but from the natural world. Only then can we take our place as observers, and only from this place may we begin to rewrite the narratives of place to resituate humanity into a conscious and realized relationship with the more-than-human. As exiles, we may take upon ourselves the role of the witch, to weave our words into spells, remaking the world.

Taylor's (2004) concept of the social imaginary sees it as the amalgamation of all ways in which a social subject *can* imagine their place within the world. Gibson-Graham (2006) provides a framework for an embodied approach to this through a realization of the immediacy of social relations. While we may feel helpless to engage with something so massive as a state apparatus, we may yet feel empowered to engage with the apparatus as it becomes manifest in the minutiae of our daily interactions. In the imaginary that we co-create together, Gibson-Graham (2006) proposes that we avoid engaging in "weak theory," which relegates the individual to the victim's place, creating a closed-loop for the future that represents the inevitability of failure. They suggest instead a means of embedding in the prefigurative imagination a grounded and momentary relation that is suggestive of the potential for molecular transformation, one that may take hold at the deepest levels of self, which resonates with Buber's I-Thou relation. In Gibson-Graham's view, the immediacy of being has the potential to rewrite the prefigurative imagination to reconstruct the imaginary. Thus, grounding through an interdependent centre, alive in the present moment awareness of independent yet linked selves, one may allow for the undoing of colonial structures of subjugation while also making room for an individual to grow in direct relationship with the world around them, including both human and more-than-human spaces. Reimagining the self thus, becomes a process of remaking the world.

Our stories become the primary material we may use to remake the world through our sense of what it means to be a world and what it means to be a person within the world. In Raphael's (1997) "Call of the Wild," she uses the archetype of the wolf to re-imagine the animality within the human and thus expand the affordances of identity for modern pagans, many of whom have already embraced their place in the world as witches. By embracing the archetype of the wolf, she argues that modern pagans engage in the process of bringing out resonant natural qualities to embody a new norm. In another manifestation of archetype as a transformational fulcrum, Haraway (1990; 2016) speaks about a breakdown of human exceptionalism through the archetype of the cyborg. She argues that the cyborg blends humans and technology and, in so doing, opens the door for the erosion of other boundaries. This semiotic decoupling of definitions between human, more-than-human, and machine may perhaps unmoor the stable ground of meaning and, in other ways begin to approach an embrace of the unknown. In identifying with archetypes of liminality, one looks towards the edge of meaning, where definitions become inadequate, where we can reach towards the potential of a deeper, more just civilization. In embracing the imaginative potential of these semiotic reconfigurations of the human being, we extend our vision into the space of the unknown to call forth higher-order understandings. As one of Lorde's (2018) famous books is titled, "The master's tools will never dismantle the master's house." While we may begin with the tools of Western culture, we must disassemble them and remake them into something radically new. We may use the materials of the master to make new tools, but those tools must emerge from a new logic, a new way of being, coming from a new center.

Davis and Sumara (2007) put forth the idea that all-natural systems, whether brains or anthills or otherwise, coalesce into orders that supersede the capacity of individual units, suggesting that we might wish to remain open to what they call "higher-order unities" (p. 58). These unities, they say, open the way for even more complex forms of order to coalesce. Their concept of the "not yet imaginable" or that which exists beyond the known horizon begins to open up as we feel possible. When we begin to call systemic oppression and repression into question, we inevitably face the pain Bartunek and Moch (1994) say comes from the turbulence of third-order change. Growth inevitably causes discomfort, but it also opens up the potential for a more profound sense of pleasure. It engages with a re-enchantment of the world through an embrace of wildness and chaos. Through the ability to embrace pain as a means of knowing along a spectrum of somatic sense realities, we become attuned to our bodies as integrated brains, organs that make sense of the world, and our interpretations of the world as they manifest in present moment awareness. It is through our bodies that the prefigurative imagination emerges into the light of awareness, and through the investigation of emotion, sensation, and feeling that we may begin to understand the logic that the body proposes, a logic in relation.

The logic of the body, then, brings forth the notion of the erotic, not necessarily within the limited scope of a restrictive Western sensibility but more akin to Bell and Sinclair's (2014) sense of unrestrained eroticism consists of a free flow of pleasure throughout the body. Furthermore, Bennett's (2001) expanded sense of enchantment is described as an embodied experience, putting one into direct engagement with the world. It is this form of Eros, this biophilia, this decentred love of all-that-is that is most relevant to biophilia's revolution. Brown (2019) says, in her work entitled *Pleasure Activism*, that, "Pleasure is a measure of freedom..." that may help us "understand the liberation possible when we collectively orient around pleasure and longing" (p. 3). It may seem contradictory to embrace desire as a means of undoing capitalist-materialist moralistic structures of being. Yet, it is not desires as organized and captured within common sense, but structures of the erotic that emerge as desires within present moment awareness that bring about startling new connections and relationships that emerge from within an awareness of an embodied sense in relationship with the world around us. In this way, our bodies serve as guides for embodied relation with the world and in acceptance of the emerging order from this chaotic genesis, we integrate an ongoing conversation with the more-than-human.

My thesis coalesces around the concept of unleashing the potential of pleasure without shame, creating what we wish in the world, and eschewing repression and other forms of self-denial that hinder the pursuit of collective justice, health, and freedom. The witch archetype contains within it the components of transgression, including revolutionary pleasure, creation, and destruction that may be utilized in tandem to undo systems of oppression as well as to potentially create reality into our own images, images that cater to and suit our humanity, that bring us pleasure and joy, and that lead to a healthy and thriving world, one that does not only exist in orderly creation but that exists in the messy integration of the human spirit within the material world as it continually reinvents itself with each turning of the moon and seasons, to discover and rediscover our meaning through relationships to the sense and sensation of nature.

In Bataille's (1991) concept of general economy, he proposes the idea of the accursed share, which is a representation of all of the excess energy produced by a society. He claims that in an economy, this excess must be spent on either growth or luxury in order to remain productive. Yet, he asserts that growth inevitably reaches a ceiling above which continual expansion becomes impracticable. Thus, the excess must ultimately be spent luxuriously, or else, he claims, repressed energy will be stored up until such a time that it is spent catastrophically in violent and orgiastic rites, such as in war. Thus, if we are to engage with Bataille's form of economy, it would be incumbent upon us to engage in an economy of pleasure, in which we may each individually cultivate a sense of the wild erotic, of biophilia for all life, to avoid the cataclysm of mutual destruction. In essence, to prevent war, we must make love.

Eco-Pedagogy

The concept of pedagogy throughout this piece is grounded in learning as activated through encounters with the world. In transhumanist psychology, which Davis (2003) describes as centred around "nonduality, self-transcendence, and optimal human development and mental health" with its main practices involving "meditation and ritual" (p. 7), I ground the narrative media objects in this study, centred around archetypal stories as part of real human encounters. I believe that the stories we are exposed to become parts of our cultural imaginary; they become rooted within the lifeworld of the individual, telling us what is possible, what we may become and do. I engage in the notion of transcendence within an animist tradition that engages with the material world and the sacred world as one and the same. In this way, transcendence does not become about the emergence above the natural world into a world of perfect unities, but rather, transcendence becomes about emerging into direct relation with a world of potential that manifests in a continually unfolding order that becomes revealed to humanity through present moment awareness. I wield the concept of eco-pedagogy not so much in a moral or ideological sense, but rather by a narrative situatedness within a world in which nature and humankind have become continuous. A sense of transpersonal eco-pedagogy embraces Maslow's (1959) concept of B-cognition, which he says frees a person:

> … from the deficiency problems of growth, and from the neurotic (or infan-
> tile, or fantasy, or unnecessary, or "unreal") problems of life, so that he [sic]
> is able to face, endure and grapple with the "real" problems of life (the in-
> trinsically and ultimately human problems, the unavoidable, the "existential"
> problems to which there is no perfect solution). (p. 24)

B-cognition is a type of thinking that centres around the "essence, or is-ness" (p. 25). Yet, a transpersonal eco-pedagogy is not relegated exclusively to B-cognition; it also engages with D-cognition, name-ly cognition that focuses on separation or needs and drives towards something that isn't in the now. It is on the level of D-cognition that one may engage on the level of the imaginary, in the fantasy world and in the projection of what *could be*, that one may open up affor-dances for B-cognition, for the engagement with the real and for the undoing of unjust, oppressive structures that come from an excess of culture. In the acknowledgement of the immanence of all things, there may be a resolution of the notion of separation between the real and the imaginal, when in fact, all boundaries are temporary and instru-mental. These boundaries are like the silences between notes of mu-sic; they order the world into song, into meaningful storied relations between things. Yet, music is only amusing when it creates a rhythm from which it may then depart, to surprise and delight to the ear, to challenge, awaken and engage the listener.

In the description of ecological relations, I often choose to use Abram's (1996) term, the "more-than-human world," not only as a nod to his work in the field of the somatic experience of nature but also to expand into the vastness of what that phrase encompasses, which operates from a groundwork of interdependence, of human life within a world that encompasses much more than us. In this, there is a reaching towards a state of engagement, an eco-pedagogy which, according to Kahn (2010), is a continuation of Freire's (1990) criti-cal pedagogy, going a step further through the embrace of "biophilia" (Kahn, 2010, p. 18), a love of all life. Thus, its focus is not merely on nurturing justice among people but also *between* people, beings, and senses of the more-than-human world. Thus, inspiring a love of the world and a sense of justice for all beings and things within the world becomes a central motivating force of any eco-pedagogy. It is this focus on the more-than-human that begins to welcome the disparate needs and desires of a world other than us into our own sense of what may and should be. This leads one to the process of forging these connections within the individual to the world at large. My focus on narrative identity grounds itself within this framework of of "third-order change," (Bartunek & Moch, 1994), transcending the schemata of everyday systems into a state of transconceptual awareness in which the unknown may be encountered, and new meanings may spontaneously emerge. Spontaneous new orders are then grounded in "second-order change," which address the structural foundations of culture within the lived moment. If we can change our stories and, more importantly, who we are as individuals within those stories, new concrete relations may emerge forming new positionalities.

Media narratives and archetypes may act as a means of peering into the narrative roots of the human being within a field of interdependence but also in reaching beyond the structural understandings of human beings within a world, looking towards the possible, to create new modes of being never before conceptualized. Narratives, in this view, become a hybridized form of eco-pedagogy, a form of media narrative but also as a philosophical model for human creativity. Hoeschmann and Poyntz (2012) open up critical possibilities for thinking about popular media when they speak about popular media as a form of pedagogy that can serve as a relational medium, one that situates itself in the interstice between a human being and their agency to act upon the world, creating affordances for new ways of thinking, learning, and interacting. Bandura's (1971) social learning theory also advances the notion that an individual's ability to observe behaviour in the outside world, and to represent such behaviour symbolically within the mind, allows for a meta-experience, a means of expanding one's sense of the possible. Thus, an eco-pedagogy represented through media narratives is one that offers us radical exemplars of behaviour and being that may be utilized as learning material, internalized, and applied perhaps to identity or, more importantly, to a process of transpersonal engagement.

A Biophilic Eco-Pedagogy of Immanence

A biophilic eco-pedagogy requires a total recasting of humanity's role within a natural infinitude, not only as an emergent part of nature but as an immanent one. Becoming attuned to one's nature as a manifestation of higher-order unities requires the power to transcend through transgression by grounding down into a more substantial interrelation through and with the living world. As such, narrative and archetypal tools may be used to break through the alienation of the modern to recast the human being within an enchanted world that contains within it infinitude potential for both creation and destruction. Furthermore, the adoption of the witch archetype may offer a roadmap to those seeking a being in contact with a natural flow of power that exists beyond, over, and through human conceptions of power and agency. In embracing the transgressive nature of one who has the potential to access a raw form of power, that is not 'man'-made, therein lies the potential for an autotelic relationship, one that requires nothing else to become, thus grounding into a more profound sense of individuality, and individuality that may birth profound relationships that emerge from a radically de-centered center. Human beings are in the process of being propelled through capitalist-materialist paradigms, spending their energy on the creation of a glut of empty, object-oriented totems. Biophilia allows for a de-centring of pleasure that may then arrive at pleasurable relations in non-hierarchical modes, challenging dominant patriarchal and oppressive forms of social organization and the repression of the free flow of energy or Eros within the social world. This freeing of the flow of erotic sensation may then serve as the basis for an authentic relationship with the immanent coherence of all things.

References

Bandura, A. (1971). *Social learning theory*. Stanford University.

Bartunek, J. M., & Moch, M. K. (1994). Third-order organizational change and the Western mystical tradition. *Journal of Organizational Change Management, 7*(1), 24–41.

Bataille, G. (1991). *The accursed share: An essay on general economy (volume I - consumption)*. Zone Books.

Bell, J. A. (2007). Preventing post-traumatic stress disorder or pathologizing bad memories? *The American Journal of Bioethics, 7*(9), 29–30

Bell, E., & Sinclair, A. (2014). Reclaiming eroticism in the academy. *Organization, 21*(2), 268–280. https://doi.org/10.1177/1350508413493084

Bennett, J. (2001). *The enchantment of modern life: Attachments, Crossings, and Ethics*. https://books.google.ca/books?id=WXtxenlNMXcC

Berman, M. (1982). *All that is solid melts into air: The experience of modernity*. Penguin Books.

Borden, P. (2001). Suburban Placelessness and Identity. *Oriental-OccidentalL Geography, Identity, Space*. ACSA International Conference, New York.

Bourdieu, P. (1977). *Outline of a theory of practice*. Cambridge University Press.

Brown, A. M. (2019). *Pleasure activism: The politics of feeling good*. AK Press.

Buber, M. (2008). *I and Thou*. Howard Books.

Cixous, H. (1986). *The newly born woman*. Univeristy of Minnesota Press.

Csikszentimihliyi, M. (2008). *Flow: The psychology of optimal experience*. Harper Collins.

Davis, B., & Sumara, D. (2007). Complexity science and education: Reconceptualizing the teacher's role in learning. *Interchange: A Quarterly Review of Education*, *38*(1), 53–67.

Davis, J. (2003). An overview of transpersonal psychology. *The Humanistic Psychologist*, *31*(2/3), 6–21.

De Block, A., & Adriaens, P. R. (2013). Pathologizing sexual deviance: A history. *The Journal of Sex Research*, *50*(3/4), 276–298. https://doi.org/10.1080/00224499.2012.738259

Deleuze, G., Guattari, F., & Brinkley, R. (1983). What is a minor literature? *Mississippi Review*, *11*(3), 13–33.

Deleuze, G., & Guattari, F. (1987). *A thousand plateaus: Capitalism and schizophrenia* (B. Massumi, Trans.). University of Minnesota Press.

Deleuze, G. (2001). Pure Immanence: Essays on Life. Zone Books. (Original work published 1965)

Ezzy, D. (1998). Theorizing narrative identity: *The Sociological Quarterly*, *39*(2), 239–252. https://doi.org/10.1111/j.1533-8525.1998.tb00502.x

Forbes, J. D. (2008). Columbus and other cannibals: The wetiko disease of exploitation, imperialism, and terrorism. Rev. ed. Seven Stories Press. Retrieved from https://books.google.ca/books?id=l-BrEuAutGwC&lpg=PA1&pg=PT18#v=onepage&q&f=false

Freire, P. (1990). *Pedagogy of the oppressed* (M. Bergman Ramos, Trans.). Continuum

Gibson-Graham, J. K. (2006). Affects and emotions for a postcapitalist politics. In *A postcapitalist politics* (pp. 40–59). University of Minnesota Press.

Goffman, E. (1961). *Asylums: Essays on the social situation of mental patients and other inmates*. Anchor Books.

Habermas, J. (1987). *The theory of communicative action, lifeworld and system: A critique of functionalist reason* (volume 2; T. McCarthy, Trans.). https://uniteyouthdublin.files.wordpress.com/2015/01/4421-the_theory_of_communicative.pdf

Hall, S. (1986). On postmodernism and articulation: An interview with Stuart Hall (edited by Lawrence Grossberg). *Journal of Communication Inquiry 10(2):* 45–61.

Haraway, D. J. (1990). A manifesto for cyborgs: Science, technology, and socialist feminism in the 1980s. In L. J. Nicholson (Ed.), *Feminism/postmodernism*. Routledge.

Haraway, D. J. (2016). *A cyborg manifesto: Science, technology, and socialist-feminism in the late twentieth century*. University of Minnesota Press.

Heidegger, M. (1953). *Being and time* (J. Strambaugh, Trans.). State University of New York Press.

Hoechsmann, M., & Poyntz, S. R. (2012). *Media literacies: A critical introduction*. Wiley Blackwell.

Jameson, F. (1991). *Postmodernism: Or, the cultural logic of late capitalism*. Duke University Press.

Jung, C. G. (1981.). *The archetypes and the collective unconscious* (H. Read, M. Fordham, & G. Adler, Eds.; R. F. C. Hull, Trans.; 2nd ed., Vol. 9). Routledge.

Kahn, R. V. (2010). Ecopedagogy: An introduction. In *Critical pedagogy, ecoliteracy, and planetary crisis: The ecopedagogy movement* (pp. 1–33). Peter Lang.

Laing, R. D. (1967). *The politics of experience*. Ballantine Books.

Lorde, A. (2018). *The master's tools will never dismantle the master's house*. Penguin Classics.

Luhrmann, T., Padmavati, R., Tharoor, H., & Osei, A. (2015). Differences in voice-hearing experiences of people with psychosis in the USA, India and Ghana: Interview-based study. British Journal of Psychiatry, 206(1), 41-44. doi:10.1192/bjp.bp.113.

Maslow, A. H. (1959). Critique of self-actualization. I. Some dangers of being cognition. *Journal of Individual Psychology*, *15*(1), 24.

Morton, T. (2007). *Ecology without nature: Rethinking environmental aesthetics*. Harvard University Press.

Pettitt, T. (2012). Bracketing the Gutenberg Parenthesis. *Explorations in Media Ecology* 11(2): 95–114

Pupavac, V. (2002). Pathologizing populations and colonizing minds: International psychosocial programs in Kosovo. *Alternatives*, *27*(4), 489–511.

Raphael, M. (1997). Theology, redemption and the call of the wild. *Feminist Theology*, *5*(15), 55–72.

Ricoeur, P. (1983). *Time and narrative* (K. McLaughlin & D. Pellauer, Trans.; Vol. 1). University of Chicago Press.

Robinson, L. & Smith, D. (2021, March 10). A Conversation with Loretta Robinson and Dean Smith. The National Center for Collaboration in Indigenous Education, First Nations University of Canada, Regina, Saskatchewan, Canada. https://www.nccie.ca/wp-content/uploads/2021/02/NCCIE_Virtual-National-Gathering2021.jpg

Said, E. (2013). Reflections on exile. In *Reflections on exile: And other literary and cultural essays* (pp. 180–192).

Sprenger, J. (2009/1487). *The hammer of witches: A complete translation of the malleus Maleficarum* (C. S. Mackay, Trans.). Cambridge University Press.

Strengers, I. (2012). Reclaiming animism. *E-Flux, 36*. https://www.e-flux.com/journal/36/61245/reclaiming-animism/

Taylor, C. (1995). Two theories of modernity. *The Hastings Center Report, 25*(2), 24–33. https://doi.org/10.2307/3562863

Taylor, C. (2004). *Modern social imaginaries.* Duke University Press.

Wagner, D. (1994). Beyond the pathologizing of nonwork: Alternative activities in a street community. *Social Work, 39*(6), 718–727. https://doi.org/10.1093/sw/39.6.718

Winczewski, M. J. (2010). *Consumption, pastiche and identity in postmodern visual culture* [Dissertation, University of Pretoria]. https://doi.org/F10/153/gm

Yates Sexton, J. (2020) *American rule: How a nation conquered the world but failed its people.* Dutton. Retrieved from https://books.google.ca/books?id=dbfNDwAAQBAJ&

Zuboff, S. (2019, November 11). *Shoshana Zuboff: Surveillance capitalism and democracy* [YouTube Video]. Alexander von Humbolt Institut for internet and society. https://youtu.be/fJ0josfRzp4

Chapter 2

Waking in the Dreamtime

Mythic time, immanent identity, and emergent connection

In my childhood, my mother's teachings did not distinguish between human, land, and spirit. I felt spirit everywhere and in everything. Yet, our family didn't have a tradition of stories that would help to fully make sense of this world. So, I became attracted to reading folk tales and mythologies, which spoke of a universe populated with entities, magic, and miraculous transformations. My father always seemed uncomfortable with my interest, making fun of my fascination with spirits, saying, "You know that stuff's not real, right?" He thought it was silly for me to believe in fairies, ridiculous even. The remnants of a once animist Western tradition, spirits of the land, little people, an otherworld that intersected with our own, such beliefs are properly left in childhood. The death of magic is a rite of passage into maturity, letting go of the fantasy of an enchanted world. Mystical beliefs may be seen as nothing more than hopeful wishes, and accepting their unreality is the key to moving from childhood into adulthood, being taken seriously, and becoming a person of dignity whose opinions can be trusted to be valid. Leaving my family home to study in a major city, I left a place that felt outside of time, where spirit felt manifest. Despite my father's stubbornness, a stubbornness that came from a time when his spirit was crushed, my family home felt outside of time, with bobbing lilac bushes grown well beyond their scope and sumacs left to run wild. I could lie awake and listen to the sorrowful calls of the mourning doves as they spoke to each other. There was a pregnant silence in our home, where roving herds of cats and dogs would live parallel lives, bringing chaos and joy and leaving children to roam and discover the world.

The rules of my world had been sparse, just enough to stitch together the people and animals who lived there and little more. Everyone spoke with unguarded sincerity of their deepest thoughts as casually as if that were the only subject matter. When I moved to a major metropolitan city, I felt myself in an alien place, with the natural living systems sidelined for machines, and where the most abject of places, the only wild places left, were rife with neglect. Yet, in the world of dreams, in my imagination, the creator was continually manifest, revealing the mystery that continued to exist in the cracks of civilization, like shepherd's purse growing through the edges of the sidewalk. Through my dreams, the world could come alive again; even in the city, I could imagine the wild nature that once dominated the streets, could feel into the soil where rivers were covered over, send my senses into the pulse of life that expressed itself through starlings flying in spontaneous formations overhead, in marauding raccoons, and at times at the very edge of human awareness, a fox, a coyote, a crane, a woodpecker.

In my imagination and dreams, I became initiated into a world of symbols that would intersect in the pathway between dreams and the world, in the realization of dreams within the world and the world within dreams, a crossroads where denizens could move freely, of animals and people changing shape, telling stories, becoming myths. Yet, even in this embrace of the liminal, there remain separations representing rifts in the flow between body and earth, spirit and mind. The pursuit of continuity, of motion between these states is like islands rising up in the sea of being. To teach myself to embrace my own Indigenous worldview was not simply a matter of welcoming the imaginary evoked by an integrated being straddling the divides between spirit and world. It was and is a matter of living the reality of a world inhabited by the creator (and how he/she/it/they manifest uniquely to each), by spirits of the land, and by relations who take the form of creatures, plants, and trees, clouds, and rain, moon, and sun.

I had not found myself welcomed in the stories of Christianity I learned in elementary school. I had been told that I could not become a holy person because I was a woman and the god of the Bible to me seemed cruel in killing the firstborn sons of the Egyptians. So, I began to look for another story. In my early encounters, in folk encounters with fellow students, teachers, and authorities, I felt a pressure to recognize 'Reality,' that seeing myself in the world around me would soon reveal itself to be a projection, that I would grow out of it. After all, encounters with an enchanted world only happen in stories or the fanciful imaginaries of children before they are brought to the ground of disenchantment by the bitter medicine of maturity. Yet, as Boi (2009) states:

> Many of us may recall how in our childhood the world seemed like an enchanted place, not because anything extraordinary and spectacular happened, not because we felt we were very powerful and could make things happen at will, but because we could feel the pulse of life and mystery of being in every thing and being that surrounded us. (p. 141)

I remain in contact with the resonances within my own childhood that were so potent, resonances of living encounters with the spirit of the world that could only be erased with great effort, an effort to make invisible the sensate reality of such encounters.

The certainty created by a closed universe, one in which the human story has a projected end, serves to condition the engagement of the individual by mapping out the terrain of the possible. It may be said that "the Anthropocene is misguided because it projects human methods for solving problems onto a cosmos that is still not understood" (Weber, 2015, para. 16). Without taking away any of the power or invention of human science, the Universe may still represent a mystery in ways that may not be penetrated by human intelligence, or at the very least, one that has not been. Yet in the act of penetration, in attempting to penetrate this mystery, when one puts bounds on how deeply a human *should* grasp into the essence of reality, it is not necessarily curbing one's curiosity but rather, it is recognizing the limitations and boundaries of nature in its ability to maintain balance. To extract knowledge of the world by prying open its living body, failing to recognize its myriad flows, its lust for existence or its love, I ask, is this an act of enlightenment? We may extend our lives yet through a trail of blood, left behind us with a science that conveniently moves the line of sentience here and there to justify our aims but if the world is full of our relatives if bear and mouse and otter have stories to tell, it is not an aside or an inconvenient fact that we treat their lives as expendable; it is our religion. There must be a capacity to engage through the heart, to empathetically respond to the multiplication of pain within the world as something to be minimized and to which one responds with grief. How do we peer beyond the veil? Do we look through the entrails of beagles, or is there perhaps a visionary apparatus available to humanity that does not require a scalpel? I argue that there is a logic to the mystic's gaze, to the visionary capacity of the mind as it looks at and comprehends a world of relations.

Advances in human knowledge gained during experimentation during wartime (United States Holocaust Memorial Museum, 2009; Kristof, 1995) are commonly seen as exceeding the limits of the expansion of human understanding through the systematic torture of humans in scientific experiments. Our suffering and our pain are real and the breach of limits placed upon the exception of human suffering are unacceptable. Yet, the breach of basic decency, the dignity and life of the living world is beyond consideration, inculcated in systems of exploitation and production. Their destruction is a necessary ill.

Where human intelligence may not reach, one may engage via the more-than-human capacity to reach beyond the body and into the world. Contrary to engaging with the world as an immanent part of it, "The Eurocentered scientific approach commonly entails stripping away what is considered extraneous and isolating what is considered effective. Through this process, science makes Other, or distances in a dissociative maneuver, what is essential for native understandings" (Kremer, 2006, p. 42). The act of study that makes necessary the atomization of systems is an ongoing process that grounds the fragmentation of interrelated systems of being. Macfarlane (2019) asks, "Where does a forest begin and end? Is a mountain made of the rain it draws down from the clouds as well as the bedrock that gives it altitude" (para 8)? In seeking to understand ourselves, or even one-self along the continuum of human existence, one may ask what makes a human distinct? Can a human exist without the forest, without the trees that make the air that fill our lungs, without the sunshine that grows the food that fills our bellies? Where does the line between human beings and the world begin and end?

I was told once by a science-loving friend that it was a duty for the rational mind to penetrate all the sanctums of the world, to know everything, and to leave no mystery unturned. Yet, "When we can *see* the world as a sacred space, then it is most unlikely that we would violate and exploit the world" (Boi, 2009, p. 136). A sacred world is not only a way of seeing but also a way of *being*; it demands acts of reverence towards its objects, even if they *are* objects. In seeing the world as sacred, the meanings of such a world take root in our actions. The sacred is not merely a concept but an operative component in a world machine. In a world without churches, where Forbes (2008) says, "If we tromp on a bug, that is our religion…if we cheat at cards, that is our religion…*All that we do, and are, is our religion*" (p 25-26, italics in original), cutting down trees is our religion, burning fossil fuels is our religion, the empty consumption of mass produced consumer goods is our religion, at least, the religion engrained by our socialization, the religion of a world emptied of spirit, or of anything beyond the human.

Yet this world is not a disenchanted world. We have not lost the sacred but merely shifted it onto a reverence for human invention, for the capacity of the human will to bend nature to its purposes. The question of how to find our way home, home to a living world, to a world in balance, is a journey through the mists, where the guideposts have been either moved or lost. Yet, I believe that this world may be found in the language of our stories and how those stories engage with the latent remembered relationships with the world manifest in childhood as well as in the ancestral connections to the land that were uprooted, even if that happened for some of us thousands of years ago.

In Zimmer Bradley's (1982) novel, *The Mists of Avalon*, she tells an alternative historio-mythology of the Arthurian legend from the perspective of its women. To this day, it is noted for the effect it has had on neo-pagan movements (Paxon, 1999), yet it has been slotted into the fantasy or early sci-fi genre due to its narrative use of magic. Bradley tells a story involving real-world practices of Witchcraft, drawn from her interest in occultist Dion Fortune, as well as her own practices over two decades within various religious, spiritual, and magical traditions from the Rosicrucians to mystic Christianity through the Pre-Gnostic Nicene Christian Church (of which she was a pastor), as well as her own groups the Aquarian Order of the Restoration and a women's group called the Dark Moon Circle (Paxon, 1999). The fantastical elements of the story draw on the potential of a sacred world, a world in which human will emerges from and engages with a universal connective force that is threaded between and through all things. Yet, in the story "the sacred is not a 'counterweight to empiricism,' but ultimately an effect of sustained observation of natural phenomena" (Devlin-Glass, 2008, p. 395). The characters in the story refer to the Priestesses of Avalon—and their counterparts in the Druids—as people who have studied the world and its wisdom, bringing forth that wisdom to share with the people for healing and world-building through their ability to see through the veil of ordinary reality into higher-order realities that merely touch upon human consciousness in moments of spiritual lucidity achieved through personal gnosis as well as the passing on of oral tradition. Kremer (2006) calls Indigenous forms of healing and mysticism "non-Aristotelian, homologic causality, whereby items connected to one another in a relation of underlying consubstantiality are considered capable of acting on one another" (p. 39), which suggests that there is a logic that connects the spiritual and the scientific, traditional and modern. It's just that this logic has been dismissed as superstition, a logic born out of thousands of years of silently observing the world and its pulses.

Sadly, Zimmer Bradley's posthumous character has been darkened by allegations of child abuse and enabling child abuse via her partner Walter Breen, all of which I personally deem as both credible and horrific. It's difficult to come to terms with the people behind these mythic works, works which become a very part of you, attempting to carefully sort the horror from the wonderment inspired by their words. What I have made of this work is something of my own creation, apart from Zimmer Bradley, the reality of which is darkened by her daughter's tale, a daughter who I believe and honour for the bravery to speak her truth. I include this chapter as a discussion of the roots of my magic and myth with acknowledgement of the dark legacy left by the author.

In plain truth, this book changed me, gifting me a source of self understanding at a key time in my development. Now, in full knowledge of what has happened, I can only hope that the spirit of this work, which is not Zimmer Bradley's but my own, may be transported into other better works of fiction, which can more credibly carry forward the traditions and imaginings that she brought forth so imperfectly. Leaving such a complex legacy, of having inspired so many people with the depth of her vision, it is a difficult pill to swallow but one which we much all endeavour to continually take. It is up to us to make the world a more just place and in attempting to do so, we must all face up to the truth.

Perhaps much more can be said about the quality of transformative leadership in a world where power has been so tarnished by control and domination. It is my hope that we may take the examples of the past, both their beauty and their horror, wearing their bones like hats and building with our own hands the firmament of a better, more just and more beautiful world. It is with hope and striving towards this purpose that I write these words, that I may do justice to the victims of harm, to elevate their voices and speak truthfully as I endeavor to come to terms with these events myself.

Being involved in movements inspired by the work of leaders who were in fact predators, is disheartening. When I see the work brought so low—the lowest of the low to prey upon the innocent and vulnerable—I wonder at the brokenness of the world and the potential for true transformative change. And yet, I must continue to hope that as broken and dark as it may seem, that despite all of this, change is still possible. I hope that by including this and other work by problematic figures, who have in all honesty inspired me and pushed me to challenge the injustices around me, who have instigated a passion to build in painstaking ways, new modes of being with the world, that our brokenness—and even our cruelty—may pave the way to a better future. If someone as twisted in viciousness can still envision beauty, the next among us may look at their lives with a clearer vision, one which may take up our power to heal the brokenness that creates monsters. I continue to believe that it is better to reveal the roots of our growth, to look in honesty at the things that have made us, to acknowledge and accept the monstrosity of the worlds we are born from, to truly change our trajectory.

We have been born from both petty and incomprehensible injustices and as such, must be ever vigilant of our own propensity to recreate these systems in our own lives. The monsters aren't only without, but also lurking within. It is in this capacity, that I reflect upon the sources of my inspiration, wondering at the excesses that produce such work, ever yearning for and striving for the means to create transformation without injustice, without manipulation, deceit, egoism, and cruelty. It is perhaps better to think of these figures as the myths that they have become, which hold the collective meaning of our dreams and to be wary of the subtle and overt harms that come from the very real, human, flawed, and at times, monstrous people who exist as flesh behind the myth.

In the perspective of the novel, we see privileged a sense of the Dreamtime or perhaps what might be understood in my tradition as the Astral dimension, a plane of existence that is connected with mundane reality, in constant communication with it using characters as a channel, who are able to interact with it either due to innate ability or by special training. The rules of this world do not merely follow natural laws but laws that embrace the potential for multiple modes of existence to share space without sharing the same dimensions. Avalon represents a dimensional shifting, expressed through the mists that shroud the world of spirits as well as those who are connected with them.

Thus, the material dimension is vulnerable to consciousness. The world is experienced differently by each state of consciousness; time may flow in one way or another depending on the mind-body complex that is feeling it. Yet, when many people feel and are within a particular space, one may also sense that when entering that space, one becomes touched by it. There are resonances left within objects that may be felt, echoes of the object's experiences, and the states that a place has housed. There can be perceived as a feeling of the sacred in a church or of a grove used for circle. At times, when I walk into a ritual space, it hits me like a thick cloud, nearly taking my breath away. Yet, one may not enter *my* world simply because you have to sense the world as I do. The closest that we can get is when you listen to my stories, when I tell you how the world unfolds under my gaze; you can almost feel it as if you were standing in my place. There is a spell cast where the world may reveal a different mask, a different facet to the diamond at its core.

Conversely, when I deny attention to a given sensation, my capacity to feel it diminishes. There is a logic to the denial of sense which Weber (2015) calls a new form of enclosure within the Anthropocene; one meant "To advance narrow human purposes," which he says, "not only seizes control of self-organizing creative forces in nature (e.g., genetic engineering, nanotechnologies)" but that it may also coopt "the self-organizing wild creativity within us" (Weber, 2015, para. 17). A new orthodoxy of negation has created another enclosure, in which the human senses know the world as something concrete, passive, and lifeless. In the enlightenment, when *man*kind throws off the shackles of one repression, therein they fashion themselves another prison. Prison upon prison, opens up to reveal new, larger enclosures, tempting ever towards an elusive freedom. A belief in nothing is a belief all the same. Yet, it seems that the world should be big enough for an infinite number of philosophies, perspectives, and realities.

Yet, in negation, there seems to engender a lack of curiosity in the potential for the sacred. In its somatic sense, this does not require the belief in an outside deity or spirit. Rather, reverence may be expressed as an act of respect for the mystery itself, the world being something worthy of awe. In holding an attitude of the sacred, one may engage with the world as a luminosity, a collection of beings and forces at work on the collective endeavour of being. Yet,

> Now, having left the enchanted universe behind, we disenchanted dwell within the moral and ontological parameters of an 'immanent frame': the world as apprehended through reason and science, bereft of immaterial and unquantifiable forces, structured by the immutable laws of nature and the contingent traditions of human societies. (McCarraher, 2013, para. 4)

This immanent fame suggests materiality empty of spirit, and yet, I suggest a material reality that may be *alive* with spirit. In the rejection of the sacred nature of matter, of life manifest, I see a rejection of the reverential sensation of awe that represents the human incapacity to take in all that the world (and beyond) encompasses. This may be brought on by a lack of exposure to the wild countries that have been untouched by human hands. Simply put, if you never see the Milky Way or the hidden wild terrain of the forest, can you develop an awe and reverence for nature? The first time that I saw the sky from outside of the city, I wondered to myself how people could deny themselves the daily sight of something so beautiful. One need not travel to a distant land; it is there above us when the sky is dark; it is there behind the city lights, at night when humans refuse to accept the darkness. I would welcome that darkness to be able to see the sky, but it is not meant to be, and, living in the city, I must be content with my memories.

The appeal of *The Mists of Avalon*, for me and perhaps for others, is in the unwavering confidence of the sacred viewpoint, of seeing the world through a compassionate and encompassing lens. In the Prologue, Morgaine, a Priestess of Avalon, says,

> For this is the thing the priests do not know, with their One God and One Truth: that there is no such thing as a true tale. Truth has many faces and the truth is like to the old road to Avalon; it depends on your own will and your own thoughts, whither the road will take you. (Zimmer Bradley, 1982, p. x)

There is a reverence in the story for the sacred rights of people to determine truth for themselves, allowing for and embracing a multiplicity of facets to exist side by side. Despite a distaste for the close-mindedness of the Priests, the Druids worship alongside them. While there is a monastery on the Isle of Avalon, the Priests in the story evolve to represent the will towards domination as they serve as a force of colonization in England. They are pitied by those following the old religion as needing to live in a predictable world, in which their limits are known, in which women can be kept as chattel instead of being allowed the sacred gift of the Goddess, to choose their own lovers. In this way, their reality is an enclosure, and, "Enclosure usurps the categories of existence and disparages the concept of aliveness as well as the dimension of experience linked to it" (Weber, 2015, para. 23). Therefore, the worship of the Christians is taken indoors, while the Druids believe that the sacred may not be contained. There is acknowledged a direct experience of the divine that may not be mediated by a particular person, even by the Druids themselves, even as they honour the rights of the Christians to practice in their own way.

Instead of mediating the divine, Druids and Priestesses of the old religion act as messengers of the gods, using their cultivated relationships to understand the way things *might be* in the world and yet not in such a way as to impose their will onto those around them. At the novel's beginning, Merlin and the Priestess of Avalon attempt to convince the Queen Igraine to accept a prophecy. It says that she will have a child by a man other than her husband. The Queen resists this knowledge and they remind her that she has her own will, despite what the Goddess has asked of her and they entreat her to do what she feels is right. Taliesin, the Merlin of Britain, says:

…none can be master of another's conscience. Even if you think it wicked and shameful, would you pretend to know what is right for another? Even the wise cannot know everything, and perhaps the Gods have more purposes than we, in our little knowledge, can see. (Zimmer Bradley, 1982, p. 420)

Morgaine, a priestess of Avalon, also notes that in her duties, her obedience must be tempered by her own will, which is guided by her intuition. It is shown that her inability to listen to her instincts is the inciting incident that leads to the tragic love triangle between Morgaine, Lancelet, and Gwenhwyfar. Morgaine is instructed by her Aunt, the Lady of the Lake and High Priestess of Avalon, to save her virginity for a sacred rite that is to occur between herself and the King. She is to become the vessel for the Goddess in the Great Right, an act of sacred sexual intercourse where the participants embody the sacred aspects of male and female. She might have disobeyed those orders when desiring to be with Lancelet, her young cousin and lifelong love. After spending an idyllic day together, Morgaine could have given way to her passions and when she does not, the potential of their love is ruptured when Lancelet meets young Gwenhwyfar who has lost her way in the marshes. From this day forward, Lancelet becomes tragically tied to Gwenhwyfar, a love that brings misery to everyone involved, as she becomes promised in marriage to his best friend, King Arthur.

Morgaine consistently refers to her desire as something sacred that should be honoured and allowed to take its course and in this moment and others like it, when she ignores her desires due to social conventions, whether Christian or Pagan, it results in pain. While Morgaine consistently attempts to deny the abstractions placed upon her by her world, in denying her desire for Lancelet, she undermines her own unique connection to spirit as well as to the deeper mystery of her own being. It is not her lust she wishes to honour, but a deeper feeling of self abandonment and union with the other in a kind of sacred ritual. When Lancelet and Morgaine finally give in to their passions, Lancelet is not able to give himself up to the act as he is afraid of disgracing her, making her unchaste, tainted. Morgaine finds this to be contemptible, precisely because it makes the act of pleasure into a material act alone, without the deeper personal and spiritual consequence of a true connection made out of love, even if only fleeting. Later, when she makes love to Kevin, the new Merlin after Taliesin, she realizes

This is the first time, really, that I have done this of my free will and had the gift taken simply as it was offered. It healed something in her. Strange, that it could have been so with a man she scarcely knew, and for whom she felt only kindness. (Zimmer Bradley, 1982, p. 417)

It is not simply love, not simply passion, which makes the sexual act sacred, but a free exchange between two consenting individuals who are able to find love and beauty within each other. Kevin the Merlin was horribly deformed by fire during his youth, and Morgaine is often described as little and dark in opposition to Gwenhwyfar's tall, bright beauty. Yet, Morgaine is able to find the beauty in Kevin's eyes, and hands, and music, and for Kevin, Morgaine is the face of the Goddess herself. It is in their sexual exchange, given freely and without shame, that they discover the hidden beauty in the other.

A central theme in this text is the ambiguity of fate and performing the will of the Gods when their reasons and rules are felt rather than documented and known. This is set against the new religion of Christianity, which brings with it established dogmas that allow its followers to understand right from wrong as separate from the felt resonance within each interaction. Zimmer Bradley's (1982) vision of the past is from the perspective of one looking back and perhaps inventing a new beginning to the story, developing untold stories that have been historically excluded. Her writing is a re-enchantment of the world through the lens of a Pagan worldview as well as an imaginary of the Indigenous people of Britain, those who are tied to the land in their worship. Yet, there is also a tacit understanding that the Christianization of the land was not a loss of the spiritual.

Instead, it poses the question, "What if those waters of pecuniary reason constituted a baptismal font, a consecration of capitalism as a covert form of enchantment, all the more beguiling on account of its apparent profanity" (McCarraher, 2013, para. 7)? Christianity in the story—and perhaps by extension, the secular materialism that arose from its ashes—were never able to remake the base matter of humankind, to erase its spiritual core, the symbolizing and storytelling center of human life. Instead, there begins a new story. In the novel, there is a small chapel where nuns worship the Mother Goddess through the Virgin Mary, and as such, there is a sense that the ultimate reality may never be destroyed. And yet, even though the seeds of the sacred may be kept safe, we see advanced the notion that "The discursive spell has thoroughly captivated perception to the point that much of our perception is an abstract conceptual exercise that bypasses the more sensuous experience of perception" (Boi, 2009, p. 143). In the novel, those who accept Christianity as their religion must continually subvert their sensual impulses for the sake of moral purity as it has been expressed to them through rote instruction. This contrasts with purity as expressed by Morgaine, which is honoured through deeply felt moral impulses that emerge from within.

The discursive morality of the colonizer is one that supersedes the individual felt notions to create a moral superstructure to which all wills must bend. In this structuring of reality, one may create or recreate a world that also upholds other matrices of power, such as the coming of Patriarchal domination as represented through Church doctrine in the novel. For, it may be known that "how the world appears to us has all to do with the state of our consciousness or the quality of our being. In the same way that, to a tired person, the world looks tired and tiring, to a disenchanted person, the world appears disenchanted and inanimate" (Boi, 2009, p. 138). Whether the world is or is not disenchanted, whether women are sacred or evil, depends very much on one's perspective. So, it may follow that perspective advocated by force may create a lens through which one perceives the world, even dictating affordances for how one may understand their own sensations. An act of re-enchantment is less an action that needs to be performed than the recognition of an erasure; it is not an act of will but of memory. As McCarrahe (2013) states, "The world does not need to be re-enchanted; its enduring and ineradicable enchantment requires our belated recognition and reverence" (para. 9). The enchantment of the world lays dormant, a latent potential to be recognized within even the mundanity of contemporary life. There is enchantment in the world to one who has the eyes to see.

The narrative presented in The Mists of Avalon is complicated by its situatedness across genres with respect to its categorization as an otherworldly text that is simultaneously informed by real-world experiences. How may a text be understood when the elements of magic and spirituality are grounded in real-world beliefs and practices? How does one resolve the tensions existing between representations of reality? Faris (2004) says that "magical realism modifies the conventions of realism based on empirical evidence, incorporating other kinds of perception. In other words, the narrative is 'defocalized' because it seems to come from two radically different perspectives at once" (Faris, 2004, p. 43). So, a magical realist text puts the reader on shaky ground, where the stability of what is, is called into question. In *The Mists of Avalon*, there is an overt privileging of these perspectives, which encapsulate different potentials of *what is*. With Avalon grounded as the center of power, other radical potentials become activated due to the perspectives and practices of the Priestesses. Their wielding of will and discipline as tools allow them to channel otherworldly forces for divine purposes. There is the potential for magic to occur in the world because their world is constructed to house it, and their beliefs and practices bring about their connection to that potential. Camelot, in contrast, represents a narrowing of worlds, a world that operates by different, more coherent, and more controllable rules. It is a Christian world, a discursive world, a world that may be captured and held by humankind. Faris says of the blending of mundane and magical that "these two modes of realism and fantasy often reflect the presence of different belief systems, which question post-Enlightenment categories of fact and fantasy" (Faris, 2004, p. 48). If I experience things that exist outside of my understanding or of what is deemed to be possible within a post-god, rationalist, empirical paradigm, I am not simply mad. Possibilities of sense are evoked or else repressed by the paradigms that categorize the possible.

Kohn (2013) suggests that there is a "living semiotic dynamic" (p. 16) within the world that suggests that meanings may emerge from within the relations themselves. Magic may be colloquially understood as a pressure release through imaginative processes of wish-fulfillment, whereas in the eyes of practitioners, it is as a praxis of engaging with semiotic curiosity. The relations of the world may be brought to life through one's relation with them, exploring and unpacking the possibilities of the mystery in a process that spills over the human empirical grasp, instead hovering at the edges of one's perception, never becoming fully transparent or opaque, simply suggesting potential connections within an ineffable patterning under the eye of the Creator. By weaving a fantastic world grounded within the possible, *The Mists of Avalon*

...combines the realism and surrealism of European origin with indigenous beliefs and practices–or at least the memory or the fantasy of them–and can be seen to be concerned with metaphorically rising up, with powers of the imagination not grounded in sensory data, perhaps even with the escape from written archives. (Faris, 2004, p. 58)

The only modification I would make to this statement is that there is a required kind of sensory leap in the remembrance of enchantment when one has been habituated to a world in which incredible things do not happen and where the imagination is a separate organ from the other sensory faculties. One must begin to engage with the world with the question of what if, to seek out and find the sensory data that would serve as the basis for a new ground for potential. There is sense and sensory data in the practice of magic, just as there is in the worship of gods. I am not simply mentalizing my world; rather, I am teasing out the somatic presence of *something* that I language into form within my own semiotic scaffolding. I call it magic because magic is an excellent word; it conjures the mystery within the world better than other words could. God might be a good word because it feels so vast, but for others, the concept is relegated to something quite limited, a Judeo-Christian framework that holds god within the hands of *man*-kind, and so it will not do. For some, it is Universe, for some Goddess, for others, it is not fit to name at all. Yet there is something described by the words that is not the words, a feeling, a sense, that may become woven into a tapestry of living relationships, evoking wonder at the mystery and grandeur of the world.

To begin this work is to loosen the semiotic mooring within a constant and stable world and to invite in the shifting and dynamic potentials of unknown relations, living within the question as a matter of course. The word then becomes a declaration of potential, an act of repair that brings forth a reality in which semiotic connections create new networks for being and action. As such, "acts of magical speech are the highest form of healing" (Kremer, 2006, p. 29), and thus magical narratives serve to conjure "a narrative space that we might call the 'ineffable in-between'" (Faris, 2004, p. 46), which invokes an important aspect, namely, a comfort in existing within an unknown which allows for spontaneous new connections to form. Reading these kinds of narratives has the potential to open up one's perception to potentials beyond the rational, to connections that may be formed based upon heretofore uncategorized somatic data, collecting those experiences and elevating them to the level of attention that might allow for the full scope of one's experience to become engaged. In the creation of a liminal narrative, there is "a special kind of defamiliarization, not only with respect to familiar events and images but with respect to habitual realistic narrative referentiality, knowledge, and authority" (Faris, 200, p. 50). In questioning the concreteness of the real and with it, the ability for empiricism to enclose the somatic experiences of reality, one begins to break down categorizations that become enclosures of experience, engaging instead in immediate relations of sense.

The Desiring Body as Dream-site

The body serves as a focus within all this, as the prism through which the sensory material of the world flows (Witteman, 2021). The material of the senses provides the basis by which one may read the text of the world as it is encountered by the body. Thus the body is like an encryption key for the world; it becomes activated and particularized within the encounter as at the moment of encounter two objects within the world become relations. Thus, one's:

> Philosophy has to do not only with the human future, but with the cosmic future and with the destiny of the entire universe. We are not only actors and spectators of the *Divine Commedia*. We are also authors of it—co-authors... (Panikkar, 1992, p. 243)

Encounters with the world provide sensations that may then be read as texts, and it is how those texts narrativize sensation that co-writes the world. Desire is such a central somatic experience, that the practices of Witchcraft and the narratives of *The Mists of Avalon* center it as the locus of human drama, the site upon which the sensing animal seeks to assert themselves within the world, to find or to make something that was missing in the physical but not the mental. In this case, desire then is the pursuit of one's internal guidance to manifest the world as it *should* be or even only as it *might* be. To unloose a felt potential craving emergence.

In the novel, there is a repeating motif of the archetype of a young stag killing the elder once the elder has come to the end of his powers. Through this is expressed the given order of things, asserting the ultimate supremacy of the life over will. There is an attempt to organize and accept this limit through a ritual called the 'Kingmaking,' wherein a young successor to the crown must kill a stag, nude, with only a small blade, in hand-to-hand combat. In another ritual, Morgaine uses her magic to inhabit the body of a wild sow, mother to a brood of piglets. In the scene, her mate is killed by hunters. The sow accepts his death as a matter of course, yet is driven to fight back through protective instinct towards her offspring. Morgaine is forced to live through the death of the sow, becoming delirious and sickened by the experience. These rituals bring to the fore the natural way of things as they are encountered and storied, in the way that "Such encounters with other kinds of beings force us to recognize the fact that is seeing, representing, and perhaps knowing, even thinking, are not exclusively human affairs" (Kohn, 2013, p. 1).

The animals within the novel are capable of agency, yet they are also storied as being in harmony with *what is*, which is explained not as passivity but as a simple acquiescence to life and its ways. By overlaying the animal's narratives of the world onto the highest echelons of power (via the ritual of the Kingmaking), the social world within the novel attempts to intertwine the sensuous reality of the animal body into the cultural space of human relations. Humans are continually brought to face their animal nature and it is this which is presented as a sacred act through the elevation of ritual. The ritual is what stories the natural world in accord with the human body, the human life cycle, and the tides of power that ebb and flow with the health and vitality of the body, and the imaginary as populated by the spirit. In the cyclical narration of human animality:

> Peace does not mean an idyllic or idealistic view of total passivity or the static idea of Life, as if positive and negative metabolisms were not required. The animal does not 'kill,' but it eats. Man does not exploit when following Nature, it grows and evolves. The chain of being or the wheel of existence is a living thing. There is exchange, there is death. But there is also resurrection. (Panikkar, 1992, p. 244)

The passive acceptance of animal agency encapsulates a narrative in which eating and being eaten are part of the story. Death may be narrativized as tragedy just as it may become a natural flow, an end without end, a transformation of the material body into the earth, and an escape of the spiritual in the form of energy being released.

Within and beneath the cycles of life, death, and resurrection is the symbol of the Holy Grail, an ontological bundle in which life and death become merged in the sense of a non-dual, ultimate reality. When one touches the grail, one is instantly killed but in such a way that one's body is transformed into a luminous object with the face taking on a mask of perfect beneficence. It suggests that within the materiality of the body "is simply an organization of layers of luminosity (or a cluster of awarenesses or feelings)" (Kawin, 1982, p. 87). Encounters with the grail evoke deep somatic experiences. A coalition gathered under King Arthur witnessed a manifestation of the grail during a feast. When they see it, each person tastes a perfect meal, and smells something that evokes a positive memory. They see a vision of divinity that captures their own notions of the divine and yet, these visions are brought about by the Priestess Morgaine, dressed in the disguise of a peasant. This momentary energy opens a space for divinity to manifest, in which a miracle takes place. It is because of her training and because of the training of Raven, her fellow Priestess, that they may channel this energy for those who were present to witness. Morgaine is an earthly presence; her physicality is always referred to like darker, like the 'little people' or tribespeople. Yet, her role as a conduit for the Holy Chalice signifies a doubling that may be made singular. For, "when soul goes, soil goes, and what connects soil to soul is, most prominently and not exclusively, the sole of feet that make contact with the ground" (Boi, 2009, p. 146). It is precisely because of her groundedness that she is able to harness the energy of the divine. When she rediscovers her role as Priestess after a period of spiritual disconnection, she begins the procession to power by counting the days between the solstices and equinoxes until their rhythm becomes embedded within her body/consciousness.

Grounding down into the body is not a process of devaluing the mind, but rather occurs in reaction to an erasure of the body. Boi (2009) states that:

> When mind, or the mental faculty, is defined as the essence and perfection of humanity, it becomes therefore its most valuable possession. If matter is what mind is not, and mind is the only thing that has intrinsic value, then matter is just a stuff that has no intrinsic value and therefore has only instrumental value. (Boi, 2009, p. 137)

Thus, a privileging of mentation also diminishes matter while simultaneously materializing the world and its relations. The mind may make static objects out of moving relations precisely because it holds them within its inner world, outside of time, removing any potential for co-evolution. While the objects remain outside of the self, the mentalized object exists within. A mentalized object may be dominated and controlled in a way that remains impossible within the relation. The relation requires a bodily engagement that responds to and pays attention to an object or being, allowing the mind to respond to an evolutionary dynamic. Thus, in an attempt to capture and comprehend the mysteries of an Indigenous worldview, there is colonialism to the mentalization of these relations rather than as an encounter, which asks something of the individual to engage directly, to suspend oneself in the engagement. To learn how to comprehend an enchanted world, it is required to invoke one's remembrance of enchantment and thus to become it again, in recognition that "Psychologizing spirit amounts to the appropriation and containment of Eurasian [or other Indigenous] ancestries" (Kremer, 2006, p. 37). Thus, we must be cautious against the enclosure of the spiritual dimension within a paradigm that mentalizes objects in order to dominate them within the terrain of the imaginary.

One may understand enclosure to occur "through a type of thinking that ignores creative processes and the meanings of emotions, both of which originate in the body" (Weber, 2015, para. 24) and thus, may comprehend a pivotal aspect of the colonial to be the denial of the body and its logics. In the pursuit of an ecological attitude, Boi (2009) suggests that "the most destructive kind of crime is not the crime of passion but of *psychic numbing*" (p. 135). This is the struggle that must be engaged, to set the body into motion, to engage with the symbolic or narrative order of the world through a conscious experience of one's feelings. Stories bring meaning and may inscribe meaning upon the spontaneous luminosities of the body, but they may also suppress it. There may be no set truth that does not require balancing in its opposite. The body and the mind must speak to one other, none achieving supremacy. The storying of the world is continual, taking place in dynamic relation with the body. It can be seen in the Zimmer-Bradley's (1982) novel that

When reality is heavily mediated by the symbolic and discursive order, we lose, however momentarily or minutely, the sense of Being, or Reality—that intensively 'real,' vivid, existential feel of being alive and seeing everything to be throbbingly alive. (Boi, 2009, p. 142)

In the novel, we may see the enclosure of the embodied senses by the symbolic order in the women's denial of the sensual desires through the character of Lacelet, who is almost supernaturally handsome, graceful, and noble. Both Gwynhwyfar and Morgaine desire Lancelet and both deny these desires due to their obligations under two opposing symbolic systems, one of the Goddess and one of the God. In each, the women are asked to deny their bodies in order to fulfill a requirement of the given spiritual order. If any would have honoured their internal sensual wisdom, they might have altered their fate and brought about love in all its dimensions. In the denial not of lust but of a deeper and more lively form of embodied desire, they allow the supremacy of the discursive to win over the felt sensuous reality of their embodiment. One can see here, "The totality of one's being is a relationship between the organized self (tonal) and the indescribable colony of awarenesses (nagual)" (Kawin, 1982, p. 89), which is the crossroads that the individual must continually mediate, ever storying into relation the past, present, and future.

It is precisely at this crossroads that we encounter the immanent self, the self which becomes constituted by relations as, "Our identities arise through that which we are not: through impressions and touch, through sensory exchanges with that which is stone and water, molecule and light quantum, all of which somehow transform themselves into the energy of the body" (Weber, 2015, para. 2). It is at the limits of the body that the identity becomes constituted through relationships with the other, which throws into contrast that which I am not. In reading a text, there is the potential to prepare an individual for this relation by instigating reflections brought on by the text itself. Kawin (1982) suggests that, "A text's awareness of systemic limitation can engage the reader's sympathetic identification and stimulate an investigation into how his or her [sic] system understands what is within and without itself" (Kawin, 1982, p. 82), and the primary investigation thus, becomes the engagement of a body within a world, a mortal world in which there is a continuum of life and death, birth and renewal. Such an engagement becomes key, for "No ecological renewal of the world will ever succeed until and unless we consider the Earth as our own Body and the body as our own Self" (Panikkar, 1992, p. 244). Where is the line between mountain, hills, and forest, between life and death? There are no limits in the world except sketches and luminosities, collections of collaborative molecules working towards an end, but even so, those same molecules become soil, move into the air, and are born again into new configurations, again and again.

Materiality and the Dreamtime

The Mists of Avalon is approached by many as a sacred text, supported by the notion that Zimmer Bradley was later harangued by fans, hoping for her to become their personal priestess (Paxton, 1999). Reading the book instigated me to tattoo a crescent moon on my forehead at the age of 23, a sacred contract that I made with myself at the end of a problematic relationship. As such, the text stands as something that people may draw into the world, in and through the spell woven by Zimmer-Bradley's words. It becomes a praxis, a tone that may be felt through, brought into the body and thus into an embodied relation. Through the novel, I felt "...a dimension of freedom and infinitude which impregnates both matter and spirit, the senses and the intellect, the *aesthesis* and the *noesis*" (Panikkar, 1992, p. 245). The sensibilities of the novel create a certain state of mind, which may be taken up as a kind of prayer. I asked myself, what if I could transform the sensibility of the book and adopt it as an aspect of my own sensibility, to own the ineffable perspective of the Priestesses and draw it down, aspect it (as we say, to invoke a being of power into the body), to make it a part of my lived reality? I would say that this form of reading might be called a sacralised reading of a text to elevate the narrative to the level of symbolic, ritualized, liminal dimension, one that imbues the text with a spiritual significance. This is the means by which I have read all of the texts within this book as *sacralised, mythic* texts, sacred precisely because I have made them sacred by finding the sacred within them.

The perspective conveyed by a re-mythologizing of the Camelot tale is a romantic one, to say the least. It is a tale of knights and nobility, beauty, glamour, and generous reading of pastoral countryside. Yet, one might mistake romantic sentiments with a lack of weightiness, a lack of true grounding. Yet, "Conveyed in a poetic rather than a theological idiom, Romantic ontology envisioned a reality that both transcended and pervaded the sensible world" (McCarraher, 2013, para. 31). The elevated emotionality of a romantic text is one that embraces the more-than-rational world, one in which "...the enemy was not reason *per se*, but rather what Blake cursed as 'single vision': the occlusion of the sacramental sight, the options of mastery and exploitation, the inability to see the world as anything more than material resources" (McCarraher, 2013, para. 31). In a romantic vision, the world may carry within it the emotional resonance that is derived from a personal relationship with it. The landscape does not only serve as the site wherein material resources are found but is valued for the aesthetic pleasure one may derive from its vistas, for the beings one meets within it. Thus, it is a personal relationship with the world which gives rise to a romantic sensibility. It may be that "the very metaphors we use to describe our role in the world are inadequate" (Weber, 2015, para. 8) and thus, there is a requirement that we expand the ontological human narrative object into something more, perhaps something beyond the grasp of the noesis or the discursive mode. In personalizing our worlds, we also open ourselves to the radical possibilities of recontextualizing our own place within them.

In adopting an imaginary that may encompass new frames for being and time, there is laid the foundation for new forms of being and time to be experienced within the lived relations of the moment. Where "the Dreaming is a cosmology 'without me' or, perhaps better, 'outside of time' (as we know it)" (Goddard & Wierzbicka, 2015, p. 46), there is a sense that there is a world that exists beyond, or as I see it, over top of this one. This other world is a mythic dimension wherein the normal laws of matter do not apply. As such, the imaginary may be considered an actual landscape wherein relations with the world may become modelled and carried out, where journeys may be taken and where real physical effects may be felt. This is something that requires a blurring of the distinction between imaginary and real. The astral is a name given in circle to the way the imagination touches upon the world. It is considered as an actual place without being an actual place. It is a time without having time. Things may happen there without happening, but they can also have real and lasting effects on the 'Real' world. There is no firm line between the astral and the material, and in a circle, we talk about drawing back the veil. In ritual, the tenuous boundary between material and mythic is made thin so that those within the circle may engage in mythic space/time, to interact with the imaginary as brought into the world, through systems of symbolism and emotional resonance. The self which works in the circle "…is not so much constructed as affirmed and confirmed during initiations; it is the rigorous confirmation of something that has been in the process of construction" (Kremer, 2006, p. 36). The self is made, unmade, and remade again and again. There is a continual sense of birth and rebirth, of transformation. Just as the seasons transform and come back again to a new iteration of the cycle, so too would we come together in a circle as both the same and new. It is something that would keep us in contact with the world and its rhythms, just a Morgaine would count the days between solstice and equinox, so too would we draw the procession of the seasons into our bodies through ritual and trance states brought about by dance and music. It is the continual reinvestment in this connection that would constitute a link to the sacred in my own practice. I recognize as Kohn (2013) states that:

> There are many kinds and scales of death. There are many ways of being pulled out of relation and many occasions where we turn a blind eye to and even kill relation. There are, in short, many modalities of disenchantment. At times the horror of this everyday fact of our existence bursts into our lives and thus becomes a difficulty of reality. At others it is simply ignored. (Kohn, 2013, p. 18)

This form of disenchantment feels like something which must be continually resisted through positive acts of reaffirmation of a sacred reality. If one lives in a disenchanted world through the minutiae of life, in the simple everyday acts of existence, this will be one's worship, one's church. Only in living in a sacred world in the everyday, can that world be consistently affirmed. Boi (2009) states that "there is an essential connection between psychic numbing and the kind of numb indifference that is destructive to the world" (p. 135). Enacting the sacred is also resisting the desire to numb the physical senses in response to the absolutely stultifying intensity of global environmental destruction. The pollution in the city causes me physical pain on a daily basis, but the only alternative is to give in to the desire to block out the real world and its potential. Ritual gnosis allows me to continually ground and re-ground my responses to my world, continually striving to engage with the world as a sacred space in a revolutionary act of creation. One may see reflected in the Romantic sensibility that imagination is "…the most perspicuous form of a *vision*–the ability to see what is really there, behind the illusion or obscurity produced by our will to dissect and dominate" (McCarraher, 2013, para. 33).

The imagination serves as a vital tool in the struggle against the tide of a deadening philosophy, to construct and maintain a posture, a space, and liminality that allows for embodied relations to emerge from within even the depths of the metropolis. We might accept that "the qualities that would elicit and evoke our feelings of gratitude, respect, or even reverence, fondness, care, sympathy, and so on, do not belong to, are not part of, the objects themselves." (Boi, 2009, p. 137), they are instead a part of the way we engage with the world. This is the posture whereby we come to an enchanted world, one in which we first allow for the possibility of enchantment to act upon us through our lived relations. One may see as Devlin-Glass (2008) suggests:

> *Vital* organisms and phenomena in the natural world (e.g., plants, animals, rocks, weather phenomena) may be reclassified at will (usually by negotiation) and according to circumstance as *supervital* (having sacred power) if named as such, or if they have a proper name applied to them. The semiotic charge of such organisms/phenomena may oscillate between the 'vital' and the 'supervital,' but the two states are always folded within each other rather than functioning as binaries. (p. 395)

The sacred is a perspective that may be initiated at will, and the effects may then be felt within the relation. In the lived momentary instances of sacred interaction, "…mythological meanings are embedded in the mundane and everyday real, and…this process involves continuous renegotiation" (Devlin-Glass, 2008, p. 393). Within an Indigenous or mythic worldview (as in my own footing within both an Indigenous worldviews and practices of witchcraft), the sacred world is not comprised of a network of ossified symbols but rather *supervital* forces which may act upon the self just as they are acted upon or understood. The cultivation of special states of attention becomes an integral aspect in this evocation of the sacred, enchanted world. For example:

> The nagual is a reflection of a paradoxical and all, including a category that also exists in the universe. The only way to deal with the nagual is to top or enter or synchronize with it, in some cases by tapping or entering or entering or synchronizing with the nagual that appears to be inside oneself–the *will* or arational center. (Kawin, 1982, p. 85)

The power of transformation confronts the rational, threading through the arational like a golden filament. Sense doesn't always touch every moment, but like a boat, it ferries one across the waters of the nagual, sensual dimension to make enough reason, to develop a tenuous thread of sense that draws one forward and through the world. It is this thread that serves to tie one in continuity of experience, and yet it is not a concrete ground but a tether. The ground itself is not ground at all but an unknown and unknowable ocean upon which we attempt to navigate. This ocean is a living organism; to me, it is Creator and to me, "To say all is alive is not to affirm that all is of one stuff or all alike. It affirms the moving, free, precisely living relationship to every brim of Reality" (Panikkar, 1992, p. 243). The Creator as such, is more than I could ever express, not a being but the essence of all energy, of what may be understood to be the body of Creator as a moving force, like an ocean, alive in change.

To step into this new reality is an act of initiation. One may not simply enact such a change as Kawin (1982) states:

> The verbal self cannot wake itself up (end the dream from within) any more than analysis can lead to an intuitive breakthrough. The intuition happens on its own; the higher self chooses, autonomously, to step forward. The minds only option is to step out of the way, to create a vacuum for the higher self to fill. Until that happens, 'waking up' is only another event within the dream. (Kawin, p. 134)

One may see the dream as either the imaginary or the real, or perhaps both at once. Awaking from the dream of commodity fetishism to a deeper dimension of interrelational significance is not the difference between being asleep or being awake. Instead, it is remembering that the everything is a dream, dreams, and reality become one and the other in a never-ending process of transformation.

Dreams as Resistance

In *The Mists of Avalon*, Avalon is on an island that is becoming increasingly overrun by the mists, a surreal condition that removes the island from mundane space/time. In the story, the realm of the fairies was carried away from connection with the mundane world so that days in their world become years within the human world. Much in the same way, the symbolic ground of Avalon cannot exist in the same space/time as Camelot, which does not mean that it ceases to exist, but merely becomes obscured by the inability to perceive it—except during instances of exceptional perception where the mists become penetrable. We may see in the mists the notion that "Every physical enclosure of wild and emotionally unbridled reality can be traced back to this separation of living entities from the living context of which they are a part—a separation that neutralizes the generative power of life itself" (Weber, 2015, para. 19). Avalon is the living spirit of their Goddess as manifest in the world. Through the ideological enclosure of women via the patriarchy, the world that Avalon represents, the unbridled wild feminine, becomes subsumed. Thus, with the birth of a religion contained within a book, where the churches are walled in, we have a systematization of the world, where the authority of the priest supersedes the felt, intuitive wisdom of the individual.

On what one may call a continuum, in contemporary society, we face the "Complete monetization of the world and our lives," which may be said to spell "the ultimate reification. That people should almost imperceptibly lose their health, happiness, relationships, friendships, connections with the land, and even their actual lives, for the gain of money should tell us just how thickly the spell of the discursive has been cast over us" (Boi, 2009, p. 142). 'Spell' is a good word to use here because it is not as though our world lacks enchantment but rather, we are not able to see that enchantment for what it is. The spell cast by visions of material wealth reaches towards the level of a suicide cult, bringing the entire globe to the brink of utter annihilation for its sake. Thus, "If the proletariat is thoroughly permeated by pecuniary enchantment, why would the oppressed ever desire the transcendence of alienation and servility" (McCarraher, 2013, para. 21)? It thus becomes important that people do not realize that their reality is a spell. If one were to realize the spell of the contemporary world, one might break it, or cast a spell of one's own, to remake the world in one's own image.

Weber (2015) argues "that reality, from which we are descended and through which we experience and engender ourselves, is itself a commons that must be understood and connected to as such" (para. 10). Each individual must remember that the world is enchanted, awakening from one dream into another, one spell into another deeper spell. In discussing the mystical traditions of Eurasia, Kremer (2006) notes that "the völva in Völuspá is raised with spirits in such intensity and to such depths that she sees through time and remembers the beginnings of things, the center of her traditions (the tree of fate)" (p. 36). The völva may be understood to be another word for witch and/or shaman, as each tradition has a word to describe these practices, which are particular to the tradition itself. The witch, thus, has the ability to know things about the world in a different way, one that is continuous with a mythic tradition that becomes entwined between and in both inner and outer worlds. The world becomes more than a "regressive repository for nativist truths or buried treasures; it is volatile, and commotion causing" as Macfarlane (2019) states, instead the land "bristles'; it morphs and causes metamorphosis" (para. 13). The narrative text of the novel is not one thing and the reader of the novel another. The words, the body, and the land are one, and they interpolate one another, causing shifts, disruptions, and ruptures. Thus a novel in which magic operates might be seen to carry, as Slemen (1995) states, "a residuum of resistance toward the imperial center and to its totalizing systems of generic classification," which recognizes that "Established systems of generic classification are complicit with a centralizing impulse in imperial culture." (p. 408). The revolutionary act is in taking apart the sense of imperialism to suggest radical new possibilities for action and imagination. We are caught in a torrent of history where people and human activities become equated with material accumulation, human life robbed of its humanity, with people being given the roles of labourer and consumer through "the construction of a gorgeous symbolic universe of advertising, marketing and entertainment, the arsenal of what Graeber has characterized as capital's 'war on the imagination" (as cited in McCarraher, 2013, para. 23). It is a process of immense effort to keep the public enthralled by the spell of the material devoid of spirit, for spirit is often felt, unbidden, and freely roaming within the hearts of humankind, elicited by the sky, by the folds of the landscape stretching out to the horizon, by the vast ocean, by the sunrise.

Entering into a process of re-enchantment is remembering—where one enters into "an ontology of relations that is at the same time existential, economic and ecological. It emphasizes a process of transformation and identity formation that arises out of a mutuality that is not only material, but also experienced" (Weber, 2015, para. 12). It is not merely imaginary or embodied but a breaking down of the barriers between, where one may begin to experience the self-made world that reflects and acts upon the emotional body, the embodied psyche, to make a living relationship. We may begin, as Boi (2009) suggests, to "not compromise and destroy children's native capacity for participatory consciousness—some call it the 'aboriginal mind'—by forcing on them early, in the name of modern science education or progressive education, the mechanical worldview that objectifies the world and sees it in mechanistic and quantitative terms" (p. 146). If we never forget our connection, we will not need to remember it again, instead striving to contextualize and understand it as it develops throughout the course of our lives.

In this, a collective vision may be developed as Kramer (2006) suggests, an approach to healing via the imbalances of the world, to approach the rifts in the world's fabric to re-establish wholeness on all levels. Thus, the holism of the world may be taken into account, dealing with all fractures at the sites in which they occur, a fractal, a spiral, a continuous thread of cracks that may be touched by human hands and brought back into alignment.

Real Magic

When we have a novel like *The Mists of Avalon*, we may be tempted to place upon it a bias that trivializes magic as a lower form of religious practice (Devlin-Glass, 2008). Yet, the sacred knowledge of magic in the story captures the logic of magic as a real system, albeit in an imaginary fashion. Its realistic elements engage the reader into a temptation, a temptation to see that the world is, in fact, enchanted. It may be that the loss of the sacred has erased the potential of human inventions in labour, art, and science to serve as methods of contact (McCarraher, 2013). In recognition of a chaotic unity, one may also recognize the constituent reality that "spirit is everywhere, spirituality is everywhere, everything is spiritual. Everything is immanent; the spirit is immanent, not separate or transcendent (immanence and transcendence are more like poles on a scale with many thick and thin places of connection in between)" (Kremer, 2006, p. 39). There is no away, no out; it is all here, creator, god, goddess, spirit, human. To become present in this reality is to open up to latent potentials that have become subsumed by an overarching reality in denial of their potential. As Boi (2009) suggests, "It is when we are fully and completely present in the moment to the phenomenal-material world that we are able to tap into what may be called the psycho-physical energy of the universe" (Boi, 2009, p. 143). We all have the potential to tap into vast resources, resources of wisdom, and connection. There is no separation between the self and the world; in fact, the world permeates our being at its deepest dimensions. As we are immanent, we are a part of the world, never able to separate from it, emergent as children of the world, returning to it when we die. In opening our eyes to the world, we may see that "the root of the violence wrought upon the planet lies in an ontological blindness" and that "our capacity to act well relies on our capacity to see what is really there" (McCarraher, 2013, para. 45). In this, I contend that magic is not something beyond the world to be seen as a supernatural force. Rather, in recognition of the power latent within every moment, magic is an act of reaching out to grasp it.

References

Boi, H. (2009). Reanimating the Universe: Environmental education and philosophical animism. In *Fields of green: Restorying culture, environment, education* (pp. 135–151). Hampton Press.

Bollier, D. (2020, January 29). *The New Animism and Commoning*. Resilience. https://www.resilience.org/stories/2020-01-29/the-new-animism-and-commoning/

Devlin-Glass, F. (2008). A politics of the dreamtime: Destructive and regenerative rainbows in Alexis Wright's Carpentaria. *Australian Literary Studies*, *23*(4), 392–407.

Dreams_and_visions_in_initiati.PDF. (n.d.).

Faris, W. B. (2004). *Ordinary enchantments: Magical realism and the remystification of narrative*. Vanderbilt University Press.

Forbes, J. D. (2008). Columbus and other cannibals: The wetiko disease of exploitation, imperialism, and terrorism. Rev. ed. Seven Stories Press.

Goddard, C., & Wierzbicka, A. (2015). What does Jukurrpa ('Dreamtime', 'the Dreaming') mean? A semantic and conceptual journey of discovery. *Australian Aboriginal Studies*, *2015*(1), 23.

Kawin, B. F. (1982). *The Mind of the Novel: Reflexive Fiction and the Ineffable*. Princeton University Press.

Kohn, E. (2013). *How forests think: Toward an anthropology beyond the human*. University of California Press.

Kremer, J. W. (2006). Dreams and visions in initiation and healing. *ReVision*, *29*(1), 34–45.

Kristof, N. D. (1995, March 17). *Unmasking Horror—A special report.; Japan Confronting Gruesome War Atrocity—The New York Times*. The New York Times. https://www.nytimes.com/1995/03/17/world/unmasking-horror-a-special-report-japan-confronting-gruesome-war-atrocity.html

Lincoln, B. (1986). *Myth, Cosmos, and Society: Indo-European Themes of Creation and Destruction*. Harvard University Press.

Lowan-Trudeau, G. (2015). Teaching the Tension. *Education Canada*, *55*(1), 44–47.

Macfarlane, R. (2019, November 2). Should this tree have the same rights as you? *The Guardian*. https://www.theguardian.com/books/2019/nov/02/trees-have-rights-too-robert-macfarlane-on-the-new-laws-of-nature

McCarraher, E. (2015). We Have Never Been Disenchanted. *The Hedgehog Review*, 13.

Ogilvy, J. A. (Ed.). (1992). *Revisioning philosophy*. State University of New York Press.

Panikkar, R. (1992). A Nonary of Prioritiees. In J. A. Ogilvy (Ed.), *Revisioning Philosophy*. State University of New York Press.

Paxon, D. L. (1999). Marion Zimmer Bradley and The Mists of "Avalon." *Arthuriana*, *9*(1), 110–126.

Rosenfeld, G. (2002). Why Do We Ask 'What If?' Reflections on the Function of Alternate History. *History and Theory*, *41*(4), 90–103.

Slemon, S. (1995). Magial realism as Postcolonial discourse. In L. Parkinson Zomora & W. B. Faris (Eds.), *Magical realism: Theory, history, community*. Duke University Press.

Unites States Holocaust Memorial Museum. (2009, April 2). *Josef Mengele*. Holocaust Encyclopedia. https://encyclopedia.ushmm.org/content/en/article/josef-mengele

Weber, A. (2015). Reality as commons: A poetics of participation for the Anthropocene. *Patterns of Commoning*.

http://patternsofcommoning.org/reality-as-commons-a-poetics-of-participation-for-the-anthropocene/

Witteman, C. M. (2020). Body as Prism: Somatic Pedagogy in the Development of Embodied Ecological Awareness. *Canadian Journal of Environmental Education (CJEE)*, *23*(3), 74–91.

Zimmer Bradley (1982) The mists of Avalon. Knopf

Chapter 3

Building Utopia

The Eco-Pedagogy of Collective Imagination

I read a short story as a child about the experiences of a child trying to find her parents after the bombing of Hiroshima. There was a time I lived in the world where people weren't incinerated in their homes, where people doing their shopping didn't have their skin singed off, and where children and their families didn't die of radiation poisoning. In the space of one moment, I moved from one world into another. I watched videos on TV of nuclear bombs that would haunt my nightmares. I grew up during the tail end of the Cold War, watched the second plane hit during 9-11 after they wheeled televisions into the lobby of my high-school. I remember the feeling of moving between worlds, passing through the veil of ignorance into knowing. I remember moments of awareness when I awoke to the complex, multi-layered, and interlocking upheavals of global social and environmental crises, at once coming to an awareness of my inheritance within the contemporary human collective. The ripples of past projections create forecasts of a shared future and as the recognition of a slowly dying planet begins to dawn on one's awareness, there is a weight to projections of the future, anxiety that presses down on the body's movements as it bears the burden of unlikely seeming hopes. In witnessing the world as it has been known, unravelling in unprecedented storms, economic instability, and global social unrest, it has become increasingly difficult to set my sights on a hopeful future, even one so modest as represented by home ownership, children, retirement, or even basic access to water, food, or stable employment. States of precarity exert pressure, slowly seeping into the collective dreams of our culture until the very act of imagination becomes yet another source of apprehension.

In the hours before dawn, I find myself bracing myself against the onslaught of seemingly insurmountable obstacles, and in those same moments, I draw on my ability to dream of providing an egress from present states of misery. Our collective vision is what allows us to build upon radical solutions to the unique problems of our age, brought into being when the hope of a solution may lift the weight of inevitability, of doom, from the shoulders of those struggling against the creep of a future that seems all too certain.

Van Der Kolk (2014), in *The Body Keeps the Score*, states that our "Imagination gives us the opportunity to envision new possibilities— it is an essential launchpad for making our hopes come true. It fires our creativity, relieves our boredom, alleviates our pain, enhances our pleasure, and enriches our most intimate relationships," he says. "Without imagination, there is no hope, no chance to envision a better future, no place to go, no goal to reach" (p. 17).

It is our hope that helps us believe in change and our imagination that gives us the possibility of hope, especially in a world where hope may be a radical act, to stake one's belief in the transformative power of humanity. In envisioning utopia, one could say that "imaginative, discourses justify or challenge the discursive 'is' to envision the world as it ought to be" (Brownlee, 2018, p. 223). Our ability to envision a world as it *ought to be* is at the core of re-establishing a holistic and interdependent web of life. It takes into account the injustices of the world in all of their permutations, envisioning divergences from orthodoxy and extending these into the realm of the possible.

In Starhawk's (1993) utopian society, captured in her trilogy beginning with *The Fifth Sacred Thing*, we may see an imaginative vision of a social order that projects a potential utopian praxis, engaging with the very real human frailties that have created the environmental and social ruptures of our present world. It seems that "The total absence of an adequate study of imagination in our most influential theories of meaning and rationality is symptomatic of a deep problem in our current views of human cognition" (Johnson, 1987, p. ix), especially because our imaginations have the potential to create the ground for new future potentials, new routes of meaning, and new forms of sense to take form. The imagination is the ground of such a praxis; it is the means by which we create the structures of utopia, beginning to weave the threads of belonging and connection upon which it may rest. If we believe ourselves to be a reasonable species, taking pride in the accomplishments of the homo sapien towards higher cognition, it seems that we might also need to take stock of the potential of such cognition, to take stock of our ability to project unforeseen configurations to generate new life. In order to solve the global problems we are facing; such geneses are essential. To birth ourselves as new humans into an age of peace and justice will require a fuller understanding of reason, cognition, and imagination as formative and interrelated wholes within a larger process of change and discovery.

The process and practice of creating a collective hopeful futurity may be helped along by reckoning with works that engage in such generative acts as the birth of new worlds. In Starhawk's *Walking to Mercury* (1997), *The Fifth Sacred Thing* (1993), and *The City of Refuge* (2015), a hopeful narrative of a future humanity that is free from domination and free to engage in consensual relations, has presented an ovule, a vision that engages in the hopeful projection of human potential, one that may lead to fertilization through our creation of a hopeful present, one in which we may engage in the process of continually stepping into the unknown with courage and the creative capacity to enact new futures within the now. In hearing it spoken, the hidden and suppressed pains of my own existence are unleashed, allowed to turn their faces to the sun, to be seen. In being seen, our desires may become elevated into conscious awareness, their suppression becoming problematized by even the most cursory visions. Those who are unable to suppress their latent human desire become unfit for the current social order while becoming innately fit for a world to be, a world in which a human being may express their mortal frailty, receiving care and empathy from a loving world. I owe my own happiness to a gentle line of caretakers and healers, to those who have offered me the permission to liberate my desire by whispering to me in quiet living rooms, 'me too.' Being born into a world can have the effect of making the rules of that world seem immutable. In the quietude and isolation of my own mind, a strained, desperate, and lonely suffering—the child of our present world—remains as a hidden stain.

In an experiment on the topic of learned helplessness and superstitious behaviours, Matute (1994) theorized that people only began to become passive in the face of phenomena that they *know* they have no ability to control. In the experiment, subjects who did not know whether or not they could control a light that was turning on and off and even when their actions had no effect, believed that they did and would continually try to figure out how it worked. In past experiments, subjects who definitively learned that they could *not* affect a phenomenon subsequently remained passive even as it became possible to change it. Yet, when there was no evidence of helplessness, even though the subjects were *not* able to control the light, all claimed that they believed there *was* a method to do so. It didn't matter whether or not the subjects could control the blinking light in her experiment. The fact that they believed that it might be possible allowed them to keep trying to find a solution.

Holding onto hope in the face of a social order many magnitudes beyond our own scope, seems to lie in opposition to reason. In colloquial terms, calling oneself a realist often infers a perceptual skew towards the dismal. Yet hope is something that may persevere even in the face of contradictory evidence as it exists somewhere beyond reason. As argued by McGeer (2004), hope exists as an integral part of what makes us human. Friere and Friere (2000) in their work, *Pedagogy of the Heart*, suggest that "Hope is an ontological requirement for human beings" and warn that, "The more of a sombering present there is, one in which the future is drowned, the less hope there will be for the oppressed and the more peace there will be for the oppressors" (p. 44). In this way, if humanity can find a way to hold onto hope, despite or perhaps because of the sombering present moment, this presents a revolutionary possibility for change. It empowers the drive to keep trying, despite evidence of our own ineptitude, despite continual failures, despite lacking any concrete vision of the way forward.

Yet, however indelible the human spirit, hope is also fragile. One may easily succumb to the peace of the oppressors, floating into a drowned future and like a screen that lies over every facet of the concrete, observable world, imagined and deeply held contextual interpretations of helplessness may take root through the senses. If we believe, as in Matute's (1994) study that there is no way to alter the circumstances of our lives, we may become passive to the feeling of helplessness even in circumstances where we *can* make a difference. We may look to our lives and see no way to interact with the very real and concrete relationships that face us in everyday moments. These matrices of felt meaning, of the prefigurative reality of the body, the area of the felt that precedes thought, overlay the material world so that when we engage with the world, we engage both symbolically and sensually. That feeling of heaviness that comes with a lack of hope may colour our sensory experience of life. If the 'I' is laden with grim hopelessness, all experiences are be touched by it. One may become so inured to the experience of injustice that one may become like Seligman's dogs who, when exposed to electric shocks without the possibility of escape, learned not to try to escape their cages even when they were freely able to leave, even as they continued to hurt (Maier & Seligman, 1976). Those creatures became accustomed to a world where there was no recourse, no freedom, no hope and it was human intelligence that created the world that did that to them. We are not so different from the intelligences around us. We, too, can lose the ability to see the potential of the moment, helpless in the face of our own pain, even when egress is possible. Human cognition without the wisdom of its animal intelligence, the intelligence of the body, has created many clever forms of torture for animals and humankind alike.

Perhaps the battle for the human soul does, in fact, occur on the playing field of our imaginations, in the creation and interpretation of our dreams and in dreams, the symbolic language. Symbols create the foundation upon which a hopeful imaginary flourishes. They can start and end wars, populating the imaginings of lovers and scientists, poets and politicians. In ritual, symbols are potently experienced, acted upon as realities unto themselves and in this space, symbolic relationships can be both rehearsed and transformed. In the 1890s, a group of captured Lakota performed The Ghost Dance; a ritual spurred on by the visions of an Elder named Wodziwob. The participants hoped that the dance would allow them to return to their way of life, to stop the spread of White settlers and create harmony between the Indigenous tribes. Yet, the ritual made the surrounding settlers afraid, so afraid that they slaughtered over 200 men, women, and children at Wounded Knee. Short Bull says,

> Who would have thought that dancing could have made such trouble? We had no wish to make trouble, nor did we cause it of ourselves...We had no

83

thought of fighting ….We went unarmed to the dance. How could we have held weapons? For thus we danced, in a circle, hand in hand, each man's fingers linked in those of his neighbour…The message that I brought was peace. (DeMallie, 1982, p. 396)

The Lakota were creating symbolic egress for themselves in a situation without hope. The dance allowed them to envision a reality in which their people were no longer imprisoned on a reservation, where the settlers' cruelty was no longer dominant over their way of life. Despite the seeming impenetrability of their prisons, they were constructing a collective vision for a hopeful future. That future was so powerful that it survived the massacre at Wounded Knee, continuing to powerfully speak to a vision of Indigenous resurgence, honoured in the form of contemporary dance and theatre (for example, see Robertson, 2010). The power that the dance created was real, powerful enough to reach beyond the confines of the reservation and to rattle the hearts of the settlers even as they slumbered in a dream of cultural superiority and dominance.

Our imaginations hold the power to generate transformational action, to incite violence, and to inspire peace. Imagination eludes the straightforward order of conscious reason precisely because it lies beneath it. It is the canvas upon which we paint our reason; it is a gateway wherein the world becomes crystallized within the body and the body, the world. Reason may be seen as a dialogue between sensation and the imagined, systematic, and symbolic understanding of our material conditions. The dialectical nature of reason thus keeps us in touch with the world as it is, while continually moving towards what Sameshime, Wibe, and Hayes (2019) call the world as it *may be*.

Transformative Community Practice

In circle, we lay in a pinwheel with our heads pressed together at the center, our eyes closed, breathing deeply. A chosen leader with a melodious voice would set the scene, a winding pathway leading up a mountainside, iridescent clouds that envelop your body, a fathomless ocean, a tranquil meadow. We would journey together through our minds, listening to the guiding voice, and yet the world populating itself through the visionary eye, playing across our minds as an immersive waking dream. There would be moments when we would walk together and moments when we would walk apart, but the journey was a collective one; the purpose was to harmonize the group mind, to help us to share our visions not only within the circle but also after it. Working in such intimate spaces with a group of people changes you. The act of harmonizing one's rhythms to the rhythms of the group, each person in the circle becomes an intimate friend, entering into the inner circle, the circle of trusted others. With my eyes closed, I could hear their voices speak out during the visioning. We would each describe nascent images emerging within our mind's eye and those pieces of the collective dream would then infuse the world of the whole. It felt like a group dream, like we were a part of each other's visions and it was in moments like those that we learned how to dream together, how to construct a world with others, one that would weave the visions of each into a coherent whole, where each individual would be distinct and yet welcomed, embraced. Our dream was made up of each of its parts, the visions of each person writing the story of our progress and it was in this way that I learned how to stay with the moment and delight in the creativity of others, owning nothing and contributing everything.

I learned in circle how to be a part of something other than myself. The work of the imagination may seem like a clandestine effort, veiled off in the secret corners of the mind, but it is deeply connected with and threaded through the world, its events and the characters that inhabit it. One's imagination is impressed upon by dealings of significance in the world that are fit into the matrix of one's values. An interaction has meaning due to the clandestine efforts of a body that becomes aroused to its import, going on to populate both imagination and dreams with latent potentials of sense and connection.

Dyke, Meyerhoff, and Evol (2018) see imagination as having significance as "a collective social process" (p. 174). Their approach invites us to interrogate the commonly held notion of the imagination as an isolated, inward-looking, and contemplative space alone. Beyond the individual, imagination becomes "an ongoing relationship and material capacity constituted by social interactions between bodies" (Shukaitis, 2009, p. 10). It occurs within living systems, emerging from within environments. There is a continuity between the world and the imagination that does not privilege distinct boundaries. We impress our dreams upon the world just as the world impresses its drives and passions onto us. We are in a continual process of attempting to manifest the world that happens inside of our bodies into the world outside of them and what we desire in our most secret dreams becomes informed by that which we encounter. I am sure that the little stone cottage that I imagine as a place of tranquility has been informed by every little cottage that has ever made me gasp, with their delicate lines and tiny inviting windows complete with shutters, gardens, and little fences. Why would I want a fence unless impressed by such a thing as fences, to keep the rabbits out of the lettuce, after all, because I am aware of lettuce and rabbits, and homes, and cottages and that is what I dream of now, because it is just at the edge of what is possible. I could build a cottage with my two hands, placing stone upon stone. I can see it, smell it, feel the texture of it.

If we want the most profound transformation, to build a world with each of our hands, such a world, such a change must emerge from within a network (McCaslin & Kilrea, 2019), from within communities of people building things together, stone by vivid stone. In Starhawk's (2015) novel, *The City of Refuge*, we are introduced to the characters of Bird and Madrone, a pair of revolutionaries from a Utopian city called Califia. In this city, the essence of all law is based upon the idea that the elements of Earth, Air, Fire, and Water are free for all to use and share. Food, water, air, and power are the collective inheritance of all people and as such, it is built with the collective effort of all who live there. Their governance structure is comprised of a group of representatives from various guilds, who meet at a central council whose membership rotates depending on the situation at hand. There is a universal basic income that can be supplemented by work, even housework, and all money expires after a year. The defence of the city is ruled by Elderly women, who are trusted to react wisely. There are stunning innovations that may be recognizable to a practitioner of Reclaiming Witchcraft; there is a temple where those harmed by sexual violence may heal their sexuality in the presence of loving others, and there are temporary places of song and food and sharing emerging from the joyous engagement of a free people. There are fruit trees growing in the streets and rivers running through the city that was once called San Francisco. There are no cars, schools, no military and yet there are ample opportunities for learning; there are methods for travel and deeply knit communities who live close at hand, so nothing is very far away. It is a beautiful vision, threaded through with innovations meant to satisfy one's deep human longings.

In the story of *City of Refuge*, Bird and Madrone travel to the Southlands, to a place where all resources, including water, food, housing, and medicine are strictly controlled by an elite ruling class. The Southlands feel lurid in its familiarity when juxtaposed to the idyllic Califia, just barely beyond the touch of the real world where I currently live in contemporary Canada. In the Southlands, water is owned and so when the characters reach the city, their goal is to locate a clandestine spring, one that will allow them to nurture gardens, giving birth to a thriving oasis within the otherwise arid wasteland birthed by a hegemonic social order. The linchpin in their creative vision is an ability to connect directly with the land and to establish a relationship there that circumvents socially mediated methods for the distribution of the land's wealth. Their intent is to reach out directly to the water, to draw upon the earth in violation of the law. Their vision reaches into the water of the world itself, drawing it up and into the city, creating an oasis that is physical, emotional, and spiritual at once. To attract inhabitants to the refuge, Bird composes a song that goes like this:

> Come all you hungry, all you weary,
> All who toil without reward,
> Come take the road to the place of Refuge,
> Through the way be long and hard.
> Find the spring of endless water,
> Where all people can be free,
> There all debt will be forgiven,
> At the hearth and the sacred tree.
> (pp. 322 – 323)

His song inspires people to join in the dream, to create a temporary autonomous zone (Bey, 2003) within the cultural ruins of a despondent and hopelessly subjugated land. Those inspired by this vision are the ones who build it. As was the plan, the subjugated are the ones who create the refuge. They populate it with their dreams and their visions speak most powerfully to the potential of freedom. It is the dreams that we ourselves generate that have the greatest potential to serve as templates for personal and social transformation. Utopia, after all, cannot be contained within a singular dimension. It expands fractally, moving towards the goal of social and ecological integration, yet approaching it from the multitudinous facets of individually embodied experience, from a limitless amount of directions, from near-infinite centres.

As firmly as our imaginative potentials are situated within our social and ecological networks, they are also contingent upon what Davis and Sumara (2018) call the "not-yet-imaginable," a space that contains all potential knowledge, in fact, everything that lies beyond what one may apprehend within the moment. When the unknown emerges into awareness, it becomes known and a new unknown is formed at a newly formed and continuously re-forming edge. We live in the tiny pool of light cast by the intelligence of humanity amidst a sea of darkness and can only see beyond the limit when we can go *to* the limit and adjust our eyes to the outer darkness, peering beyond the light cast by the comfortable and known. Reaching into the darkness at the edge of knowledge engages our ability to reach beyond the realized. Our potential to move bodily into new utopias means continuously adapting and reforming an ever-expanding sphere of awareness. It means reaching towards the unknown, the formless, and the unknowable, that which will forever elude capture, that which exists beyond the capacity of human awareness. In getting access to Starhawk's vision of a potential future utopia, my own mind is expanded beyond the limit of the not-yet-imaginable, setting a new limit that now contains within it the revolutionary possibilities of a new relation. It creates a pool of light beyond the confines of my own imaginary, creating the potential for hope based in a world of mutuality, health, and care.

Bock (2016) suggests that engaging in transformative practice, the practice of reaching towards the embodiment of our ideal potential means doing a kind of taxonomical work, interpreting our everyday experiences within a new network, one of the personalized meanings. It has been my experience that engaging in these kinds of collective processes has the potential to create a collectiv*ized* sense of meaning and purpose. As a collective vocabulary of stories, myths, and songs are built up between people, we create a common language which can aid in creative action. When I said that Starhawk's vision might be recognizable, it is because the seeds of her vision are practiced every year at Witchcamps across the globe. I spent a lot of time at the Temple of Love at Vermont Witchcamp, where my friends were grounding the temple that year. We created a group "puppy puddle" where dozens of people lay splayed across the padded floor, touching ways that felt safe and loving, reaching into those spaces of harm that had been torn by rape culture, soothing those parts that were broken. 'Peer scaffolding,' or a system of peer support and motivation, helps the individual to grow, allowing for meaning-making to occur while also achieving personal and group actuation (McGeer, 2004). We buttress each other, both pushing and supporting our steps into the unknown. Within a forest, we see the individual trees growing up towards the sky but underneath there are roots, stretching into and twining amongst each other. The trees are stronger together; they hold the soil to prevent erosion, they hold on to the precious water and they share nutrients between themselves. A forest is not just a collection of trees but a collective of trees, stronger precisely because they are together.

In Starhawk's (1993; 1998; 2015) trilogy, a central element of the philosophical core of her vision is the presence of a collective of individuals, free to choose their own destinies. Califia is a culture where individuals may revoke consent at any time and it is this very freedom that strengthens their will to collaborate. In *The Fifth Sacred* Thing, individuals from the water council disagree with other members' insistence on peaceful resistance against an invasion force brought by the Southlanders, who want to capture and control their water. Yet, there is nothing the council can do to force the water council to abide by a strategy of passive resistance. The invading army has dammed the rivers that once flowed freely through the city and the water council decides to continually blow up the damns, continually unleashing the water, not allowing their resources to be held, throttled, or controlled. In the Southlands, the refuge built by Bird and Madrone becomes a refuge only because those who live there are empowered to collectively practice their power of creation. This supportive network of peers continually redirects the individual towards their agential power (McGeer, 2004). So long as I grow in respect of the well-being, health, and strength of those around me, I can be supported through mutuality in my own well-being, health, and strength. The limits of the community are my container, like the chosen form of a poem. They are not limits imposed by violence or coercion; they are limits created in joy and pleasure.

When one finds a supportive community, one may be continually redirected towards the "not-yet-imaginable," where we may challenge ourselves to bring into being what is beyond our capacity as individuals, continually buoyed by both individual and group processes of hope. It is through the cultivation of hope, both individually and collectively tethered, that we remain fixed upon that unknown destination, one that carries within it the constant evolutionary potential of change. More so than even this, we are buoyed by the creation of meanings that project beyond the scope of our individual lives into the potential futures of our grandchildren and grandchildren's grandchildren (Bock, 2016). This is reflected in the Haudenosaunee Seven Generations teaching as told by Mohawk (2016). In the story, Peacemaker tells of a hopeful future with no wars, in which all power would come from righteousness, which he defines "as the result of the best thinking of collective minds operating from principles which assume that a sane world requires that we provide a safe environment for our children seven generations into the future" (p. 80). The health and well-being of our descendants are one of the forms of the world poem, a delightful way to organize and structure the meanings of the human project, to offer pleasure in human form to the pursuit of world health, in collaboration not only with our grandchildren but also our relations. For there is no point in passing down a world to our children if that world has no relations, no plants or animals to populate it and to make it grow. The world only delights when it is alive, and this is the worthiest gift, a relationship with a thriving world.

The Imaginal Machine

The world of Califia might be described as an "imaginal machine…a particular arrangement or composition of desires and creativity as territorialized through and by relations between bodies in motion" (Shukaitis, 2009, p. 13). Drawing the imaginary of such a machine into the world is a process of drawing out the current composition of desires that might work together to constitute a relational matrix. The embodied imagination can be understood as emerging from within a concupiscent frothing of sensation, relating with and against the other. Through this confrontation, a drawing into embodiment occurs, which Bock (2016) suggests is a process of activating meanings that were previously only internalized. It is when the imagination comes up against and performs *with* others that it becomes realized. Gibson-Graham (2016) proposes that through these processes of collective imagination,

> … we can work in the conscious realm to devise practices that produce the kind of embodied, affect-imbued pre-thoughts that we want to foster. And in the daily rehearsal of these practices we can hope that they will become part of our makeup, part of a cell memory that will increasingly assert itself without resort to conscious calling. (p. 7)

Even while we engage in the process of collective visioning, practices within the present moment project into the not-yet-imaginable; our rehearsal of future movements suffuse the pre-conscious. Co-creative practice may form a bridge between the conceptual and practical realms, creating space for work that transforms the mind and body, individual and society (McCaslin & Kilrea, 2019). In *City of Refuge*, citizens of the refuge must learn how to embody new relationships with each other, with authority, as well as with power, outsiders, and dissent. They are taught these new ways of being heuristically, through doing. It is in doing that their unconscious assumptions are dredged up. For example, Bird refuses to take on the role of leader because he thinks people are giving him too much importance. The gathered council almost cannot fathom what to do without a leader. When they ask him what they should do, he suggests that they learn to lead themselves. In the rejection of the accepted role of leader, Bird actuates his theoretical beliefs about power. The agitators Bird and Madrone cannot force people into their vision of the future simply because the transition that they have envisioned necessitates a movement into agency with and through non-hierarchical, collective action.

This process is similar to collective world-building through Indigenous theory, which Simpson (2014) states is "generated from the ground up and its power stems from its living resonance within individuals and collectives" (p. 7). She further explains that such a theory "isn't just an intellectual pursuit—it is woven within kinetics, spiritual presence and emotion, it is contextual and relational. It is intimate and personal, with individuals themselves holding the responsibilities for finding and generating meaning within their own lives" (p. 7). The imposition of theory cannot offer true emancipatory potential. It is only through the meaningful generation of commonly held values that we are able to honestly remake our worlds. Yet, this kind of work is not efficient nor straightforward. It would be difficult to imagine the arrow of progress through a collective storying of humanity. Such a road is winding, perhaps looping in on itself in formulations that fail to move in one solid direction, one particular kind of sense. To take account of the people of the world, forward progress cannot be a driving force. Human achievement must not become an arrow. Instead, it might look more like a Taurus, an eternal circulation of energy outwards, then gathered in and brought close to be understood, processed, and then released.

The Physical Space of the Imagination

When seen from the perspective of unity and interdependence, firm boundaries between body, mind, and spirit become something to be seen as largely conceptual. When I see the sky, there are myriad networks activated by the light, colours, and movement of it within my being, and as the sky moves me, mechanisms beyond even my conscious perception come into play; my body is moved by the shape of the sky just as I shape the sky with my vision of it. The body, mind, and spirit are thus continuous, in that they participate in one's perceptions of the world, one's experience of it. Furthermore, as each moment bends into the next, our bodies take up the space of action to move into a dynamic of interaction suggested by deep structures within the brain, or moral structures within a system of values, or deeply felt instinctual drives as felt from the body, or perhaps, all of these at once. The imagination does not simply take place within the mind because the imagination plays a part in the creation of acts within the world, of responses to the world and its players, making sense of each new dynamism as it emerges from chaos and becomes incorporated into sense. The task of taking up new dynamics is an act of making new senses, patterns within the rational courses of the world.

In *City of Refuge*, Madrone goes on a journey to the hills outside of the Southlands to meet a temple where the priestesses practice the worship of bees. She learns from these women the practice of connecting with the hive mind, with their collective intelligence, how to understand the world of smell, of chemical compositions, and she becomes capable of producing medicine in a droplet that emerges from a depression in her forehead. There are boundaries of sense broken here, between human and insect, between material being and natural force, between material and spirit, between intuition and science. Madrone becomes something more than human by entering into a relationship with the bees, and in the description of their communication as a communion through the body, she is able to grasp a deeper understanding of matter. In this turn, there is a temptation to enter into the imaginary, into the play between feeling and possibility, between what seems to be possible and what is unknown and beyond the ability to know. Such imaginings may be fanciful, but they tempt one into sensual engagement with the world as something one may reach out and touch, to know and become one with. It suggests that mind, body, spirit, and world may have bridges between them that we may traverse and explore. It engages sensually with the desire to engage poetically and to perhaps test hidden and unknown depths of human potential. How deep do our senses go? Do we know, can we know, when their limit exists somewhere beyond the periphery of the known?

Murray (2018) suggests that transformation through learning is best applied through an engagement with a mixture of action and emotion, noting that this is what brings about an environment that supports imaginative work. Critically, he underscores that it is the engagement with emotion that allows participants to feel safe enough to engage in excursions into the unknown. Having space for all felt dimensions of growth provides the most fertile ground for discovery, especially discovery in unknown territories, as yet unexperienced lands of being. Dyke et al. (2018) further suggest that a radical imagination is one that engages "with alternative, horizontalist modes of study" and that it is the "communizing praxis of visioning and realizing new futures" that may allow "boldly imaginative projections into the unknown void of what-is-to-come" (p. 176). Not only must the boundaries between emotion and action be softened, but also boundaries between leader and follower, between self and other. Radical imagination is "a collective practice that arises from within social movements against imaginaries that uphold the status quo" (Dyke et al., 2018, p. 160). Its radical-*ness* comes from its excursions into the unknown but not into the original for its own sake. Rather, the unknown territory being explored in this work is one that incorporates mind, body, and spirit alike. It is work that brings into the known the realities of the human, in all of its capacities, into immediate, felt praxis. The radical imagination brings into being practices that actuate the theories upon which they are established, built upon a ground that is open to emotion, that is safe, non-hierarchical, and communal.

It is just this imagination *with* others that constitutes the radical imagination, and it is this which is demonstrated in Starhawk's trilogy. She describes this process as a process of collective becoming, of emerging from a radical centring of the heart. In the story, their utopia springs from the choice of a small group of old women who take up pickaxes, upending the pavement of a road. From an act of loving destruction, their society is able to collectively build a world in which the elements became the domain of all people. Food grows where once cars dominated, clean drinkable water flows through the streets. It is a world where human life has become entwined with environmental health, where human needs and the needs of the world become synergistically connected. It is this engagement with human needs, the validation of human life, that holds power to inspire and motivate. For, it is radically imagined that human life and human happiness are intertwined with the well-being of the world, that human health is located in environmental health and in the stewardship of the land. The creation story of this society hints at the notion that if people can *feel* into this potential, they may be inspired to take the first tender steps toward change. It is a radical act of transformation that stems from a deep love of the Earth that inspires others to act, to take up the process of change in their own worlds.

Ecological Futurity and The Practice of Hope

It must be said that "it is a mistake to consider issues of human welfare and justice without regard to nonhuman beings and in isolation from our broader life context" (Bell & Russel, 1999, pp. 68 – 69). Bell and Russsel (1999) claim that domination is reflected in all forms of oppression, saying that, "The global ecological crisis *is* a social and political crisis" (p. 69). In this way, we may see that efforts towards liberation from oppression, of imagining pathways other than domination, have the potential to reverberate beyond their original contexts. Brown (2016), in her book, *Emergent Strategy*, says that we are currently experiencing what it feels like to be caught up in someone else's imagination. The work of seeking justice for both the human and the more-than-human world means discarding the oppressive visions we have been sold, replacing them instead with our own dreams, feelings, needs, and desires. The work is a recognition that the world has become one inhospitable to human life just as it is inhospitable to the lives of those beings with whom we share this world. It is the recognition that the oppression we experience is reflected not only in the world but also in our own imaginaries of what we understand to be possible.

Walking the path towards remaking the world begins with creating what McCaslin and Kilrea (2019) call a "community of practice," described as "the joint enterprise within a collection of human potentials...that creates a sense of accountability and engagement to the collective's body of knowledge" (Integral Meta-Theory/epistemology, para. 6). The radical imagination must take place in the community precisely because it is a networked imagination, an interrelational imagination. No one vision is given the opportunity to dominate or destroy another precisely because no one being is elevated above another. While one idea may better serve the collective, may be more practical, or more inspired, it does not become so through a process of force. In the practice of collective agency, notions must serve the whole but *also* each individual within the whole. There is no collective good without individual good; it is not either the collective or the individual but the harmonious alignment of each within a whole. It may be said that "the co-created truth is epistemologically valid because it is co-constructed by the collective experience" (McCaslin & Kilrea, 2019, *Locating Transformative Inquiry as a Viable Research Method*, para. 7). The openings that we make for individuals to wield their agency allow for communities to reflect the felt values of their members and to create structures that reflect an elevation of care. In allowing our systems to reflect our hopes and dreams, we instil within our societies a sense of collectively fed hope, which ground our relations in our collective mental, physical, and ecological health. Creating social movements impressionable to the needs and desires of their constituents means not only engaging in radical imagination but also practicing those alternatives through mutual respect and collectively held power. As Bock (2016) suggests, "Just as portions of humanity have enforced hierarchies of domination and control on one another in the form of class, race, gender, and nationality, we have also attempted to dominate and control the natural world" (p. 12). The injustices occurring within the human world are replicated both up and down, into the minutiae of our everyday lives and into the macro-interactions of humanity within a global ecosystem.

Thus, in recognition of the animal intelligence within humanity, we recognize the good of the relations around us. The human animal in me recognizes the damage of pollution through the intelligence of my body. The smog of the city and the lack of trees create a subtle ground of anxiety that threads through my life. As much as I might get used to it, escaping for breaks into the natural world in order to reconnect, I am able to feel the imbalance of the human project within my body. It is obvious that I may not drink from the rivers, that I may not take food from the trees because I don't own them. My disconnection is obvious when reading through my animal intelligence, and in elevating such intelligence non-hierarchically, I may recognize the relative limits of so-called 'higher' functions in rationalizing away such concerns as pollution, inequality, and ownership. The things that feel bad in the world are not necessarily meant to be borne as fundamental forces and it is the animal in me that balks against these restrictions. It is my reactive bodily impulses that think through oppressions, that seek the course of pleasure and that question the impediments to an animal happiness that is found in simple contentment, in being fed, warm, and among loved ones. I am not debased by the animal inside of me (or that I am inside of); I am elevated by it, it is a sacred piece of me as I am a sacred piece of the world, working in harmony between its many pieces, voices, and drives.

Gibson-Graham (2016) suggests that our sense of melancholia in thinking about the future is an attachment to past theorization that precludes a sense of potential for "mobilization, alliance, or transformation" (p. 5) in the present moment. Hope has the potential to draw humanity deeper into connection with one another but also with the natural world by allowing the individual to transcend their paralysis, to open their perception to the potential within each felt moment. Working with communities of practice, ones that support and encourage the expression of agency towards justice, peace, and ecological healing, may lead us to what Bock (2016) refers to as "orthopraxy", which is "right living relationally, in immanent context, and with an epistemology that is intensely personal as well as universally connecting" (p. 26). For example, in talking about one of their actions that they call "Black Table Arts", Dyke et al. (2018) say,

… we are not only attempting to announce our love for Black people but announce the possibility of arriving to a new land, one we hold in common and in relation. A land where it doesn't make sense to be capitalist or racist or sexist or transphobic not only because it's not in one's self-interest but because it's not desirable or practical for futurity. (p. 173)

The practice of radical imagination is a process of developing clandestine pockets of new, utopian realities. Lived from one moment to the next, our collective imaginations can exercise our hope, drawing us back into connection with each other and with the living world. These practices create potential egresses from patterns of dispossession, meaninglessness, and wanton destruction. It is through our connections, of imagining new worlds *with* each other, that we are able to tackle the problems of our current day as they arise in each new moment, in each unfolding potential. Through practices of hopeful futurity, we may learn to make our own way forward, together.

The Potentiating Arts

Yet, our utopias are never complete precisely because they are formed out of relationships. As such, holistic utopian processes must continually reformulate a collective concept of the just. As leaders, teachers, and facilitators of these connections, our role lies in the ability to encourage a sense of infinite time, moving ever forward into new relations, new hopes, and new worlds. McCaslin and Kilrea (2019) call teaching, leading, and community building the "potentiating arts." There are those who are able to gather together the strands that we create, weavers of our collective visions of the future and while there may be fewer weavers, we create the threads together.

Third-order changes, those that which occurs on the level of profound ontological and fundamental change, come from the connection to that which forms between people, coming from instances of shared resonance (Bartunek & Moch, 1994). Teachers, researchers, academics, and activists engaged in transformative processes, must ultimately engage in acts of "deep heuristic research" (McCaslin & Kilrea, 2019) that emerge from within an embodied experience of change. Our feelings and experiences engage and potentiate us not only as professionals but also as people. We must take the risk to involve ourselves in the work precisely because it is more than an intellectual posture but rather a deeply felt and embodied shift that occurs on levels far beyond the conscious.

I take inspiration from the life and work of Starhawk herself. Her utopian vision emerges directly from her activism. Yet, her imaginary allows for the extension of this experience into spaces not easily accessible within the individual life. She engages in an extension and experimentation in non-violent philosophy in *The Fifth Sacred Thing*. The characters are subjected to a military occupation and decide in council to collectively approach individual soldiers, part of the invading army, saying, "There is a place set for you at our table, if you will choose to join us" (Starhawk, 1993, p. 234). The soldiers kill some who approach them, and the community decides to 'haunt' them with what they called ghosts. These ghosts are the family members and friends of the dead who follow the soldiers around, telling them stories about their loved ones. It is a bold vision, one not easily accessed without giving one's own life. It is a vision of a people so committed to the way of peace that they would give their own lives rather than participate in violence. One of the elders in the book, a character named Maya, quotes poet Diane di Prima in a meeting, saying, "The only war that counts is the war against the imagination" (p. 238), and it is in the imagination that the residents of Califia stake their resistance, in the embodied imagination that includes a heart and a soul. In the afterword of *City of Refuge*, Starhawk (2015) says,

> While I remain personally deeply committed to nonviolence, I believe the job of fiction is not to espouse a position but to deeply explore a question, through the actions and behaviours and realizations of the characters, lived through incidents of the plot. I hope readers will understand that *City of Refuge* is not meant to be prescriptive, but rather, to experiment with possibilities that are easier lived in fiction than in real life. (p. 662)

She mentions how her strict adherence to nonviolence was challenged by the question, "Can our strategy of peaceful resistance work against a truly ruthless opponent" (p. 662)? This emerged from lived experiences of police violence, of Palestinian struggles against occupation, of the struggle to organize amidst an oppressive force blinded to the lives caught within its gears. Thus, her later visions are coloured by her immersion in the world, a fully active participant within it. The movements which move and shape her imagination, sculpt her belief in the possibility of change. To follow her example, community leaders must help to open up those around them to an emergent picture that exists beyond the scope of individual suffering (Bock, 2016), to witness possibilities within the moment that may not easily appear when facing an oppression that seems like a natural force, an avalanche, a glacier, moving with an unfeeling, unstoppable progression to crush you. This oppression is not a glacier. Our suffering is not inescapable; it has a thousand human faces, each with eyes, a mind, a heart. We may not reach out to the glacier to stop its course, but we may speak to another human being, saying, "There is a place set for you at our table, if you will choose to join us" (Starhawk, 1993, p. 234).

Exercising our imaginations as engaged processes in and of the world may help us to create connections between larger social and environmental processes. One may see the role of a leader as facilitating the extension into the unknown, creating an opening whereby one's community may transcend the habitual. This, by necessity, implies a means of assessment that allows for the unfolding of unknown potentials (Murray, 2018). To find the path of a new humanity, there can be no predetermined outcome. Rather, the work must be allowed to run its course. It is a phenomenon that comes into being radically dependent on the personalities and experiences of those involved. When we are immersed in the work, we cannot shape it from above. Instead, we must surrender ourselves to the process and, in that surrender, find meaning collectively. Doing so changes the purpose of leadership, shifting the role towards one of grounding group processes, inspiring, and participating in collective horizontalism. I may become a leader in one moment, a follower in the next.

I experienced the idea of a Quaker religious service in an episode of the HBO TV series called *Six Feet Under*, in an episode titled "Singing for our Lives" (Ball et al., 2005). At the end of the episode, there is a scene the characters attend a service. I was taken by the way in which the community sits in silence, waiting for revelation to occur. A man stands up, expressing his appreciation for finally having found a place where he feels at peace. Everyone waits for a moment, allowing his statement to stand and then one of the people in the congregation begins to sing a song that goes,

We are a gentle, angry people
And we are singing, singing for our lives

We are a justice-seeking people
And we are singing, singing for our lives
(Ball et al., 2005, 18:00)

The others in the congregation seem to know the words and they join in. They begin to sing at that moment almost as a response to the spontaneous gratitude, to speak to the collectively held feeling that they shared. There is no teacher, no leader per se. Those who become full of the spirit may share that wisdom with others. This episode shared with me a piece of this community, and I carried that message with me as a potential, as a known means by which a community may connect and hold in their collective vision, a seed of the sacred. I believe that holistic leadership functions in a similar vein, that a leader is one who has the relevant knowledge to facilitate group processes and only leads when their gifts are useful. In this example, there was a person in the congregation who knew what song would put into words the feelings of the group, and this is what facilitated their leadership at that moment, and the collectively recognized and shared feelings of the group are what led them to follow. Leadership, in this way, is not some special distinction or title but rather is a lived praxis in which the gifts of the community are put into service of communal processes. This work, the work to build a collective vision, becomes transformative in the very means of its accomplishment. In the expression of each unique voice, unfolding in myriad directions, we may find a force for grounding change in the intelligence of mind, body, and spirit.

Hope and The Future Imaginary

Gibson-Graham's (2016) "weak theory" posits that there is a tendency to ideologically distance ourselves from power in order to avoid its corrupting influence, consequently setting up a binary in which the powerful may wield influence, being bad, while the good may not wield power, remaining good. In shifting the locus of power from dominion to cooperation, the process of collective creation serves to undermine this aversion to power, embracing it as a natural right of all people. Within the community of Reclaiming Witchcraft, there is an exercise called the Iron Pentacle (p. 115), set out in Coyle's (2004) book, *Evolutionary Witchcraft*. In the exercise, the five points of a pentacle are named from the top and moving clockwise; they are sex, self, passion, pride, and power. One 'runs' the pentacle through the body, starting with the head (sex) and drawing into the body the meaning of the word, invoking depth as experienced through the felt sensations. One moves from the head to the left foot (passion), the right hand (power), the left hand (self) and the right foot (pride). The concepts contained in the iron pentacle are considered those that are most problematic to the Western mindset, and the process of 'running' the iron pentacle is a process of untangling the knots in the Western psyche, to clear these concepts of their negative baggage and to embrace the liberated positive potential contained in each. In the Reclaiming community, power is approached as a process, a movement with and through people. As I have run the Iron Pentacle through my own body, I engage with power as alive in an experience of the present moment, neither a force for good nor evil, merely a force, one that may be directed in concert with the will. Thus, I believe that the radical imagination is one that allows us to revitalize the notions contained in the Iron Pentacle, to investigate and locate the sacred within them, but also to engage in positive aspirations toward both our collective pasts and futures (Dyke et al., 2018) through an engagement with radical possibility. In creating healing in the now, I may not only engage in the creation of a hopeful future imaginary but also a reinvigoration of a collective past, re-examining and recontextualizing the gifts of the past so that they may lead to new present moment potentials. This work gives communities the power to create definitions and systems of value that situate their own needs at the centre of their collective universe, with their own feelings and desires at the fulcrum of a network of felt meaning and purpose. The fractal work of transformation occurs in a myriad of centres and sites. It is from these sites that lived transformation may demonstrate new potentials, new links, new networks of relation and meaning.

Decolonization is part of the work here, to engage in the creation of what Bruyneel (2007) calls the 'third space' of Indigenous identity. This is one that rejects the settler imaginary of who and what constitutes Indigeneity, pursuing instead a process that he describes as defying superficially applied external boundaries and instead creating space that exists strategically within and outside of settler realities, contingent upon the complex lived realities of real Indigenous people. An even broader conception of colonization, suggests that modern systems alienate *all* within them, that all are made to feel unable to either move or comprehend the boundaries of the systems that colonize their lifeworlds (Habermas, 1987). While one can and *must* recognize the privilege of White naturalized settlers, one can simultaneously recognize the failure of settler cultures to serve even their elect, harming all and serving none. There can be a sense that the individual cannot hope to fathom nor change the machinations of society, which exist far beyond the scope of our individual lived presence. Yet, it is not through navigating oppressive systems, nor in resisting them, where we find freedom. Instead, it may be found by following the advice of Bruyneel (2007), by consciously engaging in a third space, we might establish a new centre not as a binary in opposition to an other but as a connected process of feeling and relation emerging from within an individual life. In the novels, Madrone and Bird did not travel to the Southlands to fight the power of their political leaders, rather, they create another option which is enough to cause a revolution. The threat was not constructed in opposition to the powers that be, which is precisely what made it so much of a threat. It was a threat because it planted the seed in the imagination of the people that the power of the oppressors was not absolute, and that a different world was possible.

At the center of the storying of a new Earth, is the process of fabulation, which allows for the lie that tells a deeper truth (Garoian, 2018). It is an act of resistance that does not speak only in opposition to a current state of being but that speaks a new way of being in relation. This makes way for "an incipient storying of political fiction that occurs from an emptying out of the self to allow for ideational encounters and alliances from outside the confines of one's learned understandings" (Garoian, 2018, p. 192). One may speak into being the potential for new relationships to form from within the lived experience of the now. Imaginative fabulation gives us the tools to take apart our social imaginaries, each symbol becoming a building block that may be rearranged, and recontextualized into new meanings and relationships. We need not tell the 'truth' as it has been given to us to arrive at the 'truth' we know it in our bones. Take, for example, the belief in magic. Starhawk, for one, does not only write utopian fiction. She also publicly expresses her belief in the reality of magic and writes books about the spiritual practice of magic, which is where I first encountered her writing.

In my own life, I have often been told that magic is *not*-real, and yet practitioners of magic are engaging in something that they both feel and experience *as* real. Practitioners of magic engage in something that has been determined to be *not*-real to get at something that is profoundly real, deep, spiritual, and human. This is not a reactive process but rather one that "resists punitive judgments that are driven by social and historical norms. It is a legending process that in falsifying normative, majoritarian predilections affirms thinking and living life as a creative force" (Garoian, 2018, p. 192). Garoian posits that creative processes of fabulation open the door for collective meaning-making in ways that think, say, and do *with* one another. Because this process makes use of traditional symbolic understandings, it may also serve to bring forward perspectives that have experienced less mainstream representation. Much like the "not-yet-imaginable" (Davis & Sumera, 2018), the roots of our desires often lie somewhere beyond the limits of our understanding, nebulous and, as yet, unformed. Through fabulation, we may put substance to the prefigurative desiring forces that reside within us. Yet, putting form to the formless may require one to step outside of the confines of the strictly rational in favour of a more intuitive form of meaning-making, one that makes use of non-traditional relationships between symbols in the form of pastiche, to express more nuanced meanings, meanings that exist between and beyond symbols, reaching towards and into the unknown.

In Starhawk's (1993; 1998; 2015) trilogy, the markers of Western culture are strategically rearranged into a new symbolic network. The Southlands, for example, seem very much like a not-too-distant future for the West and in othering this society, we are able to identify with the utopic, to stand in the place of the liberated and look back at ourselves. It is through the conceit of the other that we may more clearly examine our own faults and potentials. In this narrative, the expression of power that has become untethered from a purpose dictated from on-high, expressing a subversion of the structures of domination we may take for granted in our everyday lives. As such, there is a subtle call to take the meanings that we are given, rearrange them, restage and restructure them for our own purposes. We don't need to wholly reject the culture of domination in which we find ourselves but may instead *construct* a third space, neither fully in line nor fully out of line.

We may begin the process of undoing the knots of hegemonic control through the assertion of our individual and collective will, not just in the mindless consumption of material goods but in the creation of truly satisfying personal realities. We may continually turn towards hope, as tied up with the processes of resistance and creation both, serving as a support during the disentanglement from oppressive structures as well as in the pursuit of a dream of social and ecological healing.

Hope has the potential to extend our consciousness beyond our individual lives (Bock, 2016), allowing our communities to actualize change that must, for the sake of global wellbeing, occur on a more-than-human scale. In cultivating a connection to what Ella Baker describes as "democratic time" (Dyke et al., 2018), we take into account the need for an organic temporal scope that doesn't respond to the immediacy of our yearning, but rather, to the space required for processes to take place in their own ways and according to their own scales. To face issues that exist beyond the limited sense of one human life, we need to develop a sense of "hope that is deeper than desire, broader than the individual, and that contains the transformative power to change suffering, injustice, evil, and apathy into meaning" (Bock, 2016, p. 15). We need a sense of hope that exists beyond even our capacity to rationally conceptualize the notion of utopia. We must believe, somehow, that there is a potential reality that exists beyond even our wildest dreams and we must continually orient ourselves towards its unfathomable realization.

Yet, the pragmatic question remains of how to arrive at this place, especially in the face of an ever-increasing sense of impending global calamity. Murray (2018) suggests that an emphasis on meta-cognition, on thinking about thinking or alternately, on an awareness of process may aid in the development of the imagination, and perhaps this emphasis on process might also lead to the spontaneous comprehension of global structures of power, which is what I am attempting to achieve here. In understanding ourselves and how we are doing the work, we may actuate a theoretical ground that may be moved into actuation through praxis. Murray (2018) recommends a sense of fun, playfulness, and risk-taking in this endeavour. These skills all lead towards confidence in venturing into the unknown, where a sense of the ludic may add to the anticipation of positive outcomes.

It is through solidarity in the collective mission of expressing and fulfilling our desires within a community of practice, of continually buttressing each other with expressions of hopeful futurity, fun, and pleasure, that we create right relation, where we discover the paths towards orthopraxy. The act of fun and pleasure easily invites one into the present moment, where the acknowledgement of pain is a useful tool merely in the pursuit of increasingly deep states of pleasure and contentment. Buber's I-Thou relationship (Blenkinsop & Scott, 2017) is an expression of pleasure in relation, a form of non-reductive direct contact where both parties retain their separate and individual essence, coming into relation without one or the other being absorbed. This form of encounter might be described as an opposite to the process of dominion, whereby the 'weak' become absorbed by the 'strong.' The I-Thou relation is a radical realization of the other, one that fails to consume or be consumed, where we may begin to recognize the kind of connections required for a healthy, sound, and mutually integrated lived relation, one emerging from a state of engaged pleasure. It is this form of relation that allows for near-infinite centres to act towards a shared goal of mutually held power and agency. We may see this relationship reflected in the construction of the refuge in Starhawk's (2015) *City of Refuge*. Those who come to the sanctuary are asked to imagine a different life and in so doing, to become different, but this process does not erase who they are. In fact, it elevates the individual and their will within a new structure of relations. One may witness the other in motion and align oneself with it, through a will that is free, without coercion, without control or domination.

Of Collective Transformation

When facing the complexities of interlocking global systems of life whose realities span across multiple human lifetimes, one must be able to access both hope and imaginaries of the future as a means of connecting individuals across spatio-temporal distances into a community of relatives spanning the planet, across the eons. It is when we are able to unite our visions, creating meaningful connections within our communities that then extend out into the world, that we can address the disconnection that comes from being trapped inside someone else's imagination. The process of building collective hopeful futurity allows us to own the process of our own becoming, investigating and reaching into the spaces between the known and the unknown, to grow into hopeful visions of what we may become. In the practice of creating meaning collectively, reaching towards and bringing into the world the realization of our deepest desires, we are not only projecting our hopes into the future, but we are also bringing that hoped-for future into our midst.

It is in the practice of justice that we experience justice, and in the practice of care that we feel care. The idea of utopia is not just an idea; it is a reality that we must feel in our bones and express through every fibre of our being into the most mundane reaches of life. Thus, utopia itself may not be a place, but a state of being, a practice. In this way, we may begin to live utopia by developing orthopraxy, which is not just a means but also a posture, a stance towards life that is the point of departure from which all of our actions emerge. By looking towards the life forms around us as active agents, capable of defining and acting upon their own sense of internal meaning, we begin to raise those around us to the dignity that comes with agential power. We empower ourselves through engaging in collective processes of mutual respect, of listening to and responding to the needs of those around us; we too may find a place in this world, a lived utopia in the present moment.

Yet, we may also seek to expand upon the realm of the possible by engaging in imaginative excursions into what may-be, entertaining new potentials and adding to our own expanding understanding of the known in our engagement with imaginative potentials, in the serious consideration of hopeful futurity, even though it may seem naïve, even though the way towards the creation of such realities may be winding. In entertaining the possibility of worlds that fulfill deep human needs and desires, allowing for human agency and will to be expressed in harmony with living systems of care and mutuality, we feed the living centre of our hope, linked in a forest, to feed each other on tender dreams through our held hands. We sustain each other by passing on stories of hope, taking those stories into our bodies and playing them out in our lives. We may begin to construct our utopias in the now strengthened by our visions of a collective future made more profound and deeper by their poetry.

References

Barker, A. J. (2014). "A Direct Act of Resurgence, a Direct Act of Sovereignty": Reflections on Idle No More, Indigenous Activism, and Canadian Settler Colonialism. *Globalizations*. http://dx.doi.org/10.1080/14747731.2014.971531

Bartunek, J. M., & Moch, M. K. (1994). Third-order organizational change and the Western mystical tradition. *Journal of Organizational Change Management, 7*(1), 24–41.

Bell, A. C., & Russell, C. L. (1999). Life Ties: Disrupting Anthropocentrism in Language Arts Education. In J. P. Robertson (Ed.), *Teaching for a Tolerant World, Grades K-6: Essays and Resources* (pp. 68–89). Illinois: National Council of Teachers of English.

Bey, H. (2003). *T.A.Z.: The temporary autonomous zone, ontological anarchy, poetic terrorism.* Autonomedia,

Blenkinsop, S., & Scott, C. (2017). Becoming Teacher/Tree and Bringing the Natural World to Students: An Educational Examination of the Influence of the Other-than-Human World and the Great Actor on Martin Buber's Concept of the I/Thou. *Educational Theory, 67*(4), 453–469. https://doi.org/10.1111/edth.12258

Bock, C. (2016). Climatologists, Theologians, and Prophets: Toward an Ecotheology of Critical Hope. *Cross Currents, 66*(1), 8–34. https://doi.org/10.1111/cros.12171

Brown, A. M. (2017). *Emergent Strategy: Shaping Change and Changing Worlds.* Chico, CA: AK Press.

Brownlee, K. (2018). Collaborative Imagination: Earning Activism through Literacy Education. *International Journal of Communication (Online)*, 2922-. Retrieved from Literature Resource Center.

Bruyneel, K. (2007). *The Third Space of Sovereignty: The Postcolonial Politics of U.S. - Indigenous Relations.* Minneapolis: University of Minnesota Press.

Coyle, T. T. (2004) *Evolutionary witchcraftI.* Jeremy P. Tarcher/Penguin.

Davis, B., & Sumara, D. (2007). Complexity Science and Education: Reconceptualizing the Teacher's Role in Learning. *Interchange: A Quarterly Review of Education, 38*(1), 53–67.

DeMallie, R. J. (1982). The Lakota Ghost Dance: An Ethnohistorical Account on JSTOR. *Pacific Historical Review, 51*(4). https://www-jstor-org.ezproxy.lakeheadu.ca/stable/3639782?seq=1#metadata_info_tab_contents

Dyke, E., Meyerhoff, E., & Evol, K. (2018). Radical Imagination as Pedagogy: Cultivating Collective Study from Within, on the Edge, and Beyond Education. *Transformations: The Journal of Inclusive Scholarship & Pedagogy, 28*(2), 160–180. https://doi.org/10.1353/tnf.2018.0010

Freire, P., & Freire, A. M. A. (1997). *Pedagogy of the heart.* New York: Continuum.

Gallagher, M. W., & Lopez, S. J. (Eds.). (2018). *The Oxford Handbook of Hope.* Retrieved from https://books.google.ca/books?id=W3s7DwAAQBAJ&pg

Garoian, C. R. (2018). Performing Art and Its Pedagogy of the False. *Studies in Art Education, 59*(3), 185–200. https://doi.org/10.1080/00393541.2018.1476950

Gibson-Graham, J. K. (2006). Affects and Emotions for a Postcapitalist Politics. In *A Postcapitalist Politics* (pp. 40–59). Retrieved from https://books.scholarsportal.info/en/ read?id=/ ebooks/ebooks2/ pda/2011-12-01/1/9934.9780816648030

Habermas, J. (1987). *The Theory of Communicative Action, Lifeworld and System: A Critique of Functionalist Reason* (Vol. 2; T. McCarthy, Trans.). Retrieved from https://uniteyouthdublin.files.wordpress.com/2015/01/4421-the_theory_of_communicative.pdf

Johnson, M. (1987). *The body in the mind: The bodily basis of meaning, imagination, and reason.* The University of Chicago Press.

Maier, S. F., & Seligman, M. E. (1976). Learned helplessness: Theory and evidence. *Journal of Experimental Psychology: General, 105*(1), 3-46. https//doi.org/10.1037/0096-3445.105.1.3

Matute, H. (1994). Learned helplessness and superstitious behaviour as opposite effects of uncontrollable reinforcement in humans. *Learning and Motivation*, 25, 216-232.

McCaslin, M. L., & Kilrea, K. A. (2019). An Introduction to Transformative Inquiry: Understanding Compelling and Significant Relationships for Personal and Societal Transformation. Retrieved July 29, 2019, from The Qualitative Report website: http://link.galegroup.com/apps/doc/A588342545/AONE?sid=lms

McGeer, V. (2004). The Art of Good Hope. *The Annals of the American Academy of Political and Social Science, 592*, 100–127. Retrieved from JSTOR.

Mohawk, J. (2016). Origins of Iriquois political thought. In S. Lobo, S. Talbot, & T. L. Morris (Eds.), *Native American voices: A reader.* Routledge.

Murray, G. (2013). Pedagogy of the possible: Imagination, autonomy, and space. *Studies in Second Language Learning & Teaching, 3*(3), 377–396.

Reinhardt, A. D. (2008). The Third Space of Sovereignty: The Postcolonial Politics of U.S.-Indigenous Relations. *Journal of American History*, (2), 512.

Robertson, R. (2010, July 21). *Ghost Dance.* https://www.youtube.com/watch?v=eA0zpemMUow

Sameshima, P., Wiebe, S., & Hayes, M. (2019, April). Imagination: The generation of possibility. In B. Andrews (Ed.), *Perspectives on arts education research in Canada, Volume 1: Surveying the landscape* (pp. 19-35). Brill Sense

Shukaitis, S. (2009). *Imaginal Machines: Autonomy & Self-organization in the Revolutions of Everyday Life.* Retrieved from www.minorcompositions.info/wp-content/uploads/2009/ImaginalMachines-web.pdf

Simpson, L. (2014). Land as pedagogy: Nishnaabeg intelligence and rebellious transformation. *Decolonization: Indigeneity, Education and Society, 3*(3), 1-25.

Starhawk. (1993). *The fifth sacred thing.* Bantam Books.

Starhawk. (1997). *Walking to Mercury.* Bantam Books.

Starhawk. (2015). *City of Refuge.* Califia Press.

Van Der Kolk, B. (2014). *The body keeps the score: Mind, brain and body in the transformation of trauma.* Penguin Books

Chapter 4

Immanent Imaginaries

Pedagogies of Wildness and Enchantment in *The Craft*

Our family garden had many different faces, but it was the wild one that I loved the most. My father saw it as neglect, as if leaving nature to take its course was some kind of moral failing, but I saw the sumacs, the lilac trees, and the wildflowers as ferociously beautiful. I could bring the soft, cloud-like seeds of the sumac to my mouth, their tartness alive on my tongue. Black-eyed Susans would bob their heads from amidst the purple-furred trunks, rustling in the wind. This wild country, untouched by my father, became a refuge to me, a place where I could be still and listen to the hidden music of the forest. This is where I learned how to love the world, where the trees and flowers taught me to feel pleasure, to be with them as they danced and grew. It is barren soil there now that my father has tended to it, the sumac trees are gone, and not even dandelions grow in the patches of dirt scattered with construction debris, but the forest lives on in my heart. I tend to it in a way that it cannot be destroyed.

To make a new humanity, we must open a place, like Pandora's box—one that contains the energy of wild Eros, daring to love and take pleasure in the living world, giving license to the animal within the human, the feeling heart and the center of a lived biophilic connection. We must dare to feel for a world that is dying, feeling grief in its humiliation and despair. There is something dangerous about eroticism, at least to the Western mind. In this mind, you might shield the eyes of a child from a breast, giving living sustenance to a baby, but not from a person tearing into a person's body with a machine gun. Shielding children from the wonderment of life, keeping them trapped within an imaginary of brutality, oils the gears of a war machine. One must consider the latent freewheeling connectivity of the erotic, carrying within itself the capacity to remake the world while also serving to undo the current human order altogether, making it into something new, something felt not only in the heart but in the stomach, the loins, in the reaches of the fingers, the lips, the intaken breath, the embodied life.

In an ancient Greek play entitled *The Bacchae* (Euripides, 1905/405BC), the queen, a character named Agaue, drunk with erotic power, tears the head off of her son, who is spying on the Bacchae in secret. In a moment of frenzy, she hallucinates that her son is a lion and parades his severed head around like a trophy. The Bacchae, followers of Bacchus, the God of wine, engage in wild revels at sites where Bacchus would strike rivers of wine from solid rock and around whom men should be wary to tread, lest they be beheaded. The women became forces of nature, wild, untameable, and feared. Here, the erotic has the character of a force of electricity, a streak of lightning tearing through the sky, setting fires. This is a power that resists human attempts at control and conformity.

Eroticism, in a more classic understanding, has poetic associations with the feminine polarity, as a pleasure expressed through Cixous' (1986) concept of jouissance. It might be more adequately captured in a word like rapture, entering into a state which unites all aspects of the self into an ecstatic union between self and world. This view of feminine pleasure—not contained neatly within the feminine body at all, but any body embracing the poetic capacity to enter into a state of pleasure without aim—calling into mind the natural and spiritual world, a world that exists as a synthesis between body and earth. Yet, there also exists a divide where we see "rationalist traditions that have policed the mind/body, culture/nature divides," and it is here that "thinking has been seen to operate in a register above and separate from untamed bodily sensation" (Gibson-Graham, 2006, p. 1). It is the well-crafted world of order that attempts to separate humankind as a mind perceiving a body and a body separate from nature in an attempt to transcend the chaotic force of eroticism and to maintain predictability, safety, and closure. Yet, the body, as "a locus of freedom, pleasure, connection and creativity" (Shapiro, 2005, xviii), continually reinvents itself, resisting attempts to neatly classify its desiring machinations. Therefore, any "critical pedagogy of the body means to understand not only how it is socialized into heteronomous relations of control and conformity but is also a site of struggle and possibility for a more liberated and erotic way of being in the world" (Shapiro, 2005, xviii). We cannot approach the healing of the world while we atomize ourselves as structures outside of the moving, physical, pleasurable, and connected world from which we emerge. Power, in the sense of a felt force within the body, is linked directly to our ability to channel wild Eros. Through embracing undercurrents of desire, we are able to access a greater depth to our humanity, one whose dark, incipient flows may awaken us to our connection with nature through an understanding of our shared roots.

When one seeks to uncover the processes of healing justice towards the health of both human and more-than-human, one must consider need, desire, emotion, and feeling holistically as they operate within the body. "To be rooted," Weil (2003) claims, "is perhaps the most important and least recognized need of the human soul" (p. 40). We require the roots of community, kinship, meaning, and pleasure too. It is in the ruptures between mind and body, human and nature—and perhaps also the rupture between mother and child, self and other—that continue to define our alienation, dislocation, and up-rootedness. As Bové (1982) suggests, "Desire for the mother and identification with her oppose the religious belief that such desire is impure, a transgression against the male God and the society built upon his authority" (p. 152). We are alienated from the fundamental source of desire within the body as we are directed away from the purest and immediate expression of that desire. As such, the productive feminine body becomes "a powerless, impure body", according to Kristeva, and "patriarchy produces a figure of woman who simultaneously offers life…[and] death (she represents a life that is mortal)" (Bové, 1982, p. 154). It is the materiality of the gestational parent that makes them so threatening, the giver of life but in so doing becoming the inciting incident of one's mortality, for in birth there is implied death. Yet it is precisely this power that makes the generative capacities of the body so compelling, continually drawing humanity into relation with the mystery of creation, as a site of both one's birth and destruction, offering both succour and poison. The world, then, as understood and expressed collectively in human society, is a confabulation, a shadowed reflection of the immense and frighteningly elusive *world* as it exists beyond the realm of the known or know-*able*. Yet, even the subtlest reaching towards a collective grounding is severed through the will to control. Habermas's (1987) notion of colonization, of the lifeworld becoming colonized by an impossibly complex, untouchable, and distant state, is a colonization of the wild erotic, the human animal, by the orderly and containable structures of an order created by the human mind. Not merely conceptual in nature, "the productive and restrictive function of the social structures, as well as of the subsequent emotional dispositions, strongly link the emotional habitus to social relations of power" (Leledaki & Brown, 2008, p. 310). The embodied narratives of social order may originate in the mind, but this power quickly becomes imbued into the flesh and acted out in the life of the individual. This includes structures of meaning, of what it *is* to be a person.

In my own life, my family is one of social outcasts who inhabit a world of mystical and unconstrained libidinal forces that eschew the orderliness to be found in many (if not most) family homes. At times, we would eat a sit down to eat a home-cooked meal but at others, we would pile cakes and brownies up onto the bed in a mountain of sugar or in other (more distressing times) there would be no one there at all to make food and I would bite directly into a block of cheese while sitting on the floor of the kitchen. My world was one wherein expectation would often be disappointed in favour of new and potentially interesting or challenging arrangements of sense, and as such, I attempt to capture in words my world, one where language isn't needed to communicate with others, sound and movement uncoupled from meaning could and would be understood by those who were connected in ways deeper than language. My foundation in life, as I describe it to some, was like being raised in a very small and insular cult, one which made it difficult for me to learn the ways of the modern world, which seemed strange and nonsensical to one so accustomed to living through feeling. I understand my parents much as forces of nature; their sense moves with time and desire, telling one story and then the next, each with engagement and earnestness. As I understand their gifts, even as they may have been born out of trauma, I understand the ways in which they taught me to connect with my body, with my desire, and with nature. It wasn't merely coincidence or serendipity that brought it about. My mother was raised without guidance either, by a woman suffering from schizophrenia who had six children. She dreamed our life when she herself was a child. Her connection to spirit threaded through our home and helped us to survive. She taught me how to live and thrive in places where there are no limits, of how to create my own path, my own boundaries.

Firth (2016) believes that modern society puts forth a limited and limiting idea of what it means to be human, which "lays the ground for the production of conformist neoliberal subjects with truncated hopes, dreams and desires" (p. 126). A society filled with subjects pursuing intangible outcomes through art and other forms of spontaneous erotic expression would be much more difficult to govern. Without the need to engage in conspiratorial thinking, a centralized state apparatus whose task it is to govern some millions, if not billions of subjects would undoubtedly pursue the standardization of modes of interaction that would make a more efficient apparatus of control, not even necessarily for the means-to-power but even just in the pursuit of the methodologies of order, which in the end may not be all that different. Furthermore, in the Western ethos, the focus on visual forms of engagement also predisposes one to a passive reception and spectatorship (Lewis, 2000, p. 67), serving the added purpose of distracting and distancing modern subjects from their messier, embodied, a-rational drives contained within and expressed through the body. As such, the mechanism for actuation becomes participation in the modes at hand, the imaginaries of others that are made palatable for ready consumption. In a world such as this, methods and routes of escape may appear hidden or even more, "the theoretical close of paranoia, the backwards-looking political certainty of melancholia and the moralistic skepticism toward power, render the world effectively uncontestable" (Gibson-Graham, 2006, p. 6). There is a tidy kind of closed-loop wherein one becomes a passive channel to take in the social imaginary and to output productive labour, take-in channels that terraform the desire for methods of materialist consumption and participate in ways that are systematized, procedural, and economic.

When we become implicated within systems involving reasonings and purposes outside of our own, when we are colonized by a social order, we lose touch with the *authentic* core of life, that of one's pursuit of an actualized internal order. We thus are "[n]ever fully responsible for our actions" (Lewis, 2000, p. 68) and this does not satisfy us; in fact, it serves to nullify our desire through the creation of an expected outcome to life, a sense of certainty in its result. There is neither a sense of fulfilment nor completion; it is a stunted order without orgasmic release. Yet, the realization of our embodiment also carries within it certain implications, namely that "capitalism as a set of economic practices scattered over a landscape, rather than a systemic concentration of power" (Gibson-Graham, 2006, p. 2). We are not untethered signifiers, we are participants within an embodied social order who have access to the systemic interactions within each lived moment, and it is here that our greatest potential for transformation lies in the engagement with the fractal, the infinite centers from which new orders may emerge.

In the 1990s teen horror flick entitled *The Craft* (Wick, 1996), Ceccarelli's (1998) notion of polysemy allows for a gently resistive reading of the popular reception of the film during its time as "a political act that involves making ethical choices for one reading or another, for one reality or another, for one set of options or another world of possibility" (Gibson-Graham, 2006, p. 11). Rather than approaching the film through its status in the genre of teen horror, I approach it instead as a revolutionary eco-erotic text that re-situates the narrative of the self, liberating desire and thus serving as a narrative of re-forging the connection between body and mind, human and nature. In all honesty, I read it in the ways that it spoke to me as a young person, hungry for meaning and willing to participate in a generous interpretation of a text that spoke to my hidden desires, liberating those feelings and giving voice to needs that had previously been suppressed. At the time, I felt alienated from my own agency, lacking an understanding of how to mobilize my own will within the social world in which I was embedded. Part of that alienation, it would seem, is that in "fearing implication with those in power" (Gibson-Graham, 2006, p. 6) we simultaneously reject our own connection to the source of our own power, which I argue lies in our connection to natural forces and the pleasure we find in our engagement with them, in our connection with erotic rapture. As such, *The Craft* has the potential to offer a pedagogy, a means by which one may pursue a liberation of the erotic through a narrative tethering of both desire and the fulfilment of a desire to the spiritual ground found through contact with the source of all life.

We Are the Weirdos, Mister

The Craft (Wick, 1996), in its essence, is a story about a group of teen outcasts at a Catholic high school in Los Angeles. At the beginning of the film, we see our protagonist, Sarah, starting life in a new school. Three other girls notice her and wonder if she may be a potential fourth in their group, completing the circle, completing the elements of Earth, Air, Fire, and Water. Occurring almost entirely within the context of a school, we can see the institutional setting as one where

> … one is no longer at the helm, making decisions. No physical effort is required, for we are now being carried by the modern tide. Self-propulsion, self-determination, freedom even, have all been left behind or lost. Mental and physical exertion has been superseded by an all-pervading passivity. (Lewis, 2000, pp. 66–67)

The experience of high school portrayed in the film has a reminiscent odour of the mundane, procedural, and formulaic, a banality that the characters seek to escape. It is a banality that many of us can relate to, school as training ground, bells signalling our daily activities, habituating one to the automation of one's impulses, the ordering of one's desire. It is an excellent setting for a revolutionary text as it exists at a time when the individual is in a process of coming into the agential power but has not yet succumbed to social conditioning. A person could leave for the summer wearing khakis and loving Christian rock and come back as a goth with a love for Slayer. Transformations can be as startling and rapid as they are profound, the world a testing ground for identity, experimentation, and confrontation.

Each character in *The Craft* is revealed to have an identity formed around an experience of trauma. Nancy lives in a trailer park with a stepfather who crosses her boundaries by making sexual advances on her. Bonnie was burnt in a house fire and was consequently scarred over the majority of her body; she covers herself, and her classmates tell stories about her hidden disfigurement. Rochelle is one of the only people of colour in a primarily White environment. Lastly, Sarah lost her mother during childbirth and is implied to suffer from psychosis. Having survived a suicide attempt, Sarah reveals that she suffered from an acute episode in which she saw all-consuming hallucinations of bugs, snakes, and rodents. The girls seem to bond through a sense of shared grief but also through a shared dislocation as the Othered. In their school, their role as outcasts is culturally constituted, as represented by the reactions of a group of teen boys to the girls walking down the hallway. The boys pretend to tremble in fear, crossing themselves, thus encoding the girls as both outcasts but also as carrying their own symbolic power through their existence at the boundaries of social and religious norms. There are rumours that the girls are witches, which is the reason behind the mockery but also, potentially, their fear. Yet, even if the girls pretend not to mind when they are faced with ridicule, "the cultural constitution of bodily experience may be a particularly effective mechanism by which a society's meanings are internalized by its citizens" (O'Connor, 2016, p. 6). Their differences torment them, and their suffering is seen at various points in the film. As much as they are inculcated within a social norm, submitting to school uniforms as well as the rules of the institution, it is clear that "common points of reference do not necessitate consensual agreement" (O'Connor, 2016, p. 10). The world that they are a part of is not their own. Jodelet, (1984), in her study of the bodies of the mentally ill, found that "female associations yield a body 'cut up into small pieces' where anatomical elements are juxtaposed" (p. 8). The feminine body is inherently the body of the outcast, alienated not only from the world but also from itself, itemized into parts. Furthermore, the girls' trauma represents "a kind of 'unclaimed experience' in which the wound does not heal, but remains still festering beneath the scar" (Jay, 2002, p. 66). The girls' stories are not unique but rather encapsulations of various narratives of oppression that exist within society, as bodies of oppressed classes, of the poor, the disabled, the racialized, the ill, and the grieving. It is these groups that have the greatest potential in establishing alliances with wild nature, the more-than-human. Identities formed within rupture are better able to reach beyond the container of the human, into the beyond.

As we are led into the story, we find ourselves at a precipice. Each girl faces a particular socially mediated blockage. Freud, Reich, and Lacan each approached blockages as a cause of dis-ease. Reich believed that the body held blockages within the tissues themselves

(Freire & da Mata, 1997), and Lacan that they were held in the "imaginary" (Firth, 2016), in that which lies beneath our conscious experience. Freud thought that these blockages could be the cause of what he called "hysterical paralysis" (Firth, 2016), of shutting down and disconnecting from the world entirely. The reactions of the girls' peers serve as what Shilling and Mellor (2007) call "body pedagogics", which are "the central means through which a culture seeks to transmit its main corporeal techniques, skills, dispositions and beliefs" (p. 533). These pedagogics cause blockages in the girls due to the circumstances of their lives, which situate them within Othered classes. "[T] hey are blocked because of meaning or images which shut them off or exile particular energies or parts of the self, whist separating 'inside' from 'outside' through processes of alienation" (Firth, 2016, p. 130). Their suffering comes from the ability to freely access and express their authentic identities, to discover and pursue their desires within the world.

Furthermore, each narrative of trauma serves to blind the girls to the potential choices they may have in order to extricate themselves from the positions they are given by their social context (Niwenshuti, 2008, p. 127). We may see that:

> ... if an individual has been subjected to continual situations that involve fear or insecurity since childhood, the physiological transformations start to crystallise in the body. A response that should be specific to certain situations becomes continuous, and creates a posture and neuromuscular armour which determine a person's way of being in the world; or, in other words, their character. (Freire & da Mata, 1997, p. 6)

As such, each character that we are introduced to is like a bird in a cage, defined by their trauma and existing by way of their socially constituted position as an Other. They exist without grounding, without center

> Because *nothing* is secure. Exile is a jealous state. What you achieve is precisely what you have no wish to share, and it is in the drawing of lines around you and your compatriots that the least attractive aspects of being in exile emerge: an exaggerated sense of group solidarity, and a passionate hostility to outsiders, even those who may in fact be in the same predicament as you. (Said, 2013, p. 184)

Before Sarah arrives, the three girls have each other, but as they are, they do not have enough power to be able to emerge from their state as exiles, still defining themselves in contrast to what they have lost. In the story, it is said that their group requires a fourth member so that they may each represent a classical element: Earth, Air, Fire, and Water. Thus, with Sarah's coming, they may begin the task of "de-identification," which is "a form of emotional rehabituation" (Leledaki & Brown, 2008, p. 304). As exiles, they are tasked with the necessity of "compensating for disorienting loss by creating a new world to rule" (Said, 2013, p. 187). Their privilege is an inversion of the privilege located in the centre. Through their exile, they are released, to discover definitions and values for the new world into which they are thrust.

In one of the most powerful scenes of the film, we see the girls on a bus heading outside of town. As they step off of the bus, the driver warns them to watch out for "weirdos," to which Nancy replies, "We are the weirdos, mister" (Wick, 1996, 00:28:50). They are heading into the forest to perform a ritual, one in which Sarah will be welcomed into the coven of witches. With them, they take their abject bodies, "the body of base materiality, the body invaded by technology, ravaged by disease and unable to maintain its normal boundaries" (Jay, 2002, p. 62). Their "'abjection' is the simultaneous attraction and repulsion for the body that derives from the moment when the child's symbiosis with the mother is interrupted" (Bové, 1982, p. 151). The mother's body is impure and in their pilgrimage, it is this abjection that they seek to transform. They will unite themselves in a covenant of the blood, symbolized through an act of pricking their fingers, the blood of which filters into a chalice from which they drink. This act is completed directly after they hold a ritual dagger to each other's chests, saying, "It is better to rush upon this blade than to enter the circle with fear in your heart" (Wick, 1996, 00:29:00). The performance of these symbolic acts serves as the creation of a temporary space in which meaning can be encountered, confronted, and shifted. They drink the blood of their 'sisters' as a means of establishing a bond that incorporates the materiality of the other into the self but that also ritualistically purifies and elevates the feminine body, for, of course, "estrangement from the world is to be expected when one is already estranged from one's body" (Lewis, 2000, p. 68). In these acts of symbolic material incorporation, they come up against the physical stuff of nature, forced into a confrontation with their "organic nature" (Lewis, 2000, p. 61).

We experience an act of creation, a chosen family coming into being. Embedded in their creative act is a belief in the power of this connection to raise them above their suffering. They "draw on the pleasures of friendliness, trust, conviviality, and companionable connection" (Gibson-Graham, 2006, p. 6) to form an emotional link whose immediacy is experienced within the felt moment. As Gibson-Graham (2006) would suggest, "In this utopian atmosphere, distrust, misrecognition, and judgment are temporarily suspended and a solidarity develops that is based not on sameness, but on a growing recognition that the other is what makes self possible" (p. 20). No longer are the girls exclusively defined by their otherness, they have become *something*. They are part of a coven, part of a newly formed symbolic order, without boundaries that may hold up against a world that seeks to destroy them. Whether this new order will manifest goodness and repair or more evil is not known and is, perhaps, beside the point. It is through the potential for creation where new possibilities are magnified, where the marginalized may find opportunities to step into their power, for good or ill. They become the creators of their world and may do with it what they will.

In the coalescing of a group, a clique, or a gang, there is the potential for a coalescing of a new social order. Each member brings into the social container certain expectations and norms that may then be directed, negotiated, mediated, and transformed by embodied relations within and between the members of the group. As such, a coven may become a testing ground for new dynamics. What one *does* in a group becomes a new social norm, presenting new dynamics and definitions of the real. As such, ritual may become a formalized space wherein the group may enter into that negotiation with given tools that serve to codify the dynamics and symbols of engagement. The materials of the ritual become the symbols themselves enacted within and against the bodies of the participants. Transformation is the expected result of the ritual form, especially in the case of Witchcraft. In drawing back the veil we may look underneath the habitus that shrouds dynamical forces under the systematizing of the banal, to take up, to examine and own one's relations as texts that may be both read and written.

Enchantment and Eco-Spiritual Eros

We may consider that "on one level, the crisis of modernist class politics is a crisis of desire" (Gibson-Graham, 2006, p. 13). Unmediated desire may interrupt the smooth functioning of the capitalist-settler state, which may seem to fly in the face of the conventional wisdom of environmentalism, that humanity requires a tempering of desire in order to live within the limits of the natural world. Yet, I argue that it is a desire that is unnaturally funneled through a mediated and narrow channel which so perverts humanity's relationship with the world. In the act of materialist consumption as a means of self-actuation, we have an unmet hunger being continually met with the wrong food. Perhaps, if human desire could be satisfied, if the holes inside of our hearts were able to be closed—healed as all wounds should be healed—desire might take on a different form. In the world as it is, one must be inculcated not only into the functioning of the state but also the multitudinous and perhaps conflicting narratives that give the state its grounding. The experience of exile, according to Said (2003),

> … is predicated on the existence of, love for, and bond with, one's native place; what is true of all exile is not that home and love of home are lost, but that loss is inherent in the very existence of both. (p. 191)

The girls in *The Craft* are not merely motivated by pain and anger but by a love for a storied experience of contentment and a lost state of innocence. It is doubtful that a return to such a state is possible, yet eroticism allows for a form of return since it "is related first and foremost to love, rather than sex or calculations of sexual appeal… Eros as sensuality, connection and love has been lost within the dominance of a capitalized market discourse that defined eroticism as sex and erotic as sexy" (Bell & Sinclair, 2014, p. 269). We cannot return to innocence, but we can return to an experience of erotic love that has no centre, a love understood through the notion of jouissance, "a state of blissful freedom and pleasure that arises when sexual activity is no longer centred on the genitals" (Bell & Sinclair, 2014, p. 269). So, desire in this context is not the fixation on a certain goal but rather an opening into a formless sense of the erotic potential of each moment.

In the forest, the girls experience a moment of enchantment, which is defined by Bennet (2001) as "a mood of lively and intense engagement with the world" that consists of "a mixed bodily state of joy and disturbance, a transitory sensuous condition dense and intense enough to stop you in your tracks and toss you onto new terrain, to move you from the actual world to its virtual possibilities" (p. 111). Suddenly, the clearing is full of butterflies. The girls are surrounded and look at the spectacle with wonderment, reaching out to have them land on their hands. They understand this experience to be a direct response from the ground of nature. They refer to this as the deity 'Manon', who is beyond good and evil and who supersedes the Devil and God alike. This event could be considered to be what Berger (2011) refers to as a "marginal experience," one that "radically challenges *all* socially objectivated definitions of reality—of the world, of others, and of self." There is a shift from one world into another. All of a sudden, it is apparent to the girls that the spirit of all-being is real and that it has the ability to communicate with them. Their communion with the ground of being is realized through this encounter. This is a form of eroticism that Bataille (1962) refers to as the spiritual erotic, a connection formed between the individual and a "limitless being" (p. 21).

In the pilgrimage to the woods, we can see what Connolly, as quoted by Gibson-Graham (2006), calls "experimental practices that we can employ to re-educate ourselves, to convince our bodies to adopt fundamentally different attitudes 'that we intellectually entertain as belief,' thereby producing new affective relations with the world" (p. 7). When the girls entered the woods, they entered into a mode of expectation and possibility. It is in our "refusal to recognize our relatedness to others [that] makes projections upon them inevitable by making identification with them impossible" (Holler, 1989, p. 82). The moment that nature is able to respond to the girls, through the vehicle of the butterflies, they "become whole" by what may be understood as their "dialogical encounters and relationships with others, whether human or not" (Blenkinsop, & Scott, 2017, p. 456). Their rootedness is established through a dialogical encounter with nature itself. Their being is confirmed through the acknowledgement of their desire for connection.

In modernity, "as we are severed from the community of diverse being, we are unaware of our own being, and, like Narcissus, we will see that community only in our own image: the image of objects divorced from the being in relation to which they have selfhood and value" (Holler, 1989, p. 83). It is through the dissolution of socially mediated reality that the girls are able to enter into direct relation with the world, and thus to restore their sense of selfhood, a selfhood in relation. In essence, in going to the forest, they are returning home, which is also

> … in a sense recovering or at least becoming aware of life-giving interactions and reclaiming the freshness of what has been lost in our best shared humanity, and allowing it to fill our whole being and life. Going back into the body, (re)inhabiting the body, and letting the body inhabit us again, involves challenging a discriminatory, boxed-in logic… it challenges and overcomes the Cartesian dichotomy and anxiety, finding our way through destructive binaries, alienating dualisms and similar modes of thinking. (Niwenshuti, 2018, p. 124)

There is a moment, if only a moment, wherein the girls become whole, transfixed by a direct relation and communication from living nature. This is a recognition of life itself, a sense of meaning made in erotic dialogue with limitless being. Blenkinsop (2017) says of these experiences that "What becomes evident is that the self is now open, flexible, and dynamic—responsive to similarly dynamic others and present to surrounding dynamic ecologies" (p. 463). In turn, it is the achievement of a state of fluid openness that allows the girls "to cultivate a potential for choosing to change" what up until this point has been a "habitual experiencing and enactment of oppression and repression" (Leledai & Brown, 2008, p. 316).

Jay (2002), in discussing Dewey's aesthetics says that the aesthetic experience is a "model of that self-realization…best expressed in the sensually mediated, organically consummated, formally molded activity" (p. 55). What is interesting about this theory is that Dewey believed that the aesthetic experience could extend beyond the practice of art into a felt activation of the democratic social order. Furthermore, he saw in body art an "insistence that even the body is a process, not a fixed object in the world," which he thought "powerfully instantiates the way in which democracy is always in front of us, never fully achieved" (Jay, 2002, p. 65). The experience of a bodily mediated symbolic act performed with others might constitute a form of self-realization, a democratic process in itself, of reconstituting the body as an unfixed object, in dialogical relation, both *in* and *of* the world. This calls into question the fixity of the body but also the fixity of the world from which it emerges. It is what legendary Chilean filmmaker Alejandro Jodorowsky (2004) calls "trembling reality." Jodorowsky believed that symbolic actions could engage with reality in ways that would reveal its flexibility, engaging in the world of acts much like a kind of embodied poetry. He believed that healing could be achieved through living out the poetry of one's life, activating the symbolic and engaging with the implicit logic of one's world in order to see what would happen. In the act, the symbolic would then become tethered within the material world, informed and transformed by it. Binds that existed within the body as potential forces could then be tested, investigated, and ultimately understood through the lens of an embodied, mortal, and human existence.

In the performance of the "poetic act," the act of symbolic completion, we are able to liberate repressed energy from the body through processing and resolving an internal symbolic order. In turn, Leledaki and Brown (2008) suggest that "This change of [one's] embodied perception through physicalisation feels like connecting with the sacred and acquiring a new sense of belonging and ontological security that we might describe as a sense of empowerment coming from a state of immanence by connecting to... the 'core self'" (pp. 322 — 323). As the girls seek the ground upon which they are rooted, we see that "for the exile, habits of life, expression, or activity in the new environment inevitably occur against the memory of these things in another environment. Thus both the new and the old environments are vivid, actual, occurring together contrapuntally" (Said, 2003, p. 191). We see here, a union of an "early symbiosis as memory... that early moment of pleasure" (Bovè, 1982, p. 156). We have a return home, a symbolic reunion with the mother, the source of life, through the girls' direct connection and communication with nature and, in that reunion, a revolution of the wild erotic that asks us to look towards the interconnected source of all life. It suggests a return to "the origin and essence of our wealth," which is given to us through the sun, the earth, and nature, "which dispenses energy—wealth—without any return" (Bataille, 1991, p. 28). Relation with the world demonstrates orthopraxy in that the world and its living-*ness* responds to relations of balance and return. The world gives to its living children freely and in an abundance that exists in accordance with cyclical balance. In taking, we must give because the cycle demands it of us. This belief is grounded in the ritual form of gifting tobacco. It is an acknowledgement that taking without return is a disruption of the balance. In our participation in the balance of nature, we freely reap the rewards of that relation, being offered up the bounty of a thriving world as gifts freely given, without expectation. The world is not a fool for offering up these gifts without expectation. To take beyond measure is to destroy the balance and thus, impoverish ourselves.

Sorceress and Hysteric

As Cixous (1986) puts it, the sorceress "is able to dream Nature and therefore conceive it, [she] incarnates the reinscription of the traces of paganism that triumphant Christianity repressed," while "the hysteric, whose body is transformed into a theatre for forgotten scenes, relives the past, bearing witness to a lost childhood that survives in suffering" (p. 5). When the girls are in their circle, expressing their desires, each asks for a gift from the spirit. Bonnie asks for beauty, Rochelle for revenge on a White woman who is being racist towards her, Sarah for the love of a boy named Chris, and Nancy for all the power of Manon. Nancy goes further than any of the girls towards the realization of her desires; she is also the one who exhibits the most power. When they collectively decide to "invoke the spirit," Nancy becomes the only one of them to successfully embody the spirit of Manon. She is consequently able to walk on water—an obvious allusion to the story of the Christ—and in addition to this, she is able to catalyze a mass beaching of sea animals, primarily whales and sharks, which she refers to as her 'gifts,' consequently representing Nancy as a figure of both creation and destruction. Cixous (1986) writes,

> This feminine role, the role of sorceress, of hysteric, is ambiguous, antiestab-lishment…because the symptoms—the attacks—revolt and shake the public, the group, the men, the others to whom they are exhibited. The sorceress heals, against the Church's canon; she performs abortions, favors nonconjugal love, converts the unlivable space of a stifling Christianity. The hysteric unties familiar bonds, introduces disorder into the well-regulated unfolding of everyday life, gives rise to magic in ostensible reason. (p. 5)

Nancy represents the power to embrace more than just the healing aspect of direct connection to power; she represents the total embodiment of aspects of both light and dark, creative and destructive. She sees beauty in the mass death of sea life, presented as though for her pleasure. Her pleasure resonates much more with Lacan's reading of jouissance, as existing when one's desire becomes transfixed on the limits of what one is not, perhaps transforming pleasure into pain through the pursuit of what may not be obtained, a self with no limit (Feldstein, 1996). Nancy recognizes no limits to her will, desire, or power, as demonstrated through her wish.

We see in her an embodiment of the chaotic, uncontained erotic, like Aguae beheading her son. And yet we also witness her in contemplation, chanting alone by herself in her bedroom, focused and intent. She is willing and able to discipline her body to achieve her desires and as Leledaki and Brown (2008) state, "the cultivation of inner stillness (calm and concentration) is in itself an achieved unified body-mind experience of non-reactive engagement with personal and social life" (p. 316). It is through the power of her conviction that the girls are able to achieve a collective sense of purpose, even though they consider Sarah to be the source of their power since she is a 'natural witch.' Nancy and Sarah represent two halves of a coin. Where Nancy is fast, extreme, passionate, and hot, Sarah is slow, considerate, cool, and melancholy. In their dynamic, we see played out "the cultural ethos of self-control" which

> ... is enacted in prescriptions to regulate bodily desires regarding sexuality, food and substance use. Restraint in these domains signals discipline and self-mastery, traits which are valorised in developed Western societies. In contrast, yielding to sensory indulgence is represented as a moral failing and serves as a basis on which traditionally stigmatised outgroups—including those who are overweight, sexually atypical or struggling with substance addiction—are derogated. (O'Connor, 2016, p. 9)

Nancy has the ability to discipline herself, to practice the sustained connection with her desire and purpose. However, she also admits to sleeping with the primary male protagonist/antagonist Chris and is punished for it, being labelled a slut. Sarah, on the other hand, even though she purports to be in love with Chris and asks for Manon to gift her with his love, resists Chris' advances and is punished for her resistance through his attempt to rape her. There is no safe way to wield feminine sexuality. The feminine body is not her own, and the girls are punished both for the act of succumbing to pleasure as well as the act of denying it.

Yet, in Nancy's response to the attempted rape, we experience a sense of Bahktin's (1984) carnival, an upending of the social order to one of spontaneous creation of, perhaps perverted but nevertheless, immediate orders of sense expression. Nancy uses magic to pose as Sarah to seduce Chris, who is under a love spell towards Sarah. When she first tries to seduce him as herself, we see him reject Nancy and in a moment of uncanny revelation, she transforms herself. As he begins to make love to the person he believes to be Sarah, Sarah herself bursts into the room, therefore rupturing the fantasy in which they were immersed. Nancy is then able to drive Chris towards the balcony by levitating off of the ground, and in his panic to escape her, he falls to his death. As a sorceress and hysteric, Nancy is able to upend the order of things, to externalize the rupture of her own trauma and create the potential for transformation. In the sense of the grotesque (Bahktin, 1984), she is able to make right Chris's transgression against both Sarah and herself instead driving him into the abyss. In his desire to find union with the object of his desire through sex, and perhaps in his own way to complete the symbolic journey of reunion with the mother, he is instead swallowed by the void, welcomed home into the realm of chaos. Instead of being tragic, his death serves as a kind of catharsis, the righting of a wrong. Despite the fact that death is an inversion of the potentially life-affirming and giving act of sexual love, his death also feels like a renewal. It is in acts such as these where the potential of the Carnivale is brought to the fore; in upending the order of reason, one may witness the power of the double-bind, the autotelic loop, of life and death, good and evil contained within a moment, the dialectic that may not be resolved except in the acceptance of chaos.

Yet, Nancy cannot continue to harness the power to which she has gained access. She has gained a sense of liberty through the act of doing, which Foucault (1984) believes requires "exercise." She expresses her freedom and liberty through the pursuit of her desire, and yet she is not capable of expending the energy she has harnessed. As Bataille (1991) believed,

> ... the living organism, in a situation determined by the play of energy on the surface of the globe, ordinarily receives more energy than is necessary for maintaining life; the excess energy (wealth) can be used for the growth of a system (e.g., an organism); if the system can no longer grow, or if the excess cannot be completely absorbed in its growth, it must necessarily be lost without profit; it must be spent, willingly or not, gloriously or catastrophically. (p.

21)

As we see towards the conclusion of the film, Nancy transforms more fully into the hysteric as she reaches the limits of her ability to contain either her power or her pain. She exhibits an end that Cixous (1985) refers to as "*conservative* because every sorceress ends up being destroyed, and nothing is registered of her but mythical traces. Every hysteric ends up inuring others to her symptoms, and the family closes around her again, whether she is curable or incurable" (p. 5).

Organic Boundaries: The Coalescing of New Orders

We see in Nancy's downfall "the belatedness of a traumatic event or events that have not yet been assimilated or reconciled. As such, it brings to the surface these moments of founding violence that even the most democratic polity has difficulty fully acknowledging" (Jay, 2002, p. 66). Her desires could find no limits because she felt that what she wanted was unlimited power. As such, she began to erode the sense of connection to the source that had been *collectively* formed. Because she cannot use the energy she has created constructively towards her growth as a person or as pleasure, it is then exerted catastrophically through the destruction of the order that was created through the pilgrimage and the covenant of sisters. She tries to turn the group against Sarah, rewriting Sarah as an outcast in a new order that is created by Nancy. In retaliation, Sarah tries to 'bind' Nancy as a means of creating a boundary *for* her and out of concern for her well-being, saying that she binds her from doing harm to others and to herself. Nancy cannot condone this restriction of her will towards power and attempts to destroy Sarah and Sarah's only recourse is to 'invoke the spirit' into herself and to use the power to create a container for Nancy.

We see Sarah as symbolic of a kind of natural order attempting to exert a limit on Nancy's untethered expansion. Sarah is the yielding, intuitive *yin* to Nancy's energetic, expansive *yang*, and thus is forced to act as a container for Nancy's power in order to create balance. In Sarah's resistance to accepting the gift of the spirit, she faces her own anxiety about wielding her power. It is only in the moment before her death that she is able to muster the courage, after which she embodies what Bataille (1991) calls a "freedom of mind." After she anxiously relives the experiences leading up to her suicide attempt, including the hallucinations of bugs, serpents, and rodents, she pursues Nancy with "an exuberance, a superfluity" that imbues her with "an incomparable force" (Bataille, 1991, pp. 13-14). She has become liberated through the acceptance of both her shadow and her innate gift, her connection to power. She does not kill Nancy, but rather establishes limits to her power. At the end of the film, we see Nancy in a mental institution, restrained and drugged. She claims that she can fly, which in her new state of being is not believed. She becomes tethered within the social mechanisms of order that deny her agency, and her will to power.

As an audience, how then do we see Nancy's downfall? Do we read it like Cixous, as the sorceress destroyed, with nothing but "mythic traces" left behind? Nancy is indeed institutionalized in a mental asylum, yet there is a lingering impression left from her institutionalization, a nagging concern at the edges of her demise. She is not believed when she says that she can fly because she cannot fly. Her power has been restrained. As Sarah says, she has misused her gift, and it has thus been rescinded. As omniscient observers, however, we know that Nancy is telling the truth; she *can* fly because she *did* fly. There is a seed of doubt here, a wondering whether the ravings of the 'hysteric' might not connect to a socially dissociated narrative but, instead, might indicate an internally consistent truth, like what Laing (1970) asserts about the ravings of those experiencing psychosis, as forms of reality that exist as intensities that speak only to the individual. In addition, we have Sarah who, when visited by Rochelle and Bonnie to ask whether she still has her powers, can summon a lightning bolt out of the sky to strike down a tree branch that then falls in front of them. Sarah retains her power, which suggests to the audience that there is the ability to retain a gift given by the spirit of Manon, but only if one uses it with respect to its limits and in service of balance. In Sarah, we see demonstrated a kind of natural order that demands balance not through a moral order that requires the individual to restrict their passions but rather through a process of cause and effect.

The Transmission of Somatic Realties

In the images and ideologies embedded within this film, we have what may be referred to as "crystallized philosophical fragments, mind bombs that work to expand the universe of thinkable thoughts"

(DeLuca & Peeples, 2002, p. 6). We see played out our own internalized desires for connection, a return to innocence, and an expression of the repressed libidinal powers of eroticism that we are required to redirect towards the aims of capitalist commodity-driven consumerism. It may be that "a thought, either formulated to oneself or not formulated at all, works secretly on the mind and yet has but little direct influence over it" (Weil, 2003, p. 186). Whether one has direct experience or knowledge of the deeper themes contained within this film, it may plant a seed in the psyche that may become activated. There is created a question of, "what if?" This question only needs to come into contact with fertile soil in order to grow.

This film was a revelation for many young people of my generation and others beyond it. In its status as a cult film, it speaks to the potency of its images to capture the latent and hidden, to set free the desiring forces of those who may not find power in the social order of their worlds. When I watched this movie, it was the catalyzing incident in my adoption of Witchcraft as a spiritual pursuit. A film largely made in a perhaps, mawkish, drive for sensational entertainment appealed to deeply held libidinal impulses within my own psyche; it put a voice to something intensely real, a yearning that I had not before been able to understand or articulate. I have watched this film dozens of times, and in each viewing, I see new shades of significance and relive memories of my nascent drive towards magic. The conflict in the second half of the film is almost extraneous to me. When watching the first half of the film, I feel a loosening of some tightly held element in my body, the development of direct connection with spirit that I achieved through the medium of a film. The film led me to the practice of magic, to dancing in circle around a raging bonfire, to standing naked in a forest clearing, to holding hands and singing with people, looking deeply into their eyes and seeing them looking boldly into mine without shame. Schutten (2006) offers that "media can offer covert access to [a] movement's ideologies" (p. 349), in this instance, the movements of Paganism, Witchcraft, or the Occult, alongside other movements that share an ideological core in their reverence for nature or a radical belief in the power of the individual to shape reality. One may contend that "popular culture is always contradictory and will include traces of the struggle between dominant and resistant ideologies in order to increase its 'popular' appeal" (Schutten, 2006, p. 349). In an appeal towards authenticity, *The Craft* serves as a covert revolutionary text, a narrative that performs what one may refer to as "consciousness-raising… [of] validating submerged realities and constructing voice within safe space as a basis for affective transformation" (Firth 2016, p. 128).

The Wild Erotic

The erotic is not limited to the act of sexual congress but rather is a potential, an effusive energy that links one with a limitless being. When one is in contact with the wild erotic, there is a sense of continuity of all-pervasive being and doing within a collective whole. Yet, this force cannot be properly contained within the social imaginary as a limitless force; it cannot be contained at all. As such, there is need for an ability to escape, to walk outside of the limits of order, to touch upon the ground of being, to undo the social order and re-enter it as newly baptized, like one aware of the order *as* an order, as a created text in which we live and breathe. Through media like *The Craft* (Wick, 1996), we see an example of a narrative that not only sets out a philosophical framework for such a journey but that also exemplifies some of the practices that might take one there. Through acts of ritual magic, one may enter into a space of radical potential to directly engage with and rewrite the symbolic texts of our lives. We needn't experience the overt and instantaneous magic that is exhibited in the film to be able to open ourselves to the raw intensity of direct contact with nature as both a test and a home to our mortality and life as human beings. There is more to the world than what is constituted in the habitus. It is for witches and adventurers to go out and bring back knowledge from the beyond.

References

Bakhtin, M. (1984). *Rabelias and his World* (H. Iswolsky, Trans.). Bloomington, IN: Indiana University Press.

Bataille, G. (1991). *The Accursed Share: An Essay on General Economy (Volume I - Consumption)*. New York: Zone Books.

Bell, E., & Sinclair, A. (2014). Reclaiming eroticism in the academy. *Organization, 21*(2), 268—280. https://doi.org/10.1177/1350508413493084

Bennett, J. (2001). *The Enchantment of Modern Life: Attachments, Crossings, and Ethics*. Retrieved from https://books.google.ca/books?id=WXtxenINMXcC

Berger, P. L. (2011). Religion and World Construction. *The Sacred Canopy: Elements of a Sociological Theory of Religion*. Retrieved from https://books.google.ca/books?id=WcC-AYOq6Q4C

Blenkinsop, S., & Scott, C. (2017). Becoming Teacher/Tree and Bringing the Natural World to Students: An Educational Examination of the Influence of the Other⊠than⊠Human World and the Great Actor on Martin

Buber's Concept of the I/Thou. *Educational Theory, 67*(4), 453—469. https://doi.org/10.1111/edth.12258

Bové, C. M. (1988). "The Twin Faces of the Mother's Mask": Julia Kristeva's "Powers of Horror: An Essay on Abjection" (Book Review). *Discourse; Detroit, 11*(1), 151—156.

Ceccarelli, L. (1998). Polysemy: Multiple meanings in rhetorical criticism. *Quarterly Journal of* Speech. 84. 395-415, Retrieved August 11, 2019, from https://journals-scholarsportal-info.ezproxy.lakeheadu.ca/details/00335630/v84i0004/395_pmmirc.xml

Cixous, H. (1986). *The Newly Born Woman.* Minneapolis: Univeristy of Minnesota Press.

Clark, L. S. (2003). *From angels to aliens.* Oxford University Press.

DeLuca, K., & Peeples, J. (n.d.). From public sphere to public screen: Democracy, activism, and the "violence" of Seattle. *Critical Studies in Media Communication, 19*(2), 125—151.

Elias, N. (2001). *The Loneliness of Dying* (E. Jephcott, Trans.). Retrieved from https://www.amazon.ca/Loneliness-Dying-Norbert-Elias/dp/0826413730

Euripides. (1905). The Bacchae of Euripides (G. Murray, Trans.). Originally published 405 BC. Retrieved August 12, 2019, from Project Gutenberg Canada website: https://gutenberg.ca/ebooks/murrayeuripides-bacchae/murrayeuripides-bacchae-00-h-dir/murrayeuripides-bacchae-00-h.html

Feldstein, R., Fink, B., & Jaanus, M. (1996). *Reading Seminars I and II: Lacan's Return to Freud.* Retrieved from https://books.google.ca/books?id=qchW574Tpp0C

Firth, R. (2016). Somatic pedagogies: Critiquing and resisting the affective discourse of the neoliberal state from an embodied anarchist perspective *. *Ephemera; Leicester, 16*(4), 121—142.

Foucault, M. (1984). *The Foucault Reader* (P. Rabnow, Ed.). Retrieved from https://books.google.ca/books?id=HCNZgv0URa4C

Freire, R. and J. da Mata (1997) 'Soma: An anarchist therapy Vol. III: Body to body'. Trans. C. Buckmaster. [http://www.scribd.com/doc/127312160/Soma-An-Anarchist-Therapy-Vol-III-Body-to-Body]

Gibson-Graham, J. K. (2006). *A postcapitalist politics.* Retrieved from https://books-scholarsportal-info.ezproxy.lakeheadu.ca/uri/ebooks/ebooks2/pda/2011-12-01/1/9934.9780816648030

Habermas, J. (1987). *The Theory of Communicative Action, Lifeworld and System: A Critique of Functionalist Reason* (Vol. 2; T. McCarthy, Trans.). Retrieved from https://uniteyouthdublin.files.wordpress.com/2015/01/4421-the_theory_of_communicative.pdf

Hamilton, M. J. (2017). Ruptures in reformation: Embodiment revealed. *Indian Theatre Journal, 1*(2), 123-. Retrieved from Academic OneFile.

Holler, L. (1989). Is There a Thou "Within" Nature? A Dialogue with H. Richard Niebuhr. *The Journal of Religious Ethics, 17*(1), 81—102. Retrieved from JSTOR.

Jay, M. (2002). Somaesthetics and Democracy: Dewey and Contemporary Body Art. *Journal of Aesthetic Education, 36*(4), 55—69. https://doi.org/10.2307/3301568

Jodelet, D. (1984). The representation of the body and its transformations (L. Hodson, Trans.). Retrieved August 12, 2019, from ResearchGate website: https://www.researchgate.net/publication/324969329_The_representation_of_the_body_and_its_transformations

Jodorowsky, A. (2004). *Psychomagic: The Transformative Power of Shamanic Psychotherapy.* Toronto: Inner Traditions.

Laing, R. D. (1970). *The Divided Self: An Existential Study in Sanity and Madness.* Retrieved from http://centrebombe.org/Ronald.D.Laing-The.Divided.Self.(1960).pdf

Leledaki, A., & Brown, D. (2008). 'Physicalisation': A Pedagogy of Body-Mind Cultivation for Liberation in Modern Yoga and Meditation Methods. *Asian Medicine, 4*(2). Retrieved from https://brill.com/vsaidiew/journals/asme/4/2/article-p303_4.xml

Lewis, N. (2000). The Climbing Body, Nature and the Experience of Modernity. *Body & Society, 6*(3/4), 58. https://doi.org/10.1177/1357034X00006003004

Niwenshuti, T. (2018). A Critique of Embodiment. *Strategic Review for Southern Africa, 40*(1), 117-. Retrieved from Academic OneFile.

O'Connor, C. (2017). Embodiment and the Construction of Social Knowledge: Towards an Integration of Embodiment and Social Representations Theory. *Journal for the Theory of Social Behaviour, 47*(1), 2—24. https://doi.org/10.1111/jtsb.12110

Rubin, E. L. (2018). Phenomenology, Colonialism, and the Administrative State. *Washington University Law Review,* (5), 1097.

Said, E. (2013). Reflections on Exile. In *Reflections on Exile: & other literary & cultural essays* (p. 180—192). Retrieved from http://www.mcrg.ac.in/RLS_Migration/Reading_List/Module_A/65.Said,%20Edward,%20Reflections_on_Exile_and_Other_Essay(BookFi).pdf

Schutten, J. K. (2006). Invoking Practical Magic: New Social Movements, Hidden Populations, and the Public

Screen. *Western Journal of Communication*, *70*(4), 331—354. https://doi.org/10.1080/10570310600992137

Shapiro, Sherry. *Pedagogy and the Politics of the Body: A Critical Praxis*, Routledge, 2005.

Shilling, C., & Mellor, P. A. (2007). Cultures of embodied experience: Technology, religion and body pedagogics. *Sociological Review*, *55*(3), 531—549. https://doi.org/10.1111/j.1467-954X.2007.00721.x

Weil, S. (2003). *The need for roots: Prelude to a declaration of duties towards mankind*. Retrieved from https://ebook-central-proquest-com.ezproxy.lakeheadu.ca

Wick, D. (Producer), & Fleming, A. (Director). (1996). *The Craft* [Motion Picture]. United States: Columbia Pictures.

Chapter 5

Witches, Wolves, And Cyborgs

A Minor Literature of Immanence

them: every girl is into astrology and witchy shit now. basic. trendy. *eyeroll*

me: maybe it's basic and trendy. or maybe it's a global feminist awakening wherein we collectively return to our true nature before we overthrow the patriarchy and devour your very soul, KEVIN.

8:22 AM · 19 Nov 19 ·

("You Ready?" Source: Author; Original Source: @therealhighpriestess11, 2020)

The internet was an instrumental tool in my growing awareness of Witchcraft and its practices, not only in nascent websites sharing information in the early days of the internet, but in networking with groups that primarily came through the use of a now-defunct site called *the Witches Voice*, retired after 22 years of service to the community. Every coven or working group that I was a part of at that time, was formed through connections made online. In a somewhat isolated community, it was not easy to find others who shared the same beliefs and interests, but it was nearly impossible to connect with other members of a minority spiritual practice which might not have any other active members within one's community. Thus, the internet became a vital site for explorations and connections, a means by which new values were passed on, where stories and songs might be documented.

There is a vital tradition of oral storytelling and song that threads through pagan groups, one that is difficult to access for those who lack personal connections. Those too are documented and shared freely and without reserve in online spaces by users who seek to build a culture of resilience, exuberance, and generosity.

If we are to accept the world as a flow between nature and humans, we might also accept flows between humans and technology, nature and technology. If humanity is an extension of nature, a product of nature, an immanent piece within a natural cycle, technology as an extension of the human is also an extension of nature at its limit, an arm of the same being that has given birth to ant-hills, hives, nests, burrows, and dams. The internet is a collective mind as much as stories were and are a collective social mind, capturing and disseminating meaning through lively engagements touching upon the individual. As Hung (2014) suggests, "The natural plane does not seek to distinguish between natural and human, but to think about how people enter a diverse relationship with other beings" (p. 155). As desire emerges into being, acts touch upon and through the boundaries of the other. Humanity is suffused with nature up to and including its limit, touching upon and by it. Beyond the definitions, words, and concepts from which the world is built, the divisions between objects and beings of the world exist within a state of flux. What stops one from seeing human technology as a natural object, except the fact that it reaches beyond the balance of the natural world? In technology, we see the product of an alienated humanity and our products are an expression of that separation. Yet, they remain entangled with the world even in their destruction of it. Would technology itself change if seen as emergent from nature? Perhaps if we understood our houses, cars, and clothes as pieces of the world that are continuous with it, we might inevitably feel into an understanding of return, where created objects emerge from and return to the Earth. We might begin to feel that our belongings are borrowed; they are first the belongings of the planet and thus exist within a cycle of perpetual regeneration and decay.

In the 1973 film, *Fantastic Planet* (Laloux, 1973), the human race (Oms) are bought and sold as pets to a species of giant robotic aliens (Draags). In the story, the Oms learn secret knowledge, stolen from the Draags and use it to throw over their captors, installing themselves on a satellite to the planet. We see in this story an inversion of human exceptionalism and with it an invitation towards empathy with the dispossessed. We can also see the inversion of settler colonialism, an imaginary of a liberated oppressed. Such narratives draw in those without voice, the oppressed and the beings of the more-than-human both, expanding the potential for identification and understanding. To see oneself as prey, as in Plumwood's (1999) meditations on being nearly eaten by a crocodile, places human identity within the cycle of Earthly regeneration. Seeing human beings as pets or prey creates the potential for empathetic sympathies to exist between humans and those whose agency is habitually excluded from concern. Do they dream, how do they feel about our relations with them? In a teaching I received in a personal conversation, an Elder brought up the ways in which we refer to the beings of the world, suggesting that we call the trees, instead, tree people (personal communication, 2019, September 20). When I call my dog a dog person, I can begin to see the relative equality in our rights to life and dignity while recognizing the differences in our needs and intelligences, as separate but valid (as she is a person who happens to also be a dog). What would it mean to look at a chair as a person, as a form of intelligence that sees no need to move or change but to simply become acted upon and used? Through the means of simulating and experimenting via imagination, especially through the medium of technology, we are increasingly able to opt into or out of identities that also open the imaginal to new possibilities for being. We have a proliferating storying of the self, the potential of intentionality in crafting an ego that may exist instead as a network of lived relations. Freud (1960) says,

> It is to this ego that consciousness is attached; the ego controls the approaches to motility—that is, to the discharge of excitations into the external world;

it is the mental agency which supervises all its own constituent processes and which goes to sleep at night, though even then it exercises the censorship on dreams. (p. 8)

Our outer presentation exists as a site of sensual contact with the world, but not only sensual, it is the site of imaginal contact as well. If the ego has the potential to release or repress our very dreams, what might be possible if one were able to mediate the ego, to recast it through a redrawing of the boundary between self and other? If we wish to harness this potential to further embody emancipatory narratives, to bring them into practice in the present moment, especially in healing the divide between humans and nature, we may not wish to situate human invention as outside of nature. Instead, it may be fruitful to seek out a balance between the romantic narratives of past communion with nature and the transcendence of limits within the imaginal, which may be facilitated through technologies.

A Witch is one who is able to create a-rational linkages between opposing forces, opening up the spaces of conflict as an invitation to spontaneous union. I examine such links as encapsulated in the literary tradition of internet memes as artifacts of imaginative synthesis, as bundles with spiritual significance that may unfold within the individual souls of their recipients. Memes are able to encompass some sense of the identificatory possibilities of Witchcraft and have the potential to exemplify a flattening of difference between humans and nature through the possibilities of technology and its ability to radically expand the imaginal space of human potentiality. The memes of Witchcraft are a form of what Deleuze and Guattari (1983) call a "minor literature," a literature within a literature, a form of recontextualized symbolic order formed from the pieces of a larger ideational structure. They point towards the latent organic power of internet communications to spark the imagination as well as to spur the creation of new forms of social organization. It is in the expansion and expression of the imaginary where new worlds may be proposed and pursued and in the spontaneous expression of libidinal energies where hidden desires may become manifest. The spontaneous, fun, and confrontational nature of memes as a form of a literary imaginary, contain within them, revolutionary potential. Deleuze and Guattari's (1987) concept of the plane of immanence is triangulated via Haraway's (1990; 2016) concept of the cyborg as well as Raphael's (1997) image of the wolf. In each, there is the expression of a liminal identity fragment that may be proposed (baked), processed (masticated), and adopted (become) as a piece of revolutionary identifacatory potential. It is through the liminal where subjects may take up the tools necessary to confront the patriarchal drive to consume or destroy the natural world while also embracing humanity's creative potential, the pursuit of human comfort, joy, and pleasure in harmony with total ecological health for it is in the liminal that we may encounter nature as existing beyond the ideational structures of human being-*ness*.

A Minor Literature Through Memes

Brown (2013) points out that "Memes are not only funny cat photos; they are the way people think about their culture." (p. 190). When we connect to memes, it is because they express something that feels true about the way we live our lives or how we see the world. If we decide to put something on our Facebook or Instagram feeds, it reflects Dennet's (1990) assertion that our esteem for particular memes makes them the more replicable. Memes are replicable for myriad reasons. We share what we feel to be true. Their quality as amusements orient them towards expressions of fun, yet, they also carry within them discreet packages, bundles of sacred connections, perspectives. The purview of a meme carries within it a position. Deleuze, Guattari, and Brinkley (1983) call a minor literature, "the literature a minority makes in a major language" (p. 16). They turn the true on its head, making fun of it through the invention of new forms of sense. They express something that is unspoken, bringing it into the real with all its complexities, contradictions, celebrations and negations. Broadcasting memes that appeal to a subculture, in this instance, those attached to the aesthetic of Witchcraft, present a particular reading of the host culture inscribed with alternative modes of morality using an altered syntax in a dominant symbolic language. Hebdige (1987) says, "ideology by definition thrives *beneath* consciousness. It is here, at the level of 'normal common sense,' that the ideological frames of reference are most firmly sedimented and most effective because it is here that their ideological nature is most effectively concealed" (p. 11). Bringing an ideological reframing of the mundane world onto the internet is a probing of that sediment, a testing of the permeability of one's ideological perspective. If I laugh at a meme, does that mean that it is true?

It may be that, "The struggle between different discourses, different definitions and meanings within ideology is… a struggle within signification a struggle for possession of the sign which extends to even the most mundane areas of everyday life" (Hebdige, 1987, p. 17). If a meme can successfully communicate and replicate itself, it can begin to wrest away control over the meaning of things and, in the case of an ideology like Witchcraft, putting that control directly into the hands of the individual. For, in the identity of the Witch, there can be no appeals to an ultimate authority, no prescribed way of being or doing, and no ideal form or outcome. It is a definition applied to groups of cultural renegades, who coalesce mainly around their experiences of exile.

The reflexive act of absorbing, adopting, or transforming, and then sharing is the foundation of what Shifman (2014) calls "participatory culture" (p. 4). The internet is a place where ideas may proliferate, and the territory of the internet, as much as it is relegated to cyberspace, also touches down upon our embodied worlds, not only in the cables and servers that act as the embodiment of the cloud (Hoechsmann, 2021) but also through the ways in which the conceptual nature of internet culture and communications travel through the embodied systems of those inputting and outputting information from out of and into their own bodies. The concept of sharing is anchored in ways that suggest that "sharing is not only a buzzword" but "has emerged as a central cultural logic, encompassing realms such as 'sharing economies' and sharing emotions in intimate relationships" (Shifman, 2014, p. 19). The internet becomes a place of reciprocity, where we may share and be shared, where we make take in as we produce, and where meaning may become tethered and transformed and then actuated in the world through our identities, beliefs, and actions. Indeed, one may argue that the internet has revealed a latent human drive towards sharing, collaboration, and communication, offering a potential seed for a gift economy, an economy based not upon direct person-to-person trade of one good for another, but on the spontaneous generosity of sharing that comes from the establishment of a human collective, an will to growth and discovery for its own sake.

Yet, the internet also serves as a kind of shadow, revealing the deep, hidden, and turbulent divisions in our cultural psyche. The implicit moral realities embedded in memes act as forms of emotional and cultural currency that may, in turn, take root in minds that are suscep-tible to their communications (Knobell & Lankshear, 2005). In truth, even though memes are relegated to cyberspace, they still need to pass through the realm of the senses to be both processed and passed along (Shifman, 2014), and they do so by wielding the lived significations of the everyday. There is a larger cultural process happening here of sifting through, sharing, taking up and discarding cultural baggage in order to find a proper mirror of the self. In Dawkins's (1989) broader sense of the meme as a replicable cultural form, each meme carries within it a set of interlocking values and logics that extend beyond immediate signification. For example, style can have embedded deep-set social, cultural, or religious meanings. Hebdige (1987) says, "Style in subculture is… pregnant with significance. Its transformations go 'against nature,' interrupting the process of 'normalization'" (p. 18). In contemporary society, we are better able "to make choices about what we do with the cultural baggage that previous generations have left us: to use our capacity for meta-representation in order to collate and evaluate it" (Distin, 2005, p. 194). Through an ever-increasing capac-ity to both share and remix, we develop tools that enable us to pick and choose our very identities, creating channels for the expression of new perspectives. In the presentation of lived potentials, one may remake the embedded matrixes of the banal, sifting through momen-tary instances of touch wherein the human life intersects with the world, making ideational shifts in those interactions that may serve as fundamental remodulations of group behaviour and identity when translated into the macro.

In this, we may find the familiar logic of a neo-liberal focus on individual action as a means for change, which shifts the locus of pressure from the impacts of group structures—most notably corpora-tions—in terraforming the world for the benefit of the few, to the indi-vidual choices of consumers based upon their perceived ecological and social value. It must be said that change must not remain within the purview of the individual alone, but rather, it is in recognition of the individual as the building block of the collective where the realization of the individual revolutionary agency may come to bear, where col-lective structures may begin to unglue themselves from their ecocidal forms. Individual drives must not simply be funneled into convenient forms of consumerism that *buy* into new relations, but rather, they must form radically new relationships proposed within the lived moment. The ability for a logger to refuse to cut down a tree, for a worker not to work, require new forms of solidarity in the formation of new collectives, collectives of sense and health that support the agency of the individual to engage in orthopraxy, to elevate and value the natural world and to actuate new potentials within the lived moment. Placing action within the scope of the individual without taking into account their interrelatedness fails to engage deeply enough in the transformative potentials of the present moment. It is the formation of new ties that exist in mutual care where we build foundations for freedom.

Identificatory Pastiche, A Minor Literature of Self

Laing (1967) asserts that in the attempt to find an authentic form of expression, "No one can begin to think, feel or act now except from the starting point of his or her own alienation" (p. 12). To discover one's unique voice, one must begin to undo the cultural baggage of one's predecessors by examining and understanding them and then, potentially, by undoing or perhaps reinscribing them. Seibt and Norksov (2012) suggest that "personal identity is best represented by a selection function that generates identificatory narratives" (p. 286). They assert that identity is a process of sifting wherein we attach ourselves to those things with which we find identification, and from that assemblage, we construct a self. We can see this also in Bruyneel's (2007) "third space" of Indigeneity, where identity under settler culture becomes a selection of momentary instances of identification that emerge from the individual centre rather than an outer ideological or cultural center. This is not just a shallow sifting process but rather a search for identificatory meaning in the world and, thus, a search for instantaneous connections that attach meanings from within with corresponding resonances found in the other.

Through the internet, we have a space much like the imaginary, where we are able to try on notional identities ungrounded from the physical body, exploring instead the body-without-organs, a body without substance and therefore limitless potential (Deleuze & Guattari, 2003). In this way, there is the possibility of gaining access to parts of the self that would have otherwise been denied or repressed by cultural forces that place meaning upon one particular configuration of the body or another, through gender, through appearance, through race. On the internet, we can be any gender, subculture, or even species, thus liberating the imagination through a process of trying-on new ways of being, new perspectives, and new potentials for embodied expression. Turkle (2011) suggests that "when identity is multiple in this way, people feel 'whole' not because they are *one*, but because relationships between aspects of self are fluid and undefensive" (p. 194). So, when someone like Winczewski (2010) argues that the pastiche as applied to identity may result in a loss of interiority, it may be only one side of the coin. In a minor literature, one may use larger narratives and remix them in order to bring out themes that may otherwise be buried or suppressed. In this form of the pastiche, one is able to craft an ego expression that may otherwise become decimated by a dominant, oppositional, and homogenizing force.

By identifying with archetypes and symbols found in folk encounters, we may effectively remix our identities in ways that liberate repressed energies. For example, as Raphael (1997) describes it, "The call of the wild is at least a call to remember the unbounded self; a self that is not exhausted or defined by its occupations" (p. 59). Within Western epistemologies, the self may easily become identified with one's occupation; thus, one's identification with an instrumental role may create an imaginary that becomes prescriptive, stultified, or even desimated. In identifying with a narrative construct like the call of the wild or identification with a figure of the wolf, we may instead draw upon cultural narratives that undo or work against the very restrictions that bind the full expression of our libidinal energies and thus inhibit the embodiment of a complete self. Furthermore, "the phrase 'the call of the wild' reminds us that nature is conscious, that the boundaries between human, animal, and plant life are fluid, and that we must listen to nature's invitation to biophilic, ecological living" (Raphael, 1997, p. 62). In remixing human identity, the place and meaning of all other living and non-living things of the world are also shifted. The process thus becomes a total reordering of the narrative matrix of the imaginary. It is our interpretation of the real that is being undone and rewritten.

("I'm a Witch" Source: Author; Original Source: @funnyasswitch, 2020)

The witch's identity structure allows for the rejection of externally imposed identities. Particularly, in the rejection of girlhood, the figure in this meme reaches towards the witch's power that is a reconstituted wild feminine, powerful and masterful. In the case of the feminine, one's image and thus one's physical body stands as a central signifier of one's value and worth. Particularly, gestational bodies serve an instrumental role in the reproductive function of a social order. Thus the rejection of the external image, the identity of femininity, as failing to encapsulate one's being, represents a declaration of being that becomes a storying of the self. One may choose one's identity despite, and even in contrast to, the social construct suggested by one's image. In Haraway's (2016) notion of the cyborg, there exists as "a condensed image of both imagination and material reality, the two joined centers structuring any possibility of historical transformation" (p. 7). This juncture can be seen as the intersection of the imaginary and the material, the conceptual posture of the cyborg communicating across distinctions in an embrace of the liminal. We can also see this at play in the pastoral reimagining of "wild" humanity, in the rejection of socially mediated concepts of the self. One may cultivate within oneself a kind of human that may run with the wolves, much like those documented in Estés' (1992) popular survey of the wild woman archetype. One may embrace the role of the edge walker, an embracer of the wild, a worshiper of divine chaos, a lover of the Earth, a being complicated by the materiality of the body as it intersects with contemporary technological realities. It is in the embrace of the liminal where myriad new directions may be uncovered, new means, modes, and connections formed.

It must be said that as the human project continues to expand, we are increasingly confronted by the need to make sense of a world that our narrative order can no longer contain. We must contend with the fact that within the chaos of the new, we are ever more tempted into a posture that accepts the fact that, "Every encounter, contagion, or assemblage generates and brings about another difference and genesis" (Hung, 2014, p. 150). The future of the cyborg embraces a reality wherein we engage in the uncovering of our identities within the shifting and contingent potential of each moment. We each become a "naïve ontologist" (Laing, 1967, p. 142), attempting to contend with a potentially toxic intermix of conflicting and disastrous narratives of human identity while also trying to preserve and activate our own unique desires within that same world. Yet, as we witness greater and greater levels of global environmental destruction, it is becoming increasingly clear that "in order to survive, humans must constitute a new form of allying and combining with extra-territorial relations" (Hung, 2014, p. 156). How is it that we may accomplish this? We may see that "when people go beyond their limited physical form, or beyond the 'Human' form regulated by ontology" one may "constitute and create their own life." (Hung, 2014, p. 156). This does not necessitate a rejection or splitting of body and mind as in the pursuit of transcendence. Instead, I suggest a splicing of mind and body into a new world, reconstituted within a realm of relations in which the body, mind, and spirit complex become an immanent projection, function, and alignment of forces beyond the human unbounded by the human imaginary. We have the challenge of recasting humanity within a narrative that sets both our collective and individual identities within a structure of inter-being, where we may constitute each other within a web of relationships. It may seem counterintuitive to look to the internet as a place to engage in such a task, but it may very well be one of the best places for an ideological, narrative revolution to take place. The internet is both 'out there' in the ephemeral space of the imaginal as much as it is 'in here' in the situated space of the body.

As we engage in affinity spaces on the internet, where we may explore and experiment with identity, Bommarito (2014) points out that these spaces extend themselves to the desks and offices, kitchen tables, and cafes of the world. McNeil (2009) challenges the distinction between real and digital, saying, "Distinguishing these virtual spaces from 'real life is actually inaccurate – they *are* real life to the people who use them" (p. 84). Distinctions that become drawn around 'the real' reflect Laing's (1967) frustration around what society labels as "real" and what is relegated to the unreal. He contends that it is an act of oppression to situate a person's experience in the place of the unreal, rejected by the collective real and thus banished from the centre from which meaning is produced. Thus, when we encounter narratives that seek to elevate, or at the very least, validate a facet of one's actual experience that has been otherwise rejected by a collective narrative—a narrative Binning (2014) calls "consensual reality" and what Engels (1949) in a letter to Marx would refer to as "false consciousness" (p. 451) —we may find a new sense of shared affinity.

 thoodleoo

do u ever just wish u could be an ancient oracle
and your whole job was to do weed and tell
stupid riddles to rich conquerors only for them
to misinterpret your words and die

("Ancient Oracle" Source: Author; Original Source: @bewitchymemequeen, 2020)

Broader narratives of oppression rely on complicity, on the community participating in a collective understanding normalizing which realities are accepted and which are rejected. The oracle contains a wistful reference to an archetype, a figure whose role involves engaging in mind-altering substances and altered states of consciousness in order to bring knowledge back to the mundane world through the visions encountered through those channels. The meme says, "do you ever just wish u could be an ancient oracle and your whole job was to do weed and tell stupid riddles to rich conquerors only for them to misinterpret your words and die" (@bewitchymemequeen, 2020). The oracle is approached by those in power for advice in worldly affairs, channeling forces beyond human control through a unique spiritual connection. It is implied that oracles, due to the nature of their gift and office, might not be bound by relations of power, answering instead to a higher order. There is a harkening to an imagined past of an archaic social role that invokes a kind of chaotic influence, able to touch upon those at the highest echelons of power. It is the recognition that even one at the pinnacle of a human hierarchy must answer to laws that govern all living beings, that they too may be brought down by these powers and further, that it is possible for those with the gift to communicate with higher orders, ones that may exist outside of a human imposed order altogether. In addition to all of this, the meme also appeals to the countercultural use of mind-altering substances as seen through the operative lens of mystical or ritual use, as well as an appeal to a counter-narrative to order and progress, a playful imaginary wherein progress is put to a halt by a social order that gives a privileged place to the a-rational. We also see a latent sense of dis-ease with the current social order, a sense of malaise or discontent with the responsibilities and social roles of a modern imaginary. Here in this small packet are hidden the seeds of a deep, sensual rebellion against sense, against progress, against work. Memes are potent texts, alive with liberatory potential in that they connect with and utilize the imaginary to bring new worlds into the light.

When we look at our environments, both online and in the flesh, Caine (2011) asserts that our attitudes to all forms of social realities, such as "violence, drug use, and sex, as well as kindness, compassion, and even a love for reading, are 'picked up' by what important people do in a child's life" (p. 162). The important person becomes a conduit for sense, meaning, and purpose. Beyond the guardian's role as the provider of sustenance and care, a child may just as easily attach to a figure who validates and solidifies their own sense of identity than to a parent or other authority figure who does not. If those surrounding a child fail to honor and elevate their actuation as individuals, why would those people be held in great esteem? Why then should I follow their example? Lack of purpose and meaning within the home necessitates the child to engage in a pilgrimage in which they attempt to find affirming voices, messages, and people within the world. Along those lines, Watts (1966) observes that

> … our most private thoughts and emotions are not actually our own. For we think in terms of languages and images which we did not invent, but which were given to us by our society.… Our social environment has this power just because we do not exist apart from a society. Society is our extended mind and body. (pp. 64 – 65)

Our social world gives us our oppression, and it is through the social world that we move beyond. We are looking not only to those around us to take our cues but increasingly, as technology use becomes a part of the everyday flows of life (DeGennaro, 2008), the people who populate our lives are part flesh, part machine, just as we are. Increasingly, the machinic world of the internet becomes another kind of social mind, an imaginal space where mind and machine become one in an ordinary flow and where boundaries between individual and self, individual and community, and individual and world become both flexible and permeable. It is in this shifting world that we enter into a space wherein we may seek forms of identity that look beyond those given to us, reaching into forms of emancipatory identity that emerge from ecologies of the mechanic synthesis in the machinic world of the internet where I may engage in the co-construction of a new humanity engaged with and through others of value and esteem within my orbit. The internet becomes a place wherein I may travel, make my pilgrimage, and find pieces of my identity that have been either lost or erased by a social world that fails to recognize their value.

("Real Beliefs" Source: Author; Original Source: @sister_shanti, 2019)

A man dressed in formal wear stands in front of a mirror. Behind him, it is seen that his outfit is backless, and he is wearing black lingerie underneath. In front of him, it says, "My spiritual beliefs that I discuss with my family," and behind is "My actual spiritual beliefs" (@sister_shanti, 2019). There is a doubling of self that is instrumental when acceptance of the authentic, or even an attempt to locate the authentic, clashes with an overarching social expectation. We play roles in our families of origin and social world. In my own family, I was a mediator, someone who could take on and help solve the issues and conflicts within the family, doing the emotional labour of the collective. The mediator didn't receive healing in my family system; they only offered it. I still had issues; it was just that I needed to maintain the façade of wellness to maintain the social order within the family. If I started to bring my issues to others in my family, I would destroy the order, upsetting the delicate balance of emotional flows. In the social world, I play the role required of me in leftist circles, speaking the language of secular humanism, rational and enlightened. People around me understand that I am spiritual, but I keep my spiritual talk separate from most public spaces because my experiences are not considered "real." Seeing and conversing with spirits and finding and feeling meaning and life in the world is often described as 'crazy.' If I were honest and

147

authentic about my experiences, I would be put in a defensive posture and possibly lose respect from those around me who fail to understand the deep embodied meaning one gains through a spiritual existence. Yet, I also keep the truth of my painful childhood experiences to myself. I saw what happened to my mother and grandmother when they shared the story of their trauma with doctors within the Western medical establishment. They both received multiple courses of electro-convulsive therapy that did not cure them. They were denied talk therapy due to their poverty and prescribed such intensive courses of medication that they became cut off from the world, hazy, indistinct, a shadow of their former selves. To speak frankly of certain experiences might mean that you become institutionalized, where you do not have the right to choose which medications you take. If you experience a psychic break, you could be strip-searched, forcibly injected with unknown drugs, and locked alone in a room without compassionate care, without even explanation. It has happened to people I love; people have told me their stories, and I carry them with me as a caution when speaking my truth.

The consequences of the incorrect interpretation of reality are severe. Seeing this meme, I laughed because it is ridiculous but also because it feels truthful. The front-facing presentation is respectable, almost a parody of respectability, wearing a tuxedo, a signifier of upper-class wealth and refinement. It is only when we see reflected the hidden aspect of the figure, the shadow dimension of the unknown, that we can see a depth to the character that is hidden from the social world, but that nonetheless serves as an important part of that person, like two sides to a coin. This is the sexual, the kinky, the forbidden, the libidinal. When we cannot adequately exist in the spaces we are given, with the community we are born into, we may seek other forms of expression that allow for the fullness of our being to manifest. In this way, memes such as this offer a kind of validation for queer, atypical identities to exist, as though saying that the reality of the interiority of a person is just as valid as their social expression. It calls the doubling out, naming it as an external expression, a costume, a means of navigating and shielding oneself from the judgement and condemnation of a social world that cannot incorporate our being into their systems. The incipient flows of erotic potential seething under the surface of the Westernized social world (erupting only in highly crafted containers of material sensual stimulation) are dangerous, criminal, world-destroying flows. To embrace them without a containment of their radioactive nature is to invite chaos, the destruction of the social order as we know it, to bring about the last days of Rome and the death of the Empire.

Transcendence Through Immanence

To engage in the dismantling of systems is to bring about an awareness of their language, which exists as bifurcations, boundaries, limits, objects, and symbols. For example, my previously mentioned role as mediator is expressed through the emotional labour I performed. It is established upon a series of justifications, fears, and definitions that first became rooted in my identity. If someone comes to me with a problem, what is it that necessitates my solving it, of me providing that labour without question? There are repercussions to the denial of my role. Maybe I will be yelled at, banished or exiled; maybe something worse will happen. Yet, when I recognize the system as it exists by calling forth and naming my role and the ways in which that role relates to it, I begin to call up the programming language of that system. I see it laid out before me, and I may begin to rearrange its sense in ways that allow for a rebellion without an act of war. I may offer less draining forms of sympathy, reduce the amount of time I spend relating to certain people, and give myself permission to provoke negative reactions, which may result in familial healing. All becomes possible once I realize there *is* a system and, in understanding its structures, I begin to reconstruct its function.

The world is a system whose machinations may persist as something beyond my understanding, but there remain instantaneous moments wherein the word touches me and I touch upon it. In these moments, the systems and flows of the world become tangible, touchable, and knowable. Here is my work; here is the place where I may untangle the knots of the human order. Laing (1967) declares, "perception, imagination, fantasy, reverie, dreams, memory, are simply *modalities of experience*, none more 'inner' or 'outer' than any other" (p. 20). We can see here the limits that constitute objects which may then act upon other objects like a machine, as a system. In reality, one might also consider these to exist as a kind of soup, each part indistinguishable from the next, part of the continuum that is human consciousness.

There is an instrumental value to bifurcating consciousness into distinct units, fantasy/reality, real/unreal. Laing's analysis of the political aspect of what is considered 'real' is an attempt to open up the programming language of reality to demonstrate that the category of "Real" is applied as an instrumental demarcation, an aspect of a system. The unreal, then, is that which does not serve the operation of the chosen system. It is either discarded or suppressed because its integration would threaten the operation of the whole. The subjective nature of reality might be something to be considered as true, if only true for the individual. In this flattening of distinction, we might accept a more radical notion of the real as something bordering on what Deleuze and Guattari (1987) refer to as the plane of immanence in which, "There are only relations of movement and rest, speed and slowness between unformed elements, or at least between elements that are relatively unformed, molecules and particles of all kinds" (p. 266). This is the ocean of the world. It is differentiated in momentary instances of motion and alignment coalescing in dreamlike machines, dissolving once again into latent potential, which may coalesce in a maddening number of spontaneous orders. In this, there is a levelling between humans, nature, and technology as they say that on the plane of Nature, "there is no distinction between the natural and the artificial" (p. 266). Nature becomes a category that contains all. It is immanence, that which houses all and from which nothing may truly distinguish itself. It is a sensual category, a feeling rather than a notion, a way of being with the world in the present moment, an awareness of it. In this way, the world becomes, as Hung (2014) would suggest, "a world without rules, rather than the actual and striated world as it is now. This does not suggest that the world is nihilistic and chaotic but that the world is breaking out of the rules that constrain it from further expressing itself. By doing so, the world becomes an infinite singularity" (Hung, 2014, p. 147). There is not a human world or a natural world; instead, the human world may be considered an extension of a natural world that is a container for all activities and things of all worlds.

There is a potential that is limited by one's corporeality; the body's container is bipedal, reproduces, ages, and dies. Yet, within the score of human life, the potential exists for near-infinite movements. We may seek out an expanded sense of the ecological as striving "to ensure that all existents thrive in and are sustained by their habitats, that they maintain vitality, activity, and creativity" (Hung, 2014, p. 149). This suggests that as beings of nature, we may have our particularities addressed by the notion of the ecological. Technology, including the internet, is an ecological force, a habitus exhibited by human entities within nature, just as is capitalism, power, billionaires, and air pollution. It is all of one, yet so many other things are possible. This world has coalesced into a machinic system that operates to serve human desires, yet the human soup, the immanent world, may give way to many flavours depending on its ingredients. In fact, the world itself, the universe on a scale beyond human comprehension, *will* give rise to new orders of matter, new constellations of stars, new planets, and new forms of consciousness. The potential of the real is vaster than the human, multiple infinitudes touching upon each point, expanding in every direction.

Thus, when we think about a form of identity that emerges from an immanent reality, we see that, "Becoming aims not at reaching a form, but at discovering adjacent, indiscernible or non-distinctive zones" (Hung, 2014, p. 151). This reflects the pastiche of identity or of trying out or remixing what happens on the internet, a disembodied dream world in which much is possible. This is a world wherein new conditions of being may be drawn into embodiment through revisions to the individual's narrative of self, through identification as a witch or the wolf, wild-woman, cyborg. Among the community of "Otherkin," members lay claim to identities other than human. Here, "there are a variety of types of self-knowledge supported within the community, including such constructions of the individual as: a human body with a non-human soul; multiple souls within the one body, a human who is a reincarnated non-human and even, occasionally, those who claim physical status as non-human" (Kirby, 2012, p. 276). The reality of the Otherkin defies the logic of the 'Real,' but in considering that "Shamans' ritual activities and experiences (e.g., soul flight, guardian spirit quest, death and rebirth) involve fundamental structures of cognition and consciousness and representations of the psyche, self, and other" (Winkelman, 2004, p. 194), the phenomena of Otherkins might represent a fundamental human capacity for imaginative embodiment. What might we as Otherkin or Shamans be reaching for, trying to investigate, integrate, or revitalize?

There is a form of learning that is able to take place through the imaginative game of "what if?" to use the imagination to transform ordinary observation into an alternative identity, an alternative bodily formation, another means of cognition. In this form of imaginative play, one may engage in experience limited only by the boundaries of one's capacity to hold a thing within the mind. In art, we see the manifestation of these imaginaries constructed within words or images that are then given as a gift to the world to participate in imagining a new form of being. In pursuing the skill of imagination, one's expansiveness becomes a measure of prowess. To transcend the boundaries of the external world opens up possibilities in the imagination for new connections to emerge. Thus, the internet serves as a socially mediated world in which we may collectively deconstruct these limits to engage in play that may be drawn into the body. In the case of Shamanism, I know that this "play" is a very serious game where it is believed that life and death may hang in the balance, that healing may be earned, where tools may be constructed, and guides may be found. The inner world touches upon the outside world in profound ways that we may not fully comprehend but have been harnessed and used by humans since time immemorial.

The body itself is also more than a physical object. It is more than the stuff that makes it. Deleuze's (1990) notion of the physical body is something that is both grounded in the reality of the physical but that also transcends it in "the body without organs," the human soup where potentials may become manifest, and limited only by the capacity of a body to produce them whether within or without. There is the body that expresses itself through form and sensation and there is also the body as self, as identity, and even further, the body as mystery, impulse, instinct, and the spontaneous forming of sense, contact, connection. This is contingent upon not only the physical reality of the body but also of fantasy, of the imaginal realm that is complicated by the fact that, as Laing (1967) suggests, "The relation of experience to behaviour is not that of inner to outer. My experience is not inside my head. My experience of this room is out there in the room" (p. 21). There is no strict distinction or line between my inner or imaginal world and my outer, physical reality, just as there is no clear delineation between nature, humans, and technology beyond that which we create within our words and stories. There may very well be an *out there* to which we react, but as to what that *means* or how it relates with or between humans and other beings and objects in the world is anyone's guess. We are forever living in the interstice between language, form, and sensation. While we may be able to replicate material interactions in science, we cannot nail down the infinite into words nor replicate the experience of ecstasy, fulfilment, pleasure, or happiness. What we are doing then, as writers and readers of a minor literature, is "freeing life wherever it is imprisoned, or tempting it into an uncertain combat" (Deleuze & Guattari, 1994, p. 171). By toying with the narrative constructions of a world oppressing us, we may confront that very same world by reordering its sense of meaning, using its own worlds and symbolic structures to create new meanings, either obvious or discreet. We may invoke the programming of systems through their use of intensities, symbols, habits, and roles to remake the world by altering systemic relations of sense and injecting within the symbols themselves new meanings, new realities, new potentials. What would it mean to rewrite and enact the word human, the idea of a human, the meaning of a human? What kind of machine would be made of an immanent human, an ecological human, a human animal?

Each and every one of us must accomplish "an intensive discipline of unlearning" which may become "necessary for *anyone* before one can begin to experience the world afresh, with innocence, truth and love" (Laing, 1967, p. 26). Laing believed that we live in an insane world and each have our own reactions to it. Those of us who react with insanity are not necessarily unwell, but rather, are within a cultural process that touches upon our bodies and minds in unique ways. Furthermore, the sane are not necessarily well, for the ability to thrive under oppression requires extraordinary configurations. Laing (1967) says,

> From the moment of birth, when the Stone Age baby confronts the twentieth-century mother, the baby is subjected to these forces of violence, called love, as its mother and father, and their parents and their parents before them, have been. These forces are mainly concerned with destroying most of its potentialities, and on the whole, this enterprise is successful. By the time the new human is fifteen or so, we are left with a half-crazed creature more or less adjusted to a mad world. (p. 58)

Laing suggests that enculturation, the process by which we formed to confront the prevailing conditions of the world into which we are brought, considering our historical inheritance of violence, trauma, and despair, must therefore be approached with reasonable scepticism. We must consider, as Haraway (2016) suggests, "The dichotomies between mind and body, animal and human, organism and machine... public and private, nature and culture, men and women, primitive and civilized" (p. 32) to understand more about the ground upon which they have been established and promoted. Seibt and Norskov (2012) describe the notion of "strong disintegration" that they say "involves a transition from static unity to dynamic unity, where internal coherence or the compatibility of parts is no longer required" (p. 292). Winczewski (2010), however, warns us of the dangers of decoherence, which may engender a lack of centre; in the idea of strong disintegration, we can see how the transgression of boundaries might also bring about a centre that did not exist before, that was unreachable due to social and cultural conditions of violence and suppression.

Interviewee Griselda Rodriguez Solomon states, In Galer's (2020) documentary, *The Instagram Witches of Brooklyn*, that the word *bruja* (or witch) "has been used to demonize powerful women....Unfortunately, because of patriarchy, that type of woman is a bit too powerful, so that's been an identity that has been repressed" (0:04:20). There is a perception of the witch as a person of power who is demonized specifically *because* of her power. Thus, the witch becomes a source of symbolic power, a means to identity in defiance of patriarchal norms. Yet, the witch is also a dark figure, one of taboo. Raphael (1997) says that taboo acts "are inauspicious and that violations are attended by sickness, chaos and misfortune," but she also says that the transgression of patriarchal limits is not the same as a transgression against taboo in the original sense. She asserts that patriarchy was always a violation and that by crossing over its boundaries, one is only taking back what was once stolen. So, to establish an authentic individual centre that reflects the reality of one's experiences as a woman or as another marginalized identity, one must take steps to establish new limits by violating the violation, by transgressing upon the transgression. Thus, in restoring the rights of the more-than-human world to existence, including new loci for desire and fulfillment, the territories are not territories to create but to retake. These are spaces which have been colonized, upon which transgressions of colonial orders are not violations because they are, in themselves, violations. To take back the land and to give it to itself is not a theft but a return.

Yet, in resisting colonialism, there is a danger in recasting the characteristics of the old world with the flash of a new surface. As a warning, Haraway (2016) points out that the desire for a "common language" (p. 52) in feminism may establish new forms of oppression, as it is in the limiting and static delineations of identity within which we become trapped. Instead of creating a new normativity, we may establish a non-normative normativity. We can create a centre of centres where a multiplicity of shifting meanings becomes the new norm. There are not two genders, or three, or 20, but an infinite number of configurations. Haraway (2016) posits, "There is no drive in cyborgs to produce total theory, but there is an intimate experience of boundaries, their construction and deconstruction. There is a myth system waiting to become a political language to ground one way of looking at science and technology and challenging the informatics of dominations–in order to act potently" (p. 66). It is not only in addressing the obvious sense of the colonial world that we must undo the oppressions of our age but also in addressing colonial magnitudes of order within both the self and community. There are methods of wielding power just as there are ways of *being*, of seeing the world and acting as a part of it which enact settler forms of sense. In upending sense, we must attempt to ground new senses within the somatic experience of liberation, within the fearful and terrible truth of freedom.

The lack of a central totalizing definition gives this form of meaning-making its power. It is power in the flexibility to pivot, to mean many things and to shift this meaning in ways that respond to the needs of the moment. Gore (2019) states in the introduction to *Hexing the Patriarchy*, "we will use every tool in our arsenal—from the everyday to the otherworldly–to undermine them and ultimately remove [the patriarchy]" (Introduction: Magical Letters, para. 60). In letting go of the need to assert a materialist rationalistic paradigm, the witch can mobilize techniques that lie in the a-rational. One rejects the reality under which magic cannot be wielded against the oppressor, and thus, one may create new potential modes for political action. Because the state of magic cannot be captured, defined, or systematized, it exemplifies a form of shifting reality that asserts itself through changeability. In a world where there is an ever-shrinking sense of *away*, of places that may exist outside of the patriarchal order, the witch, and by association, the magician, sorceress, or oracle, provides a means by which one may recast oneself within the patriarchal order as the very person who it most fears and thus create a sense of *away*, within. As an almost mythological figure, the witch does not have definitive edges. No holy scripture, manual, or dictionary of Witchcraft is recognized as canonical. Rather, Witchcraft presents itself as a way for the disenfranchised to "'de-code or deterritorialize' as a means of affirming a perspective that is other than the normative cultural narrative to which they are subjected" (Delezue, Guattari, & Brinkley, 1983, p. 13) and it is in this decoding that witchcraft takes its practice. Its practice is an alchemy—it transmutes base matter to gold, the self to the divine, and the world to a utopia.

("It's Friday Bitches" Source: Author; Source: @magicalmoonmemes, 2020)

A casual conversation about plans for the weekend is juxtaposed against an image of a nude woman levitating in the centre of a circle of other nude women reading books. Its caption reads, "It's Friday Bitches," (@magicalmoonmemes, 2020), which similarly acts as another level of juxtaposition. Invoked is a sense of the uncanny but also the socially transgressive, of gathering in nature, of collectively practicing magic, of sharing non-sexual group experiences in the nude, of feminine bodies holding books in their hands, sources of knowledge and wisdom, them gathering together investigate and build collective truth. The body and its transgressions are casually invoked as a normal part of recreation, thus hinting at the possibility that outside of the confines of the modern mundane, there is the possibility to engage in deeply transgressive practices as an everyday part of one's function. There is a humorous inflection of hidden transgressive worlds happening all around us but in secret. On the surface, we have the assumed world of the norm, and in each individual sphere, we have a casual depth that adopts and embraces the realities of queer existence and other "non-normative" and vitally hot states of being. This meme gives me ideas for what to do with my friends on the weekend as much as it entices me to relax into a casual, safe, and embodied social norm.

I would contend that the existence of memes such as those cited in this chapter can create a shifting sense of solidarity and community without closure or definition (Delezue, Guattari, & Brinkley, 1983, p. 17). They invoke a sense of the possible through a making ordinary of the extraordinary. They challenge the normative in their light treatment of the transgressive as though saying, but of course, our entire lives are illegal.

The Power of Reformation

In Galer's (2020) documentary @chiquitabrujita says,

> When I think about what makes life worth living, I think about all the moments I am with others, right? That provides me with access to a well of energetic capital that I can then use in the moments where I encounter micro-aggressions and I encounter explicit macro-aggressions, right? When I encounter structural systems, policies, laws, patriarchy. (0:08:30)

The being-with-others that she is referring to is one that came together for her through interactions primarily through Instagram and through identification with the archetype of the *bruja*. Through the process of reclaiming an ancestral archetype in the form of the witch, people like her create for themselves new tools of resistance that they may assert within acts of ordinary aggression. They are creating identities that allow for new forms of solidarity and practice. As such, we see reflected the reality that formal processes of organization are being replaced by fluid networks (Shifman, 2014). One may gather with others who define themselves using the same pieces, such as witches or brujas, wolves, mermaids, and dragons. These are fluid networks that form organically, and that may respond organically to the mundane and lived oppressions of the everyday. Not only do memes passed around by these groups form literature encompassing new social realities, but they also hint towards a new vision of how "the world should look and the best way to get there" (Shifman, 2014, p. 120). In a clever reframing of patriarchal norms, we see hints of the world that may be, providing the scaffolding for new potentials to emerge. Even in the limited scope of those images presented here, we see a language reaching towards the non-normative, ancient occupations, illegal*ized* and amoral realities that are remixed and passed along as a form of cultural resistance. Implicit within the memes that we encounter is a subtle but pervasive questioning of given definitions, a complication of binary designations, and structures of power. Haraway (2016) asserts, "Liberation rests on the construction of the consciousness, the imaginative apprehension, of oppression, and so of possibility" (p. 6). Is it enough to introduce a question of "what if" to spur one to curiosity, to seek out the limits of the given narrative of our social world? The "what if" then becomes comingled with, as Seibt and Norskov (2012) suggest,

> Our new cultural (*qua* technological) capacity of mixing up our real and virtual lives 'on the go,' continuously as we please, creating a 'mash-up' of several lives or a 'life-mix'… allows us to vary the degree of coherence in our self-understanding—we can consciously split our personal identificatory narrative into two or more, living parallel lives guided by incompatible personal narratives. (p. 292)

This newly forming capacity allows one to bring that 'what if' into our bodies, to play with the notion of 'what if' I wasn't oppressed, victimized, worthless? What if, deep down under layers of cultural conditioning, I am a wild animal, a force of nature, a mother f*cking robot?

Within this process of questioning and remixing, we find that, as Gore suggests, "Women recover their wildness by blowing up in the face of patriarchy—a massive dramatic release of volcanic rage and defiant joy that at once blasts or curses patriarchy and blasts open the carapace of femininity, releasing the natural (that is, powerful) woman within" (Raphael, 1997, p. 57). As the boundaries between oppressor and oppressed, victimizer and victim and blurred, we may then see the release of hitherto suppressed energies that become properly directed at the forces that have been imprisoning them. By utilizing the simultaneous embrace of the imaginative potential of the internet with the identificatory process of remixing our personal narratives, we may find ways to honour the past "by *not* repeating their hurtful mistakes–and by being thoughtful about how we can best serve our changing communities here and now" (Gore, 2019, Introduction: Magical Letters, para. 50). Undoing the feminine archetype and attaching it to that of the witch, or the wild-woman, priestess, oracle, or magician, we recast ourselves in a role with power.

Tulok the BarCAREian
@tulokthe

Town Priest: The witches that control the woods are evil.

Girl: What do they do?

Priest: They aren't heteronormative or patriarchal, do lots of drugs

Girl: Omg, what specific parts of the woods are they in, so I can avoid them extra hard?
3:24 PM · 22 Feb 20 ·

("The Woods" Source: Author; Original Source: @tulokthebarCAREian, 2020)

A priest describes the evils of witches living in the woods. It is presented as a dialogue that follows: "Town Priest: The witches that control the woods are evil. / Girl" What do they do? / Priest: They aren't heternonormative or patriarchal, do lots of drugs and have sex with each other. / Girl: Omg, what specific parts of the woods are they in, so I can avoid them extra hard?" (@tulokthebarCAREian, 2020). The humour of this meme comes from the girl's veiled curiosity rather than revulsion hidden within an insincere capitulation to orthodoxy. Embedded in the joke is a rejection of the church's ideals as placed upon the feminine, an embrace of queer sexuality, pleasure, drug use as an alternative mode of being, and an embrace of 'evil' as a liberatory transgression. If social good is expressed through oppression, repression, and environmental destruction, the category of "evil" might be fertile ground for exploring new modes of libidinal expression. The territories of evil may be explored without doing harm. There is the potential for an individual to explore action through an embodied sense of empathy that engages in imaginative modes of interrogating the other. By embracing the liberatory potential of recasting ourselves within our own stories, we open the potential to create a present moment wherein a human being may live in harmony with the more-than-human world. We find ourselves moving closer to the acknowledgement that, as Hung (2014) suggests, "The power of self-preservation does not come from the destruction of nature but from the power of enabling us to be more capable of maintaining relationships with other species, which increases our dynamic loading in order to fulfill our own self-preservation" (pp. 156 – 157). Thus, in a seemingly contradictory way, by disrupting the world's order, we may invoke a sense of evolving orders, ones that may respond to the dynamic processes of life and liveliness within the present moment. By playing in the "what if", we may open our narratives to a greater interconnected order that asserts itself in the sense of nature that permeates through all things. This is not a nature relegated to the shrinking forests but one that emerges through computers, tsunamis, automobiles, cell phones, thunderstorms, chipmunks, sunshine, and perhaps most pertinent to our purposes, us.

Memes, and the networked realities to which they are tethered, can subtly prod at reality through their identificatory potential. In memes, we see the witch as one who may undo and redo the order of things, who may question and then volcanically upend the oppressions to which one is subjected through the patriarchal order. Gore (2019) says that magic is what allows her to take back the power that was first taken away by patriarchy. There is a latent seething potential for transformation that is activated through the revolutionary pastiche of identity that exists in online platforms. Through this, we can see the example of the body without organs, tethered in the physical body but also reaching beyond it into a space of flux (Hung, 2014). Haraway's (2016) cyborg is less an archetype than a mechanism, a potentiality of "possible bodies" (p. 33) that is a constitution of the interaction between our tools and our myths. We can see in these new mythological formations that, in Raphael's (1997) words,

> To speak in the language of animals is to transgress the God-given ontological boundaries between humans and other animals and, as such, it is intended as a *monstrum* or warning; an inauspicious sign to patriarchy that the female human animal has joined forces not only with the economically oppressed but also with the ecologically oppressed. (p. 58, italics in original)

This is a warning, an invocation of terror that stands in the face of patriarchal oppression and derives power from that terror. The wildness of the more-than-human is not merely something that we derive from nature; it also has its own network of meanings that may exist in relation to hierarchies, oppression and hegemony as another literature that may make its own sense of chaotic coherence. In exceeding the limits of humanity, spilling over into animals and machines, the human story begins to unfold as something not unique to the world just as it is a unique outpouring of the world. In the acceptance of the immanence of the human within a world of connections, the human story may begin to be understood as beginning and ending in the body, a site wherein the human individual may encounter a world full of radical potential for both self-transformation and encounter with wild, wondrous, and liberatory energies craving a conduit for their release.

References

@bewitchymemequeen. (2020). Ancient oracle [Digital image]. https://www.instagram.com/p/B_kccYEnLhi/

@funnyasswitch. (2020) I'm a witch [Digital image]. https://www.instagram.com/p/B-g8q9VHIcP/

@magicalmoonmemes. (2020). It's friday, bitches! [Digital image]. https://www.instagram.com/p/BmTGAI-En5Bn/

@sister_shanti. (2019). Real Beliefs [Digital Image]. https://www.instagram.com/p/B0bsSwvnTHG/?igshid=1qr-rfbgfkb3lo

@therealhighpriestess11 (2020) You ready? [Digital image]. https://www.instagram.com/p/B-csKcwD39X/

@tulokthebarcCAREian. (2020). The woods [Digital image]. https://i.chzbgr.com/full/9445901568/hC558B1BF/omg-specific-parts-woods-are-they-so-can-avoid-them-extra-hard-324-pm-22-feb-20-twitter-android

Binning, K. R. (2014). Consensual Reality. In *Encyclopedia of Deception* (Vol. 1–2, pp. 199–200). SAGE Publications, Inc. https://doi.org/10.4135/9781483306902

Bommarito, D. (2014). Tending to Change: Toward a Situated Model of Affinity Spaces. *E-Learning and Digital Media*, 11(4), 406–418. https://doi.org/10.2304/elea.2014.11.4.406

Brown, G. (2013). Web Culture Using Memes to Spread and Manipulate Ideas on a Massive Scale. *Interface: The Journal of Education, Community and Values*, 13.

Bruyneel, K. (2007). *The third space of sovereignty: The postcolonial politics of U.S.-Indigenous relations.* University of Minnesota Press.

Caine, R. N. (2011). *Natural Learning for a Connected World: Education, Technology, and the Human Brain.* Teachers

College Press.

Clarisssa, E. (1992). *Women Who Run with the Wolves*. Ballantine Books.

Damiani, S., Dauman, A., & Valio-Cavaglione, A. (Producers), & Laloux, R. (Director). (1973). *Fantastic planet* [Motion picture]. Czechoslovakia & France: Les Films Armorial

Dawkins, R. (1989). *The selfish gene*. Oxford University Press.

DeGennaro, D. (2008). Learning Designs. *Journal of Research on Technology in Education, 41*(1), 1–20. https://doi.org/10.1080/15391523.2008.10782520

Deleuze, G. (1990). *The logic of sense* (C. V. Boundas, Ed.; M. Lester & C. Stivale, Trans.). Athone Press.

Deleuze, G., Guattari, F., & Brinkley, R. (1983). What Is a Minor Literature? *Mississippi Review, 11*(3), 13–33. JSTOR.

Deleuze, G., & Guattari, F. (1987). *A Thousand Plateaus: Capitalism and Schizophrenia* (B. Massumi, Trans.). University of Minnesota Press.

Deleuze, G., & Guattari, F. (1994). *What is Philosophy?* Columbia University Press.

Deleuze, G., & Guattari, F. (2003). *Anti-Oedipus: Capitalism and schizophrenia*. Continuum.

Dennett, D. C. (1990). Memes and the Exploitation of Imagination. *The Journal of Aesthetics and Art Criticism, 48*(2), 127–135. JSTOR. https://doi.org/10.2307/430902

Develle, Y. (2017, May 31). *The Power of the Meme—An Alternative Reading of History*. Medium. https://medium.com/wonk-bridge/the-power-of-the-meme-an-alternative-reading-of-history-3b6665cd0268

Distin, K. (2005). *The Selfish Meme: A critical reassessment*. Cambridge University Press.

Estés, C. (1992). *Women Who Run with the Wolves*. Ballantine Books.

Ezzy, D. (1998). Theorizing Narrative Identity: *The Sociological Quarterly, 39*(2), 239–252. https://doi.org/10.1111/j.1533-8525.1998.tb00502.x

Freud, S. (1960). *The Ego and the Id* (J. Strachey, Trans.). W. W. Norton Company.

Galer, S. (2020, April 1). The Instagram witches of Brooklyn. *BBC World Service*. https://www.instagram.com/tv/B-byAHOgalen8n5/?utm_source=ig_web_copy_link

Gore, A. (2019). *Hexing the Patriarchy: 26 Potions, Spells, and Magical Elixirs to Embolden the Resistance*. Basic Books.

Haraway, D. J. (1990). A manifesto for cyborgs: Science, technology, and socialist feminism in the 1980s. In L. J. Nicholson (Ed.), *Feminism/postmodernism*. Routledge.

Haraway, D. J. (2016). *A Cyborg Manifesto: Science, technology, and socialist-feminism in the late twentieth century*. University of Minnesota Press. http://ebookcentral.proquest.com/lib/warw/detail.action?docID=4392065.

Hebdige, D. 9187). *Subculture: The meaning of style*. Routledge.

Hoechsmann, M. (2021, May 18) Remix literacies in the digical cage: Pedagogy, precarity and participation [Conference presentation]. DCMET Symposium 2021, Montreal, QC, Canada. https://symposium.unesco-dcmet.com/en/

Hung, S.-C. (2014). Deleuze's ethology: Plane of immanence and the impersonal. *Tamkang Review, 44*(2), 147-. Gale Academic OneFile.

Kirby, D. (2012). *Alternative Worlds: Metaphysical Questing and Virtual Community amongst the Otherkin* (pp. 129–140). Brill. https://doi.org/10.1163/9789004226944_008

Knobel, M., & Lankshear, C. (2005). *Memes and affinities: Cultural replcation and literacy education*. Annual NRC, Miami.

Laing, R. D. (1967). *The Politics of Experience*. Ballantine Books.

Marx, K., & Engels, F. (1949). Letter to F. Mehring. In *Karl Marx and Friedrich Engels: Selected Works in Two Volumes: Vol. II*. Foreign Languages Publishing House.

McNeill, L. S. (2009). The End of the Internet: A Folk Response to the Provision of Infinite Choice. In T. J. Blank (Ed.), *Folklore and the Internet* (pp. 80–97). University Press of Colorado; JSTOR. https://doi.org/10.2307/j.ctt4cgrx5.7

Milner, R. M. (2012). *The World Made Meme: Discourse and Identity in Participatory Media*. https://kuscholarworks.ku.edu/handle/1808/10256

Nagl, S. (2009). Spaces of affinity. *Technoetic Arts: A Journal of Speculative Research, 7*(2), 191–197. https://doi.org/10.1386/tear.7.2.191/1

Plumwood, V. (1999). Being prey. In D. Rothenberg & M. Ulvaeus (Eds.), *The new earth reader: The best of Terra Nova* (pp. 76-92). MIT Press

Raphael, M. (1997). Thealogy, Redemption and the Call of the Wild. *Feminist Theology, 5*(15), 55–72.

Seibt, J., & Norskov, M. (2012). "Embodying" the Internet: Towards the Moral Self via Communication Robots? *Springer, 25*, 285–307. https://doi.org/10.1007/s13347-012-0064-9

Shifman, L. (2014). *Memes in Digital Culture*. MIT Press.

The Instagram witches of Brooklyn. (2020, April 1). In *BBC World Service*. https://www.instagram.com/tv/B-byA-HOn8n5/?utm_source=ig_web_copy_link

Turkle, S. (2011). *Alone Together: Why we expect more from technology and less from each other*. Basic Books.

Watson, M. (2019). *Can the Left Learn to Meme?: Adorno, Video Gaming, and Stranger Things*. John Hunt Publishing.

Watts, A. (1966). *The Book: On the Taboo Against Knowing Who You are*. Collier Books.

Winczewski, M. J. (2010). *Consumption, pastiche and identity in postmodern visual culture* [Dissertation, University of Pretoria]. https://doi.org/F10/153/gm

Winkelman, M. (2004). Shamanism as the original neurotheology. *Journal of Religion and Science, 39*(1), 193–217. https://doi-org.ezproxy.lakeheadu.ca/10.1111/j.1467-9744.2004.00566.x

Yoon, I. (2016). Why is it not Just a Joke? Analysis of Internet Memes Associated with Racism and Hidden Ideology of Colorblindness. *Journal of Cultural Research in Art Education, 33*. https://jcrae.art.arizona.edu/index.php/jcrae/article/view/60

Chapter 6

Rupture and Repair

Purity and Corruption in the Pursuit of a Liberatory Praxis

At the age of 13, contemporaneously with a mental health diagnosis, I began to experience crippling physical pain. It was mostly located in my joints and bones, attributed by my doctor to "growing pains" that would be present well into my 30s, expanding to global nerve pain, manifesting—at its worst—in the feeling of my skin being rubbed with sandpaper, with glass granules running through my veins. I would finally be diagnosed with fibromyalgia at the age of 35, but the symptoms had been present since childhood. When I was little, I would experience a sensation that felt as if my shin bone was being strained to the point of snapping. Because my pain had been dismissed, I was left to experience it alone without any context after being told that it was a regular part of life. No matter how much I would cry, an expert had told my parents that it was normal, and my own testimony was rendered invalid. Outside of the regular dull ache, I would become completely immobilized by pain once or twice a week, unable to articulate my suffering or to get those around me to validate its importance. Instead, I was left to manage my suffering in seclusion, to understand my world as revolving around chronic pain without being able to seek redress. My posture became twisted by the experience, which caused chronic tension and dissociation, which resolved into a feedback loop that would exacerbate my physical symptoms even further. The constant experience of physical pain set me apart from others, causing a feeling of alienation which, in turn, caused me to feel decentered from my own experience of selfhood. As I got older, it, therefore, became a nearly single-minded pursuit for me to find a way to center and validate my own experience.

I first encountered TOPY in a used copy of *Re/Search* magazine entitled "Modern Primitives" (Vale & Juno, 1989). Thee Temple of Psychick Youth (TOPY) was an art project from the 1980s, described as an arts collective of chaos magic practitioners who sought to ground their art in new forms of relations between human beings and the world. I would later encounter a film which resonated similar aspects of myself back to me, namely, the film *Midsommar* by director Ari Aster (2019), a surreal vision of an insular Nordic cult. Both projects involve a sense of tribal identity channeled through familiar imaginaries of pagan rites. Yet, rather than holding up either as models for group relations—as both would be *deeply* flawed examples—I suggest instead that they both offer radical challenges to sense, creating systems of communication that serve the interests of humans as relational subjects, connecting with and creating radical affordances for identification and expression. In my own life, I have sought out pioneers in making new pathways of sense that could bring me back to myself, who could demonstrate to me the freedom of human beings to forge new symbolic connections and to make their own hierarchies of value to serve their individual and communal needs. I have been inspired by those who have declared radical non-normative centers, which allowed me to declare my own extreme experiences as central to my own lens. Instead of necessarily being a member of the abject poor, the sick, the mad, I have given myself permission to be more. I have been able to develop a clandestine pocket of wealth within an otherwise bereft landscape of madness and pain, to develop hope within the plodding of capitalist progress, to protect and house the resiliency of spirit that may be required when the effects of our collective machinations may no longer be delayed.

Embodied Narratives of Dis-cohesion

Sickness signifies a profound loss of autonomy in the sense that "Autonomy means self-governance beginning in the Cartesian sense of ruling over one's own bodily substance, and including by extension the continent management of all excretions and expression, including language and emotion" (Belling, 2020, p. 306). An experience of trauma begins a process of incontinence, where affect spills over the normative confines of the personal into the public—what was once neatly infolded inside rises to the surface, no longer able to be concealed. Yet, what is the remedy to this exposure? Within the culture of the West,

> As the child grows in the patriarchal culture of rationality and reason, natural bodily healing abilities, such as laughing, yawning, crying, shaking and spontaneously talking (babbling), are marked as inappropriate. Likewise, the ability to access altered states of trance, often perceived as and derided as being 'spacey' or wasting time daydreaming, are arational healing gifts present early in life that are most often eroded, suppressed and taken away, sometimes violently, in our modern culture. (Bickel, 2020, p. 40)

Thus, the traumatized subject, the potentially mad subject is left without recourse, relegated to a space of abjection wherein one's alienation is continuously revealed, and one's wounds are subjected to external judgment. The body is the center of this rupture and as such, it must also be the site of healing. The body becomes the place wherein the physical manifestations of trauma take place, as documented by Van Der Kolk (2015), where feeling trauma becomes a means by which one may process and release it. My own frozen body attested to trapped facets of my experiences that had taken my body hostage, revealing its private functions in an outpouring of both physical and emotional dysfunction. The arationality of healing modalities pursue their own logics, ones that access disjunctive connections that may have become fragmented through dissociation and suffering. The logic of the body has become mute, lacking a language for expression and thus, new connections of sense must be spontaneously formed through embodied reconfigurations, through soft processes of the body, the jiggling core at the center of both laughter and tears.

There is a deep need for life "to be meaningful unto itself and not rendered meaningful according to the outcomes it produces" (Wiebe & Sameshima, 2019, p. 252), making the non-linear progress of healing and social transformation viable. It is not in the outcome that such practices become manifest, but in the realization of their processes which bring about the shift in heretofore ossified relations, reestablishing their elasticity and resilience. This alienation

repeats itself in the demonization of Nature and the other, resulting in fear of and a drive to overcome natural forces, along with plundering and sacrificing the Earth's natural resources for human 'progress' at the cost of the ecological health of all. (Bickel, 2020, p. 40)

Ossified connections leave no room for life. They do not allow for growth that occurs at the limits of each, for the purposes of each. Instead, there is a sense of boundary placed upon the relation that serves a singular function. In the case of the more-than-human world, the boundary becomes an enclosure wherein the world and its beings become objects to be commodified and then exploited for the purposes of human enrichment alone. Yet the reality stands that "All components of wholes are permanently linked by virtue of common need, function, and prerequisites for survival" (Younger, 1995, p. 60). The more-than-human world is interconnected with the human world, both dependent on the activities of the other for survival. Within this dynamic, "we adapt our everyday life drama (unconsciously, or through narrative management by our silent plotters and prompts) according to *genre* intentions and expectations" (Belling, 2020, p. 308). The world is a character in our stories, a setting, an object, a being unto itself. As such, the role it has been given, that the beings of the world have been given, constitutes their place within the genre of a human-nature relation.

In the approach to the healing of fractures, the numbness and ossification of trauma between humans and nature, "our bodies are where our dignity is first constituted, and where it can most obviously and directly be challenged" (Belling, 2020, p. 306). In an assertion of the physical body as a site of relevance and expansion, the over-spilling of an untidy incontinence that suggests a human animality asserts a shared ground within nature. When one looks at affliction "seen vaguely from a distance," one may be inspired into an attitude of pity, whereas, "when it is suddenly revealed in all its nakedness, people shiver and recoil. The afflicted themselves feel the same shock of horror at their own condition" (Younger, 1995, p. 54). The body, when asserting itself in extremity becomes abjected through one's reaction to it, as other, as an outsider to normalcy through its inability to contain the excesses produced by encounters within the world. When such encounters take root within the body, the result is shame, "an experience of exposure of peculiarly sensitive, intimate, and vulnerable aspects of the self" (Younger, 1995, p. 61). There occurs a ripping "away the public, sociable presentation of self, making sociability problematic" (Younger, 1995, p. 54). When there is no space in culture for liminal states to be experienced and understood, those going through the extremity of the human condition become silenced by a dirth of narratives surrounding their experiences. Thus, these people face difficulties with the integration of their sensations within normative humanity, becoming outsiders in their own communities. As such, a state termed 'antisocial' does not abolish the subject, actually. Instead, it creates the conditions for the recreation of subjectivity, regenerating social relations into new coalitions of sense (Balinisteau, 2021). There is a need for a place where one may find footing outside of the social, especially when the social world may not contend with one's authentic life experiences. One may set oneself against the social as a means of claiming cohesion outside of states of normativity which have become exclusionary. In this light, one may consider the meaning of rule-breaking as leading "to new ways of conceiving social systems" (Balinisteanu, 2012, p. 22). Rules in this mode of inquiry become symbols of an ossified relation, one that has become static and thus unable to adapt to the relations of growth that require expansion of the normative around the integration of new modes of experience. In the practice of anti-social behaviour, "If experiences of shame can be fully faced, if we allow ourselves to realize their import, they can inform the self and become a revelation of oneself, of one's society, and of the human situation" (Younger, 1995, p. 62). Shame may be understood as a clue to new modes of being as they are brought into the light. Yet, their starkness can serve as a shock to the system, bringing to one's awareness the sometimes harsh realities of embodiment in the potential of disintegration, illness, and death.

Returning to the body constitutes a reforming of the center, a countering of hegemonic oppressions, which force disintegration and therefore shame. It is dignity that "commands respect, which in turn confers dignity in a performative feedback look of mutual evaluation" (Belling, 2020, p. 303). If one is able to confer dignity self-referentially, the judgement received from without loses some of its sting. In an acceptance of the emanations of the body there is an encountering of the physical and all that it entails, thus a deeper acceptance of one's nature and, perhaps, nature itself. In dignity, there is inferred "relational contexts. It neither inheres in any individual nor is it brought into existence or destroyed by any individual act" (Belling, 2020, p. 305). The necessity of the relation is asserted through dignity, co-constituting the subject through the witness. One may then ask, "is dignity best supported by escaping humiliation or by enduring it?" (Belling, 2020, p. 304). By what process does the self find a new coherence?

I found in performance art the means by which I could encounter the shame of my own body and its over-spilling of affect. In the space of human ritual that centers the body, there was the potential for a new encounter that resituated the genre within which my suffering was brought into meaning. I found that humiliation, as Younger (1995) asserts, was "also the condition for passing over into truth" (p. 65). In exposing the incontinence of my body, I was also able to own and process it. It was not simply in the ability to embody states that had heretofore been states of humiliation or shame but in doing so *with* others, I was able to assert new genre definitions within my own story And in this, "The purpose of sympathetically sharing in the suffering depicted in tragedy was—is—to produce a *catharsis*, the purging of negative emotional energy through feelings of pity and terror" (Belling, 2020, p. 317). My own trauma might be constituted as a tragedy, and in the narrativization of this tragedy through the body which houses it, I expose the horror of my own trapped, mute suffering for others to be disgusted and horrified and in insisting upon the confrontation, I also assert the truth of bodily suffering as a truth which must be acknowledged. The exposure of the body takes place as a process wherein "if dignity is threatened by incontinence—the uncontrolled leakage of food or urine or tears—or words—then dignity is sustained by catharsis, the composed performative expulsion of disorder" (Belling, 2020, p. 318). The chaos of my trauma is brought into coherence through communal experience, and it was through art that I was able to bring that potential into existence as in normal contexts, this aspect of the body is kept within sanitized environments, contained by hospitals, asylums, and hospices.

The potential of communal experiences of the abject or grotesque offers the potential for individual and group transformation, as "the significance of the grotesque body is that it refuses the ordinary separations between body and outer world, interior and exterior, or life and death. Instead, there is an open-ended, spectacular display that signifies the creative life-death-rebirth cycle" (Halnon 2006, p. 37).

In bringing forward the body of the sufferer, there is an embrace of the materiality of the body in a fuller way, as part of the natural cycles of birth, sickness, death, and regeneration. It may be found that "the disposition of reader or audience is, in fact, the lens that can grant respect to even the most incontinently horrible of spectacles" (Belling, 2020, p. 308). In making a spectacle of suffering, to be consumed as a narrative, to be brought into order, social order, there is a broadening of the real that may allow for those experiencing sickness and illness to be infolded within human society, no longer abject sufferers, whose pain is kept mute, internalized, and contained.

Strategies of Confrontation and Transformation

Contending with my physical pain as an artist meant exposing my experience in a bid to communicate, connect, and make sense out of the mindless, voiceless experience of the body spilling over into my public life. The sickness exposed my vulnerabilities in ways that I could not control and in wresting back the conditions of this exposure, I also owned this leaking as something that I might bring into coherence. In my private life, I had begun to process my bodily sensations by loosening restrictions on my movement, to allow myself to thrash and undulate, to verbalize, and moan as a way of breaking the process of shame that sought to keep the pain bottled up inside. I began to affirm my body by allowing it to express its internalized state, and slowly, I moved these undulations into the public space. In what I called 'dance,' I would move into the space of observation and would slowly lower the barrier that kept my inner bodily state cordoned off when in polite company. Just as I lowered the threshold of inhibitions in my private space, I began to confront the shame that I would hold, the shame that would keep my pain hidden, masked from the observation and judgement of the other. The affirmation of this controlled exposure allowed me to deal with the humiliation of a body spilling over, robbing me of my control. In this exposure, I also gave permission to the somatic realities of those observing, putting voice to the experiences of embodiment that we shared, creating the potential of a bodily reality wherein the spilling over of affective states could be embraced, celebrated even.

Sickness in the body represents the limits of control, of corporeality asserting itself against the individual will. It is in the acceptance

171

of mortality that one acknowledges the supremacy of the material in a singular condition. When the rituals of culture deny meaning to the various states of materiality, "Humanity...copes with the reality of death by constructing a pseudoreality that denies the full meaning of death" (Younger, 1995, p. 64). Death remains enclosed within sanitized modes that uphold firm barriers between sick and well, alive and dead. Confronting the suppressed material of life draws into relation felt states of reality that are not erased but merely denied. Making this into a process means stepping "out of the servile one-dimensional mind [to] turn an instrument into a creative tool" (Bickel, 2020, p. 24). The imagination as a tool becomes a key theme in occult praxis. Ritual then becomes the praxis of imagination, allowing for a:

> [...]matrixial borderspace(s) allowing one to write/draw ignored ghosts and forgotten/hidden knowledge into awareness and being. Engaging what can be vulnerable and challenging processes in a sacred ritual container, potential corrective for repressed and forgotten knowledge and knowing can be illuminated. (Bickel, 2020, p. 23)

The circle becomes a space wherein one person enters and another person exits. Within the circle, the veil between the real and the possible becomes thinned, welcoming into experience the unknown and repressed aspects of the self, inviting them into relation with the world. In this space, there is a loosening of barrier between dreamspace and the mundane world, where dreams may "provide a bridge to personal felt knowing and not knowing, along with the empathy and compassion required to connect with and process the collective grief accumulating daily" (Bickel, 2020, p. 27). Dreamspace, trance, and ritual as they interweave offer a space wherein radical potentials may emerge into new connections of sense. Trance and dreamspace have become key sites of cultural sense-making, where the culture of the West has become "savvy at employing exploitative entrancement of the masses with the lubricant of visual media, materialism and fear inducing rhetoric." (Bickel, 2020, p. 53). The arresting of the dreaming state serves to cohere the real into form. The dreaming world helps the mind to capture the world of experience and bring it into the body, resolving new felt experiences into symbolic resolution within the inner world. In recognizing the potential of trance, ritual, and dreamspace, one may also become alert to hypnotizing elements within the world as well as being able to intentionally make use of trance as a tool in the process of self-realization.

In the integration of suffering, it becomes important to transmit the knowledge gained from this process in artifacts of cultural creation (Younger, 1995), where artists "play a consistent role in bringing 'emergent ritual' into society through art and artistic performances, which act as vehicles to awaken reflexive consciousness in society" (Bickel, 2020, p. 24). Art space is one of the few places wherein new forms of ritual may emerge, rituals that seek to make sense of the new as it emerges into experience. New forms of suffering and madness lack narrative voice and artists, poets, dancers, writers, creators in general become masters of putting voice to voiceless experiences. In cohering new forms of sense out of suffering, "narration plays a crucial role in transforming the suffering" (Younger, 1995, p. 57). In telling the story, one is able to domesticate it, to make it safe, to make it normal again.

Integration through Disintegration

During my adolescence, the revolutionary potential presented by Thee Temple ov Psychick Youth set off a spark inside my brain. They seemed immune to the judgement of others, hostile towards normalcy, embracing instead a liminal quality of rule-breaking and social experimentation that seemed to continually expand the realm of the possible. One of their key instigators—and tyrants—Genesis P. Orridge (2010) said in their tome *The Psychick Bible* that "TOPY were the direct inheritors of a century's worth of occult and countercultural 'science,' and then some, a crustpunk laboratory where radical and, in many cases, previously forgotten ideas were synthesized into a way of life" (p. 19). They wanted to constitute a new form of tribal identity into modern life that might be expressed through pagan and mystic rituals. Their aesthetic was deeply imbued with a kind of affect of negation, a rebellion against the normative that staked the ground of the alienated as a new territory. In this way, their alienation comes from a "perceived association with negatively valued activity—a type of thwarting with respect to a given set of outcomes" (Younger, 1995, p. 58). There was a palpable resentment with the limitations placed upon the alienated by normative society, perhaps reflected when the house of P-Orrige was raided by "Scotland Yard's Obscene Publications Squad, who unearthed their vast collection of occult writings and graphic photos of anything involving murder, necrophilia, mutilation, sexual deviance and Nazi imagery" (Russell Powel, 2009, para. 14), artifacts of a praxis of social subversion. Enclosures realized by the Western ethos spill over into practices of art where, "Western music has at times been particularly concerned with the nullification of anything unstructured, sexually open, 'savage,' 'uncivilized,' or otherwise concerned with the joy of life or which speaks to the 'old' parts of the brain" (Orridge, 2010, p. 22). The imaginaries proposed by punk aesthetics, the social nullification that becomes a tool for new social realities, also presents opportunities for community and belonging, especially for those traditionally excluded from other spaces. The sense of the carnivale as presented in alternative music communities "breaks through the noise of commercial culture by raising the transgression ante to the extreme and challenging nearly every conceivable social rule governing taste, authority, morality, propriety, the sacred, and, some may say, civility itself" (Halnon 2006, p. 34). Thus, there is a celebratory embrace of all those things rejected by the mainstream as modes which can be explored within newly incorporated spaces of alienated inclusion-via-expulsion. This:

> [...]exposes, and transcends the limits between body and world, interior and exterior, and life and death. It celebrates body–world connectedness, inverts what is hidden, spurned, spoiled, and devalued, and liberates from truth and order and from all interior censors. Ultimately, it is a challenge to all objective reality. (Halnon 2006, p. 43).

The embrace of previously exiled states serves as a process of dis-alienation, opening up the potential for human expression into states of felt reality that have been rejected by the social world, serving as "a critical source of positive meaning for its audiences' everyday life needs" (Halnon 2006, p. 35). Orridge (2010) describes the processes undertaken in the Psychick Temple as "stripping away thee final strips of camouflage," saying, "there is nothing else we can do anymore. To be ignored or reviled doesn't matter. We shall be simply what we desire and no more" (p. 30). Desire is centered as the means by which one grounds the transgression of limits, the compass by which the process of unravelling is forded. Yet, desire may also be a way in which one loses the way, the act of transgression alone, where fulfilling desire alone is not enough to create an authentic space of being. Suffering invites revolution in that it forces the individual to "submit to some particular set of circumstances, forces to admit to an existence that is not under our control or to the intrusion of an activity operating under an other law than ours" (Younger, 1995, p. 55). Thus, acts of rebellion become a means to encounter a loss of control, which may become a pathology in itself if no new ground may be located.

While "we all too easily limit our agency by unconsciously internalizing, enacting, and reproducing the very norms that we believe need to be overcome" (Sameshima & Greenwood, 2015, p. 168) in stepping over limits and privileging the fulfillment of individual desire, the potential to violate the other is also very near. There is an eternal back and forth between desire and integration within the world, perhaps sublimating desire in an acceptance of the world's flows. One of the directives of TOPY "was discipline; that is, discipline in focusing on and actualizing the life one actually wants to live, regardless of social pressure or constraint" (Orridge, 2010, p. 21). Yet, the very ethos designed to create a community of leaders, able to create radical centers amidst social pressures leading towards alienation, became another oppressor, where its eponymous leader was alleged to be financially, emotionally, and physically abusive to other members in an inverted replication of the toxic games rife in Western echelons of power. In the abuses occurring within a community of the abject, their abuses can "fly under our collective radar because we lack the vocabulary to frame, mobilize around, and punish another species of coercion: one that infiltrates and hijacks our aspirations as a counter-culture community" (Sepmann, 2019, pg. 3). New forms of suffering, once generated, also need to find a voice. Ritual can be used for destructive, harmful, disconnecting means just as it can serve as a means to construct new forms of sense. There is a real danger of replicating the abuses we ourselves have been subjected to as our imaginaries are full of the things we believe to be possible, conveniently blind to the practical details of newly forming utopic visions. The embodiment of power relations becomes grounded in lived potentials as they are enacted. Just like anything, patterns that reside in the imaginary may be instantaneously reactivated within familiar circumstances. Thus the matrices of power reconstitute themselves in our lived relations within the moment. Once a community coalesces, one must continually seek to unsettle "a scene's unspoken groupthink, invested in protecting the sacred cows and hallowed stories that echo back the shared beliefs, identifiers, and bonds of the subculture itself" (Siepmann, 2019, pg. 4). Belief structures settle like sediment, potentially becoming ground for new emergences or else, new enclosures which must be continually overcome. In taking one step towards a new horizon, it is almost as though one invokes the hidden limitations of the imaginary to be encountered anew, with new potential to be overturned, transformed, discarded, or absorbed. Thus, despite its failures being in a state of tension with its successes, TOPY has served as a potential blueprint for new centralities to form, for challenges to hegemony to take place, and for social healing to emerge. Most importantly, it gives permission to the abject to seek their own integration, even if this goes against normative boundaries, enclosures, and modes.

My first forays into performance allowed me to take a step into my own abjection, to put a voice to the inner voiceless suffering that had kept me in shame for so many years. Yet, the practices of artists before me—who challenged the status quo and made it implicitly acceptable to bring strange states of being to be witnessed—served to create the possibility for my art within my own imaginary. Even still, I couldn't put words to the art that I was making because it emerged from a place without words. I chose dance because, in dance, I could engage with my body in an immediate way, allowing the healing undulations of grief and joy to emerge in spontaneous expression. I was also able to work out places in my body that had become frozen, places that felt disgusting because I had rejected them in the ways that others had rejected me. I brought fragmented parts of myself back into cohesion and exorcised a darkness that kept me from looking at myself, squarely and without illusions. The potential to enter into a human space where others will silently contemplate an unfolding of my childhood trauma was made possible through an extension of the imaginary that took place and was disseminated by people such as those involved in Thee Temple ov Psychick Youth. New modes of experiencing suffering have been made possible by them in ways that cannot be erased by their failures. The doors have been opened, and once they are opened, it is much more difficult to close them again.

Disintegration through Integration

The potentials of individual and social expression are held in a balance, continuously interweaving between self, other, and the world. There are momentary instances of individuation that give way to moments of immersion into the other, into the space of the world as a container of the self, which at other times spills over into space, uncontained. In social rituals, this spilling over is held by the social world in a container constructed for this purpose. There are moments when this spilling over is invited, where a confrontation with the incontinence of the body is confronted. These instances bring forth the materiality of the body, in an "imbrication of death life" (Huber, 2019, para. 11) that takes place through the invocation of liminality.

In *Midsommar* (Aster, 2019), there is the invocation of liminal spaces through psychedelic substances, these fluids "transporting the visitors either to their deaths or to hallucinatory visions (or both), [which] is indicative of mythical ordeals" (Huber, 2019, para. 11). The ordeal brings out the body's hidden states to be held in public view, encountered, confronted, and processed. The character of Dani is presented as a person with a deep well of sorrow packaged within her body, which is within a social world incapable of holding it, as those around her are not able to hold her suffering as it strives to escape its limits. In the beginning scenes of the film, we see that her bi-polar sister enacts a murder-suicide involving their parents. Dani is robbed of her social container, the responsibility left to her boyfriend Christian, who is found to be woefully inadequate. The group is invited by the character Pelle to attend a midsommer celebration taking place every 90 years in his village. Upon entering the Hårga's village, located in rural Hälsingland, Sweden, Dani imbibes psychedelic mushrooms with the others in her group. In this scene and throughout the film, Dani's emotions continually threaten to erupt, and she is forced to isolate herself, creating her own container to conceal her inner condition of suffering from those around her. In this moment and under the auspices of the psychedelic mind state, the world begins to froth with sensation to the point where she seems ready to explode, but instead of allowing that rupture, Dani escapes into a shed, holding her hand over her mouth, seeking to maintain her containmentDespite the extremity of her experiences, those around her are not willing or able to witness her suffering, desiring instead the mask of politeness that requires that social mask to hold in whatever threatens to escape, no matter the cost. When Dani covers her mouth to hold in what may be perceived to be a verbal expression of pain, we can feel her discomfort in putting voice to that pain. We see that "Most sufferers, without a language for their suffering, cannot articulate who they are, nor will they be able to discover what their suffering means or find their way beyond mute and isolated suffering" (Younger, 1995, p. 56). Dani has internalized the judgement of the others, exemplified in an earlier scene where Christian critiques Dani's over concerns about her sister's well-being, which are shown to be fully, and horrifyingly justified when he later receives a call from her that is full of animal cries of grief. We see in Dani's reaction that "The first language from sufferers is often lament" (Younger, 1995, p. 57). For the majority of the film, Dani is caught in this stage of lament, her suffering not able to find expression, most especially due to a lack of support from her community.

In Dani's grief, I saw my own. I saw how people treated me as a burden due to my sadness. Without a reliable support system, I was often thrust into the company of strangers, who articulated a reaction to me as being 'too much,' 'too intense,' and 'too needy.' This was the same reaction I got from the adults around me when I struggled as a child, only serving to deepen and codify my abandonment as a narrative tied to my deepest sense of self. My parents and others in my life did not have the capacity to give shape and form to my suffering, and so the excess that I contained was a burden that I housed inside of my body, where its toxic effects harmed me continually. Without the ability to express the excess of grief, it began to destroy me. Yet, I found a way out of this place in what Younger describes as "expression of suffering with a compassionate other (an individual or even a community) that enables the sufferer to intercept and work on the suffering within the framework of narrative" (Younger, 1995, p. 66-67). There is a requirement of presence for those who go through traumatic experiences. It flows over you like an engulfing ocean, taking away your safety, your agency, your personality. There is a need to rebuild, but the problem is that you cannot hold yourself together long enough to do it. Individuation is a powerful container only up until the point that one encounters a marginal experience, one that requires a deep restructuring of one's individual relationship to the self and, by extension, the world.

In our presence, we find "the most fundamental experience of reality, a primordial closeness" (Younger, 1995, p. 67). It is this closeness that allows a person to move beyond their individual social shell, to find themselves in the world, and it is in this presence that the rifts in these worlds may be brought together and made whole.

We see in the film a conflict set up between the two poles of the rational and arational and, "Whereas phallocentric logic privileges the rational and conflates the arational with the irrational, or hysteria and disregards the rational...Phallic logic thus remains detrimentally blind to the wisdom of the arational" (Bickel, 2020, p. 31). The narrative of *Midsommar* sets up a confrontation with another kind of sense, one of the commune and not just the commune but of people connected with primal modes of humanity. The horror of the film comes from a confrontation of the limits of the body and thus the control of the individual over its continence (Belling, 2020). The genre of horror allows the viewer to prime themselves for the experience of border-states, but in presenting the horror from the perspective of the cult, there is represented a tension between judgment and immersion. One may find that this:

> Swelling in the inbetween-ness of the matrixial realm can draw trauma and fear to the surface at individual and collective levels. The potential *encounter-event* of connection or attunement in matrixial borderspaces creates opportunity to heal and transform the very source of trauma and fear in oneself and ones' cultural embeddedness. (Bickel, 2020, p. 32).

In bringing forward alternative modes of organization for somatic materiality, there is the potential to lay bare the limitations of our own social construct. The inclusion of an abusive domestic relationship further provokes potentially hidden wells of rage, fear, trauma, and sadness within the audience. This culminates in a scene of revenge in which the roles are reversed between Dani and Christian, where Dani is given a voice for her pain and Christian has his voice taken away, where Dani becomes glorified as the May Queen, and Christian dies, immobilized, while stitched inside of a bear and set on fire. Yet, before this, in one incredibly powerful scene, we see Dani surrounded by the women in the commune. She had just witnessed Christian having ritual sex with another woman, and when she returns to her room, other women within the commune surround her. She attempts to contain her shock and grief, but instead, their touch draws it out of her. They echo and amplify her somatic experience of grief and there is an incredibly cathartic release. As Dani's sobs begin to deepen, they are echoed and reflected by the women crowding around her, crouching animalistically on the floor. This scene touched my friends and me as something which expressed a deep longing, more so than even Dani's revenge against her abusive boyfriend. The desire was to be seen by other women, not only seen but held and reflected, being given a container for the suffering we have been holding inside that has been taking us apart, slowly, piece by piece, that is the dream.

I got a powerful sense that this horror film was performing an important function for me—though this may not be the case for all viewers. For me, it proposed a powerful shape for my own grief and a kind of catharsis for the unspoken and hidden experiences of abuse. My community might not have been able to hold me in the same way that Dani was held, but in seeing *someone* being held in this way, I felt a loosening of the knots that kept my own suffering a secret. In the acknowledgement of this horror,

> [...]a mix of fear, revulsion, and grief—as unavoidable, maybe even necessary, may free the dying from an implicit responsibility not to subject their loving audience to a horror show. This acknowledgement may paradoxically shore up a sense (and definition) of dignity made stronger and more flexible by its contact with the horrible. (Belling, 2020, p. 302).

The horror presented in the film made my own horror more palpable. In Dani's journey to be found *by* the world, I was able to find pieces of myself that had become fragmented and repressed precisely because my own reception was not able to provide a container for my grief.

Proposed Confrontational Imaginaries of Disintegration-Reintegration

Confrontations with the limits of human experience bring one more fully into the world, precisely "Because the nature of suffering is to call forth deep questioning of the truth of one's being and its meaning, care becomes a midwife of rebirth" (Younger, 1995, p. 66). To be held is a vital affirmation of life and, as such, a necessary component of finding love for the world. Without care, the world becomes a hostile place, one that does not have the capacity to house a person in their fullness. How might a person see the world as a place of beauty without an embodied experience of being held? In our human community, we create environments for people to either flourish or flounder within the natural world as it extends into the human community and vice versa. What one experiences of the social extends into one's more-than-human relations. The face of those who have rejected us may be thus be projected onto nature, making it either caring or cruel.

Balinistenu (2012) defines myth as "a manifestation of authority engendered through acts of citation that reiterate subjective identities, which through these reiterations, have become naturalized and normative" (p. 17). As such, myths of contemporary societies provide affordances for how identity, including identity through pain and sickness, may be carried out. Through an engagement with the carnivale, there is a playing out of contemporary mythologies that then open up these same myths to renegotiation (Balinisteanu, 2012). There is a sense that if one plays the social role that one is assigned by birth, there will be a given path, including a social position which serves to satisfy one's needs. When this implied contract fails to come to fruition, one is forced to create alternative paths towards self-definition and understanding. This "Regeneration takes place at the level of meanings, where one's subjection to texts that convey the norms which give solidity and legitimacy to the body politic is a rehearsal of subjection to the hierarchies of the body politic itself" (Balinisteanu, 2012, p. 21). In plotting a new course for the self, one creates a new narrative to be followed by both self and other. Opening up new potentials of sense creates potential for the human community to adopt and adapt to personal needs for narrative meaning.

The body becomes the playground for enacting these new rituals of meaning; in exploring the means by which one contends with the voiceless within the somatic world, one begins to gather the material that is then narrativized. One cannot construct meanings without experience first, and the approach of the body may either suppress or draw out this material to be contented with and understood. In Somatherapy, pleasure is approached "as an antidote to the ideology of sacrifice (neurosis). We go about undoing the authoritarian knot of our bourgeois capitalist conditioning, which demanded the sacrifice of our desires in exchange for social acceptance" (Friere & de Mata, 1997, p. 2). An embrace of pleasure carries within it an elevation of the wisdom of the somatic world. Deep pleasure communicates bodily health and balance. The release of social repression offers this pleasure and, in finding a balance in which human pleasure may be sustainable, presents the potential for "nature and culture as imbricated ontological spaces" (Balinisteanu, 2012, p. 6-7). The logics of the body are the logics of nature as the human body emerges from within the space of nature in material relations with a living ecological relation. The denial of pleasure is a denial of a human relationship with the material, yet, it is not a fleeting pleasure nor a pleasure gained through transgression alone. Rather, deep pleasure becomes expressed through living ecological relationships, relationships that feed and sustain human life not only within a balance of health but also a social dynamic of love, hope, and joy.

Yet, pleasure is contested ground. It requires anti-social behaviour in the act of reclaiming spaces of pleasure potential. One must transgress in order to reterritorialize the spaces of becoming. In breaching the barriers of oppression, there is the potential to make new spaces for the body to inhabit, spaces which embrace more fully the integrated sense of a material world made up of interactions between sentient and feeling beings. The vision of this world holds on to a course that does not require a continual transgression that may turn itself away from liberatory potential into new spaces of harm. Boundaries become healthy when considered in a balance of reciprocity and health. The continual transgression of boundaries, when one steps into the homes of one's relations without invitation, that is a violation. As such, a connection with the heart becomes a vital tool for feeling through acts of transgression to engage in pleasure without domination, transgression without violence. One must wrest back control over the spaces of pleasure without losing ourselves to a process of war, as war is the logic that has fractured our spirits and made the world a dull place, filled with pollution and death. By confronting death and transforming it within an observational reality of cyclical generation, the human body within humanity may be embraced as a limitation which brings one up against an immensely beautiful and compelling world, one full of potential for celebration and love.

References

Aster, A. (2019a). *Midsommar*. A24.

Balinisteanu, T. (2012). Goddess Cults in Techno-Worlds: Tank Girl and the Borg Queen. *Journal of Feminist Studies in Religion, 28*(1), 5–24. https://doi.org/10.2979/jfemistudreli.28.1.5

Belling, C. (2020). Project MUSE - Facing Death: Performance, Dignity, and the Horrible. *Literature and Medicine, 38*(2), 301–326.

Bickel, B. A. (2020). *Art, Ritual, and Trance Inquiry: Arational Learning in an Irrational World*. Springer International Publishing. https://doi.org/10.1007/978-3-030-45745-7

Freire, R., & da Mata, J. (1997). *Soma: An anarchist therapy* (C. Buckmaster, Trans.). *III: Body to Body,* 18.

Halnon, K. B. (2006). Heavy Metal Carnival and Dis-alienation: The Politics of Grotesque Realism. *Symbolic Interaction, 29*(1), 33–48. https://doi.org/10.1525/si.2006.29.1.33

Huber, S. (2019, December 14). *Blood and Tears and Potions and Flame: Excesses of Transformation in Ari Aster's Midsommar*. Frames Cinema Journal. https://framescinemajournal.com/article/blood-and-tears-and-potions-and-flame-excesses-of-transformation-in-ari-asters-midsommar/

Orridge, G. P. (2010). *Thee Psychick Bible*. Feral House.

Russsell Powell, F. (2009, July 17). *Shock and bore*. The New Humanist. https://newhumanist.org.uk/2095/shock-and-bore

Sameshima, P., & Greenwood, D. A. (2015). Visioning the Centre for Place and Sustainability Studies through an embodied aesthetic wholeness. *Cultural Studies of Science Education, 10*(1), 163–176. https://doi.org/10.1007/s11422-014-9615-y

Siepmann, D. (2019, September 27). Groupthink and Thee Temple of Psychick Youth. *PopMatters*. https://www.popmatters.com/genesis-p-orridge-groupthink-2640631583.html

Vale, V., & Juno, A. (1989). *Modern primitives: An investigation of contemporary adornment & ritual*. Re/Search Publications.

Wiebe, S., & Sameshima, P. (2019). The Emancipatory Reaggregation of the Irrational Man: (Im)moral Possibilities of an Existential, Lived Curriculum. In D. Conrad & M. Prendergast (Eds.), *Portrayals of teachers and teaching on stage and in film: Dramatic depictions* (pp. 245–255).

Younger, J. B. (1995). The alienation of the sufferer. *Advances n Nursing Science, 17*(4), 53–72.

Chapter 7

The Manifesto of Immanence

Religious scholar Streng (1985) says, "Myth is more than a story about supernatural beings. It is a story whose symbolic creative force orders a person's existence into a meaningful world" (p. 44). Our stories contain an infinite and indivisible unity into understandable packets, using symbols, archetypes, and characters, to embody and order our sensual experience. Yet, at times, these stories fail to capture the now properly, or else they fail to inspire the hearts of those in the now as they move towards integrating the utopic imaginary. In one story, I become a character who does nothing but serve, my entire existence placed within an order in which I become an appendage of someone else rather than a being in and of myself. In contrast, Bosker (2020) says,

> The latest witch renaissance coincides with a growing fascination with astrology, crystals, and tarot, which, like magic, practitioners consider ways to tap into unseen, unconventional sources of power—and which can be especially appealing for people who feel disenfranchised or who have grown weary of trying to enact change by working within the system. (para. 11)

The world is at times yielding and at times cruel; it affords us with bounty but also challenge and misery. Yet, the systems of the West have created another layer to both the grace and the cruelty of the world. Systems of power twist people, creating entire underclasses, the subaltern (Spivak, 1988), the voiceless, who are relegated to spaces of silence much like those experiences that confront us with our humanity due to their lack of containment. There is a cultural story that says some people are supposed to spend their lives in service to the desires of others, with dreams that limit them to the notion of someday joining the class of their oppressors.

Yet, there is a choice, a wildness that lies under the stories that we are told as children. This wildness beckons us into communion with a greater reality and a greater source of strength, what Streng (1985) calls the sacred, "an original order before all worlds, and a transcendent source of all power and knowledge" (p. 47). One might think of this as a transcendent realm of flux within which we find ourselves, yet it is manifest through the world. We can see this in the story of Kwezens in Simpson's (2014) telling of Nisshnaabeg intelligence. In the story, Kwezens learns about the origin of maple sugar from watching the squirrels nibbling on the branches of the maple tree in the spring. Her story shares the power of observation, connection with the world, and community. Kwezens' community can connect through her and into the world because they listen to her. Our community may witness the power of the sacred manifest through the world if their orientation allows it. Simpson (2014) says, "To re-create the world that compelled Kwezens to learn how to make maple sugar, we should be concerned with re-creating the conditions which this learning occurred, nor merely the content of the practice itself" (p. 9). So, while we may continue to produce maple syrup, we cannot enter into the discovery of ways of living through an engaged, open, and reciprocal relationship to the land, living beings, and each other without re-creating the conditions which gave rise to it.

Streng (1985) says, "Human beings have no choice of whether they will construct a symbolic order; they must decide, however, if that symbolic order accurately reflects the Sacred Realm (Being)" (p. 48). Thus, we are given the heavy task of evaluation. It is incumbent upon us to look at the world we have created with all of its destructive potential and ask ourselves: Is this the highest order of life humans may achieve? Bosker (2020) suggests, "Witchcraft beckons with the promise of a spirituality that is self-determined, antipatriarchal, and flexible enough to incorporate varied cultural traditions" (para 14). Yet, it is merely one of the means of engaging with the baggage of our collective inheritance.

As settlers but also as the wounded, as those who have born the burden of a destructive legacy and who live within the tattered fragments of an oppressive social order, can we truly believe that the wealthiest among us are able to transcend the milieu of insecurity, misery, and environmental destruction that lies all around them? Why do they build such high walls around their compounds if they find themselves at peace? Surely, material goods are not the only requirement of satisfaction, yet the myth of wealth as happiness, fulfilment, moral good, and rightness in the world remains persistent. Streng (1985) notes that "Myths… are always true within their communal boundaries" (p. 49). We are fed the stories of capitalism, hegemony, patriarchy. These stories and their incipient values permeate the depths of our imaginary. In the folk song, "The Big Rock Candy Mountain" (McClintock, 1928), a traveller recounts his image of heaven. He talks about cigarettes growing on trees, cops having wooden legs, alcohol running down the rocks. In its humour, it points to an imaginary that becomes wedged within the injustices of the world, thinking of heaven as requiring cigarettes and alcohol, there still being cops, but who aren't very good at it. To some extent, we are all limited by the scope of our imaginary to allow ourselves to think *out* of the confines of our own mythologies.

Symbolic actions or rituals are a means of transforming the symbols of the everyday. The Women's International Terrorist Conspiracy from Hell chose the acronym W.I.T.C.H. as part of their creating attention-grabbing actions throughout the late 1960s (Schweigert, 2018, p. 2), which has inspired new groups that have brought the theatrical aspects of the former movement into alignment with spiritual values and practices, using public hexing as a means of political activism. In addition to this, the notorious Satanic Temple has recently been using symbolic political actions to challenge restrictions around the practice of religion in the United States (Laycock, 2020). Of specific note was their attempt to install a statue of Baphomet at the State Capitol in Oklahoma, meant as a challenge to an existing monument to the biblical ten-commandments under the auspices of freedom of religion. They have also recently declared abortion to be a sacred ritual, serving to provoke while at the same time attempting to protect reproductive freedoms (Cohen, 2020). We can understand actions such as these to be related to an increasing understanding of the narrative order of the world and its uses, which can be harnessed in the service of the creation of both justice and harm. In the cooption of symbols by the alt-right and white supremacist groups, such as milk, the rainbow flag, or the okay hand symbol (Ellis, 2017), we can see the shadow side to the creative pursuit of justice. The tools to tweak and alter our collective reality are becoming more transparent, and as such, we may begin to ask ourselves: If we don't use them, who else will? And to what ends?

Recently, a sensation was created when users of WitchTok, not a group but a loose subculture of witches using the popular app TikTok, claimed to have "hexed the moon" (Martin, 2020). The most notable feature of the entire brouhaha was that the authors of numerous articles felt the need to assure people that, on a scientific level, the moon would be fine (Panecasio, 2020; Martin, 2020). Can teenaged witches using an online app call into question one's confidence in the stability of the moon? Cosmopolitan talked to a Twitter user, @RodneyStubbs, who was one of the people who performed the ritual, and he simply said that he wanted to see if he could do it because people said it couldn't be done (Smith, 2020). He wanted to test whether he had the power to hex the moon. Witchcraft, as a practice, holds less to a strict standard of morality. Rather, it allows individuals to pursue their own sense of connection to natural forces and, in so doing, to engage as they will.

Cisneros (1991) says in her short story, "Eyes of Zapata", that "words can hold their own magic. How a word can charm, and how a word can kill." Our words are how we create our worlds; they make up the symbolic mythos in which we live. That is their power. Cisneros (1991) says, "The wars begin here, in our hearts and in our beds." Suppose we were to think of ourselves as continuous with the world, as immanent manifestations of it. In that case, we cannot consider ourselves somehow separate from the horror and oppression of it. We must consider how the implicit beliefs, relationships, and values we hold dear are exactly what gave rise to the world we see. If we truly wish to see a different world, we ourselves have to change. We must live through and with that change in and of the world as we wish it to be. Cisneros (1991) lures us with her poetry, saying, "If I am a witch, then so be it, I said. And I took to eating black things—*huitlacoche* the corn mushroom, coffee, dark chiles, the bruised part of fruit, the darkest, blackest things to make me hard and strong." We are able to remake ourselves as a revolutionary process, of stepping through the veil and into a world that is remade, out of words that are as familiar as our own breath and yet made into a new whole, with a new purpose.

The purpose to which all of this is leading us is to a revolution of the body in which pleasure may be set free of the shackles we place around it—the shackles that tie us to the maintenance of a system that satisfies only the most basic longings of our spirits. To be just, the world must be made just *by* us, but not only *for* us, because that kind of solipsism has gotten us where we are today and is born of a sickness that separates us from the world. If we are to remake ourselves into the image of the wealthy landowner who surrounds their property with high walls, we can never be truly at peace within the world as it is. Instead, we must live as a part of that world, as emergent from it. Our happiness, comfort, health, and happiness depend upon the health of the natural world and it to this world that we owe our true allegiance. If we can begin to accept the animal within the human, we may be able to understand that the very foundations of a way of life that sets us apart from the physical truth of the world are a lie.

We may choose to integrate our dwellings into the landscape, wear biodegradable fibres, eat food grown locally and without chemicals, and bathe naked under the stars. When talking to my peers, I often get a sense from them that nature is yucky, uncomfortable, and dirty. If I don't shower every day, my body is gross. Indeed, many women I have spoken to have told me that they feel *cleaner* when they shave their legs. We have products in our homes that purport to kill 99.9% of bacteria, both good and bad. Yet, the microorganisms in the soil are what allow things to grow. Without the microbiomes in our bodies, we become sick. The collaboration of organisms within a body leads to organisms within a world. There are systems upon systems of life that cannot be sanitized or enclosed. If we take the animality out of humankind, what do we have left? Where does the pleasure in the body come from but from the physical self in relation to the world, and without pleasure, what joy is there to life, and what purpose?

I practice Witchcraft to lead myself back into connection with the Earth because it places the locus of power back into the centre of the self, to the core of desire and feelings of fulfillment and pleasure. If one becomes tuned in, it becomes increasingly difficult to tune out the world around us and one may, perhaps, become sensitized to the resonance of the more-than-human world. In Witchcraft, the sun, moon and earth are central symbolic powers, as are the other celestial bodies. There is a deep tradition of nature worship in practices of Witchcraft. Many rituals require one to source ingredients from the natural world or attune oneself to natural cycles, such as the seasons and the movements of the stars and planets. The practice itself is deeply embedded within the world, and the power that one might derive from it comes from that same world, not merely the human world, but the world that moves from *out there* to *in here*.

The pedagogy of immanence that emerges from this work has yet to develop a solid definition. Yet, it is found in those practices that bring us into connection with the self through the body. One can find immanence in sitting meditation, in forest bathing (Fitzgerald, 2019), dance, or anything that draws one into connection with sensation. Still, I would argue particularly sensation *in* a place, *this* place. It seems that the literature and practices of witchcraft, even on the internet, have a seductive quality that entice one into connection. It is where oppression touches down upon our bodies that the destruction seen in the natural world takes root within our own lives. What could we accomplish if we just had the time, space, and energy? How many of us might take up gardening, permaculture, handicrafts, or talking to our neighbours if only we had the time and felt less afraid? In the flurry of the world we have created for ourselves, achievement and work are held up like ends in and of themselves, and it is into this story of work that we pour out our very lives. If we could take a step back without starving or losing our homes, what kind of perspective might we be able to form? It is not enough to develop the self or connect to the more-than-human world. It must be done in tandem with dismantling the systems of oppression that have taken root within the depths of our imaginary.

In 2008, in Montréal, I attended my first Soma Therapy Workshop. Soma is a form of group therapy meant to uproot the structures of capitalism in order to experience the freedom that would need to be lived through a true anarchist ideal (Ogo & Dejerk, 2008). There was a moment when we were asked to walk around the room with our eyes closed. Whenever you would brush up against another person, you would melt into an embrace with them, stay there for a moment, and then let go. I walked around the room, melting in the arms of unknown strangers again and again. There was a feeling of breaking apart, of letting down the walls and allowing in the world, of letting in the love that lies right beyond the ends of our fingers. The way isn't only through witchcraft, though witchcraft is certainly one of those ways. There are thousands of voices, linked together in a love of the world, who are fighting daily for its life. We may join this chorus, raising our voices through the love of our bodies, our communities, and our land. In the deepest sense of love, we may begin to heal our ancestral inheritance.

It won't be easy to unleash the trapped energy of so many generations of harm. There has been suffering and trauma that has been passed down through our blood, and we will have to face that as we move forward. It is a difficult path, but it is the only path we have. We must face up to the reality of our lives here upon the Earth. As we seek the answers to our questions it may be important to remember that we cannot *create* a sense of connection with nature. We are inextricably linked and always have been. We must only *remember*.

References

Bosker, B. (2020, February 14). *Why Witchcraft Is on the Rise*. The Atlantic. https://www.theatlantic.com/magazine/archive/2020/03/witchcraft-juliet-diaz/605518/

Cisneros, S. (1991). Eyes of Zapata. In *Woman hollering creek and other stories* [ebook]. Vintage Contemporaries.

Ellis, E. G. (2017, May 10). The Alt-Right's Newest Ploy? Trolling with False Symbols. *Wired*. https://www.wired.com/2017/05/alt-rights-newest-ploy-trolling-false-symbols/

Fitzgerald, S. (2019, October 18). *The secret to mindful travel? A walk in the woods*. Travel. https://www.nationalgeographic.com/travel/lists/forest-bathing-nature-walk-health/

Laycock, J. P. (2020, March 5). *What the Satanic Temple is and why it's opening a debate about religion*. The Conversation. Retrieved 30 July 2020, from http://theconversation.com/what-the-satanic-temple-is-and-why-its-opening-a-debate-about-religion-131283

Martin, R. (2020, July 22). *Novice Witches Hexed The Moon, Upsetting Others On WitchTok*. NPR.Org. https://www.npr.org/2020/07/22/894074602/novice-witches-hexed-the-moon-upsetting-others-on-witchtok

McClintock, H. K. (1928). The Big Rock Candy Mountains. In *Discography of American Historical Recordings*. Retrieved July 30, 2020, from https://adp.library.ucsb.edu/index.php/matrix/detail/800020447/BVE-46454-The_Big_Rock_Candy_Mountains.

Ogo, G., & Dejerk, D. (2008). Soma: an anarchist play therapy. Retrieved October 30, 2018, from The Anarchist Library website: https://theanarchistlibrary.org/library/ajoda-soma

Schweigert, L. (2018). *W.I.T.C.H. and Witchcraft in Radical Feminist Activism*. Arizona State University.

Simpson, L. (2014). Land as pedagogy: Nishnaabeg intelligence and rebellious transformation. *Decolonization: Indigeneity, Education and Society, 3*(3), 1-25.

Smith, E. W. (2020, July 20). *Did TikTok Witches Really Hex the Moon, and More Importantly, Should We Be Worried?* Cosmopolitan. https://www.cosmopolitan.com/lifestyle/a33370477/witch-hex-moon-tiktok-twitter-witchtok/

Spivak, G. C. (1988). Can the Subaltern Speak? In S. Hall & P. Walton (Eds.), *Marxism and the Interpretation of Culture* (pp. 270–313). Macmillan Education.

Streng, F. J. (1985). Creation of community through sacred symbols. In F. J. Streng (Ed.), *Understanding Religious Life* (3rd ed., pp. 43–62). Wadsworth Publishing Company.